A Very Strange
Way to Go
to War

A Very Strange Way to Go to War

The *Canberra* in the Falklands

Andrew Vine

Aurum
history

First published in Great Britain
2012 by Aurum Press Ltd
7 Greenland St, London
NW1 0ND

www.aurumpress.co.uk

Endpapaeres: front: Canberra departing Southampton for the
Falklands © P&O Heritage Collection
back: The homecoming © P&O Heritage Collection

A catalogue record for this book is available from the British Library.

ISBN 978 1 84513 745 8

1 3 5 7 9 10 8 6 4 2
2012 2014 2016 2015 2013

Typeset in Fournier by SX Composing DTP, Rayleigh, Essex
Printed by MPG Books, Bodmin, Cornwall

For my brother, John

'There is but one sea service. It is manned by those who use the sea. In peace-time it may be convenient to make division into Navy, Merchant Service and Fishing Fleet. In all national emergency, these services naturally become one, and serve as one.'

John Masefield

'She drove foaming to the southward, as if guided by the courage of a high endeavour.'

Joseph Conrad

CONTENTS

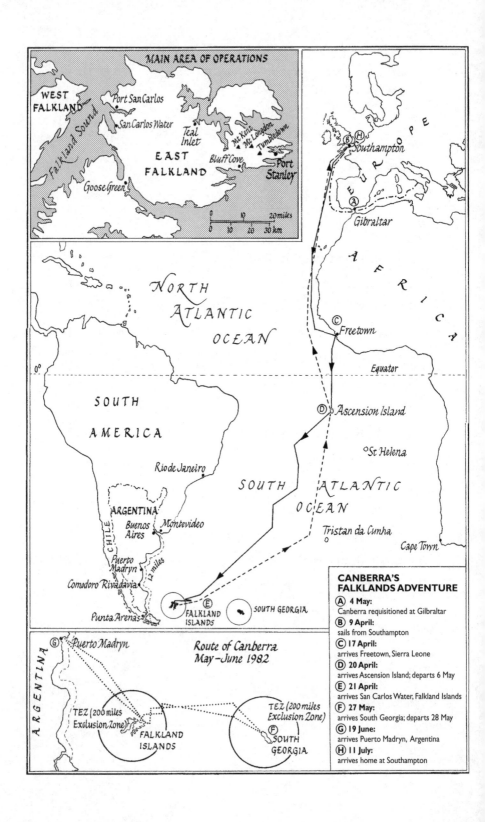

MAIN AREA OF OPERATIONS

WEST FALKLAND

Port San Carlos

San Carlos Water

Falkland Sound

Teal Inlet

EAST FALKLAND

Mt Kent
Mt Longdon
Tumbledown

Bluff Cove

Port Stanley

Goose Green

0   10   20 miles
0   10   20   30 km

NORTH ATLANTIC OCEAN

SOUTH AMERICA

Rio de Janeiro

ARGENTINA
Buenos Aires
Montevideo

CHILE

Puerto Madryn

Comodoro Rivadavia

12 miles

Punta Arenas

FALKLAND ISLANDS

SOUTH GEORGIA

EUROPE

Southampton

Gibraltar

AFRICA

Freetown

Equator

Ascension Island

St Helena

SOUTH ATLANTIC OCEAN

Tristan da Cunha

Cape Town

ARGENTINA

Puerto Madryn

Route of Canberra
May–June 1982

TEZ (200 miles Exclusion Zone)

FALKLAND ISLANDS

TEZ (200 miles Exclusion Zone)

SOUTH GEORGIA

CANBERRA'S FALKLANDS ADVENTURE

(A) **4 May:**
Canberra requisitioned at Gilbraltar

(B) **9 April:**
sails from Southampton

(C) **17 April:**
arrives Freetown, Sierra Leone

(D) **20 April:**
arrives Ascension Island; departs 6 May

(E) **21 April:**
arrives San Carlos Water, Falkland Islands

(F) **27 May:**
arrives South Georgia; departs 28 May

(G) **19 June:**
arrives Puerto Madryn, Argentina

(H) **11 July:**
arrives home at Southampton

CHAPTER ONE

We Don't Want to Join the Army

IT WOULD BE a highlight of the closing days of the world cruise as *Canberra* steamed homewards to Southampton – the crew show, weeks in the planning, in which the men and women who had pampered 1,600 well-heeled passengers for once took the starring role, putting on the greasepaint and the style, stepping into the spotlight with sketches and songs and lapping up the laughter and applause. It was a way of bidding goodbye to passengers they had come to know well, a chance also for their guests to store away another memory, take a few more snapshots for the album – perhaps to reflect that a generous tip was in order before leaving. Rehearsals had gone well and everybody involved was buzzing with anticipation. Two houses were planned to accommodate everybody who wanted to see it, climaxing with a quirkily offbeat production number, thanks to the discovery somewhere in the bowels of the ship of a cache of archaic items left over from goodness knows when.

It was nothing more than an eye-catching bit of fun, a novel idea for a finale, all part of the service across the course of 90 days of indulgence for passengers on the voyage they had promised themselves all their lives. Cold, grey, uncertain Britain, bumping on its backside along the bottom of an economic slump, beset by industrial unrest and political friction, had been left behind on Wednesday 6 January 1982. *Canberra* was the passengers' transport of delight, her own world, making their dreams of glamorous and romantic travel come true. She was the epitome of ocean-going splendour as she eased away from berth 106 at Southampton at 8pm, the deep-throated boom of her whistle reverberating across the port to announce that one of the most majestic and distinctive liners in maritime history was once more under way and setting course for the sun. A little over a month before, just before she departed for a two-week Christmas cruise, *Canberra* had undergone overhaul and refurbishment, and she was magnificent. Her hull had been cleaned and painted, so she was gleaming white; the twin funnels aft were vivid yellow. Her interiors were pristine, with new carpets and soft furnishings, her colour schemes all warm soothing tones, her armchairs deep and inviting, her cabins comfortable and welcoming, her crew smiling and attentive, her guests returning from their evenings to beds turned down, lights dimmed, chocolates and drinks set out. The wooden panelling of the public rooms was polished to such a gloss that the gentlemen could just about use it to check if their ties were straight before going into dinner and the decks were as spotless as the crew's whites. First port of call was Madeira, then on to Bermuda, Florida and into the Pacific; she would enter Sydney Harbour once more, evoking memories of her glorious maiden voyage of 1961, tour the Far East and head home via the Indian Ocean and the Suez Canal, due to arrive at 7.30am on Wednesday 7 April, having steamed more than 30,000 miles. Ten days later, her cruise programme for the rest of the year began, taking her on two-week passages to the Mediterranean, the Fjords, the Canaries, the Holy Land, Mexico and California, before she once more headed to Australia for a series of voyages out of Sydney that would take her into 1983.

The P&O brochures for the 1982 season promised 'The Magnificent World of *Canberra*', and so it was, a floating city and adult playground devoted to the leisure and pleasure of its guests, a quintessentially British ship, a corner of home cruising around the globe in style, run by the sort of men one could depend upon. 'The Bridge – Where British Officers keep watch,' declared the brochure, for the avoidance of doubt; no unreliable foreign types where it mattered here, thank you very much. Under their care, the passengers luxuriated, whether lounging in the sun around the Bonito Pool or Observation Deck, or being a little more active and trying their hand at quoits or shuffleboard on the Sun Deck. For the older ones, of which there were many, feeling the need to gently stretch their legs without unduly exerting themselves, there was the invitation to 'Stroll a Mile With a Smile', accompanied by a cheery crew member if necessary, which meant a steady four times round the Promenade Deck. Those who preferred a more sedentary cruise opted for backgammon, Scrabble, flower arranging, sewing or bridge. They browsed in the four shops for jewellery or scent, ordered a cocktail in the Crow's Nest Observation Lounge, forward of the bridge, with its semi-circular bar, spiral staircase that connected three decks, picture windows and panoramic views, where they contemplated how to spend the evening, after dinner in the Pacific Restaurant for those in the best cabins, or the Atlantic Restaurant for the rest. Would it be a show in The Stadium, just aft of the Crow's Nest, perhaps one of the themed events such as Cafe de Paris Night or Race Night, or cabaret with class acts in the more intimate surroundings of the Bonito Club? First-run films were showing in the cinema, there was a disco in the Island Room, and for those who liked their dancing rather more intimate, the Peacock Room beckoned, where, if the brochure was to be believed, Cupid was on hand as part of the service: 'Here you'll find the sort of romantic nightclub where you can dance cheek to cheek, fall in love with love all over again, and be forgiven for thinking that you're the only two people in the world.'

Life was rather less leisurely for the 800 crew. Running the ship, maintaining her immaculate appearance and catering to the passengers' whims meant hard work and long days. For all that, they enjoyed their jobs. *Canberra* was more than a workplace for many; it was home from home, as familiar as where they lived on shore. Cabins had been personalised with trinkets and pictures and curtains by crew who had served for years; they knew every inch of this ship, every creak of her woodwork when she hit a swell. They also knew her quirks and her qualities, and took affectionate pride in both. If passengers' hearts skipped a beat at their first sight of *Canberra*, so too did the crews' whenever they returned to her. This was a true community, with its characters and quarrels, its own social divisions, but above all with a real sense of identity.

3

There were parties and smiling group photos; birthday celebrations and meals together. Being at sea for long periods fostered closeness; lifelong friendships were born and lovers, sometimes soulmates, found. One couple had even married on this voyage, when the ship called at Hawaii. Nevertheless, three months away took its toll. The world cruise was always tiring, and the period of leave due at its end looked ever more inviting as the days ticked away towards Southampton. They called it having 'The Channels', the pull of home on the return leg, the yearning to be there intensifying the closer it grew. Thoughts turned to seeing loved ones again, to finding out how the kids were getting on at school, to pottering about in the garden, to just being off duty and catching up on some sleep. Before that release, though, the senior officers needed to turn their attention to how the cruise had progressed. P&O managers were joining the ship at her final port of call, in Italy, for a conference about the voyage to chew over what had gone well, or could be improved; above all to plan the future of the pride of the company's fleet, its flagship.

It was April Fools' Day, and as *Canberra* steamed towards Naples, her immediate future was to be decided not around a conference table, but half a world away, thanks to a simmering territorial dispute stretching back a century and a half that had abruptly boiled up into violence, fuelled by a toxic mix of aggrieved national pride, neglect and political ambition. In common with the overwhelming majority of Britons back home, relatively few on board knew much about the Falkland Islands, an isolated fag-end of empire nearly 8,000 miles away, marooned amid the fogs and heavy seas of the South Atlantic Ocean, where 1,800 hardy and fiercely patriotic souls eked out a living predominantly from sheep farming in an inhospitable landscape of moorland and mountains framed by a rocky and treacherous coastline. Unbelievable as it seemed, within a day blood would be shed over this tiny and distant corner of Britain as an invading army overran it, setting the country on the road to a vicious, old-fashioned colonial war that seemed to belong more to the 19th century than the 20th.

Claim and counter-claim over who discovered these islands had swirled around them since the 16th century when the logs of mariners swept east from Cape Horn by raging gales recorded glimpses of the coastlines on which their ships could so easily be dashed. It was one such British seafarer, Captain John Strong, commanding *Welfare*, from Plymouth, who indisputably set foot there in 1690, having been forced to take refuge from a storm while en route to Chile. He charted the passage between the two main islands and named it Falkland's Sound, in honour of Viscount Falkland, the then Treasurer of the Navy, whose ancestral title came from a village in Fifeshire. The French and Spanish, as well as the British, had roles in the extended drama over who ruled the islands as their empires rose and fell during the centuries that followed, eyeing them as strategic bases from which ambitions in South America could be furthered. The territorial game of pass-the-parcel had threatened to lead to war between Britain and Spain in 1771, prompting Dr Samuel Johnson to write of how odd it seemed to contemplate bloodshed for the sake of such a far-flung outpost. His words would resonate two hundred and more years later, in the spring of 1982.

'What, but a bleak and gloomy solitude, an island thrown aside from human use, stormy in winter, and barren in summer; an island which not even southern savages have dignified with habitation; where a garrison must be kept in a state that contemplates with envy the exiles of Siberia; of which the expense will be perpetual, and the use only occasional; and which, if fortune smiles upon our labours, may become a nest of smugglers in peace and in war the refuge of future Buccaneers.'

The imperial tag contest continued for 60 years after Johnson's reflections, until Britain flexed her muscles in 1833, taking the islands and holding them. This was a grievous insult to the young Argentina, newly independent since 1816, an illegal occupation, an affront to national pride that would gnaw at the country's psyche unceasingly until, 149 years later, it led to war. To her, the islands were the Islas Malvinas, unquestionably

Argentine territory, only 300 miles off her coastline and as the 19th century became the 20th, and its decades rolled by, she doggedly pursued her claim.

The islanders were no less resolute in their attitude. To them, their land was as unquestionably British as if it lay within earshot of the chimes of Big Ben. They regarded with suspicion politicians of successive governments, whom they did not entirely trust to safeguard their interests and ensure they remained subjects of the Queen. In that, they were correct. In the decades leading to war, there had been firm indications that Argentina could have her wish. The issue had been taken to the United Nations and to many impartial international observers the long-running dispute was simply absurd given the territory in question; more than one had likened it to two bald men fighting over a comb. Talks dragged on from the mid-1960s for a decade, but invariably foundered, to the frustration of all concerned.

Three days before Christmas 1981, as *Canberra* cruised around the Caribbean where the officer dressed as Santa Claus needed sun lotion as well as a long white beard, a chain of events was in motion that would run in parallel with the progress of her New Year world cruise, and ultimately cost more than 900 lives. In Buenos Aires, a 55-year-old career soldier with a none-too-distinguished record was raising a glass to himself in celebration of having scrambled from unpromising beginnings as the son of poor Italian immigrants to the very top of Argentine society. General Leopoldo Galtieri had done spectacularly well, forging alliances in the military machine that had run his country since a coup against a weak and corrupt civilian government in 1976. He had made powerful friends in the USA, who saw him as an ally against communist influence in South America. Years of plotting and positioning bore fruit on 22 December when Galtieri ascended to the ultimate prize, the presidency of his country. He was no dictator, but ruled as one of three members of a junta, the others being the Head of the Navy, Admiral Jorge Anaya, and Air Force Chief Brigadier Basilio Lami Dozo – and they had a major problem. Argentina was in serious trouble, its economy a basket case. Political unrest showed signs of surfacing against a regime beginning to acquire the same stench of incompetence as its discredited predecessor. The junta needed a rallying cry, an issue to unite and inspire that would set the flags waving and the crowds cheering. They found it in the country's longest-held grievance. The Malvinas would be returned to their rightful owners before the 150th anniversary of their occupation by Britain. Plans had long been laid for invasion by Anaya, and now they were dusted down and codenamed Operation BLUE.

The omens seemed good; Britain appeared to be neglecting the Falklands, announcing the withdrawal of the Royal Navy patrol ship HMS *Endurance* from the region as part of defence cuts, and denying third- and fourth-generation islanders full British citizenship. The garrison there was little more than a token. As 1982 dawned, the junta's plans took shape. Argentina stepped up pressure for a settlement of the sovereignty dispute and in the South Atlantic the islanders noted increasing numbers of flights over their homes and farms by military aircraft. Intelligence chiefs in London had long warned of the possibility of an invasion of the Falklands, and it seemed that now the tempo was quickening. Talks at the UN between the two sides broke down in early March, but the diplomacy was overshadowed on the 19th of that month by an incident that was seen by Britain as a deliberate provocation. Argentine scrap metal merchants landed on South Georgia, a forbidding, glacial island 800 miles south-east of the Falklands that was also under British control. There, they hoisted an Argentine flag. HMS *Endurance* was dispatched to evict the party, which had landed without permission.

Relations between Britain and Argentina were at breaking point. A little under a week later, as *Canberra* headed towards Suez, intelligence emerged that Argentine warships were on their way to South Georgia. As each day ticked by, the pressure ratcheted up. The crew aboard *Canberra* were avid listeners to the BBC World Service; it was trusted as the best and most impartial source of news wherever they went, and its bulletins reporting defiant Argentine refusals to budge from South Georgia were making it plain that a serious international incident was under way, even though no one yet dreamed that they would have a part to play in it. Calls at Port

Said, Haifa and Piraeus brought them ever closer to home, and ever closer to a role in this bewildering and unsettling crisis. It was on the evening of 31 March that firm reports reached London that Argentina was about to invade both South Georgia and the Falklands. Operation BLUE was under way, and not even desperate, last-minute diplomacy, including an emergency meeting of the UN Security Council and a telephone call from US President Ronald Reagan to Galtieri urging that the invasion should not go ahead could head it off.

The success of the operation was never in question. Before first light on Friday 2 April, troops began streaming ashore on East Falkland, followed soon after by armoured vehicles. The airport was seized and the invaders headed for the capital, Port Stanley. Opposing them was a force facing impossible odds – 80 men, 43 of them Royal Marines from Naval Party 8901, which had just arrived to begin a year-long tour of duty, plus 25 from the 1981/82 detachment about to return to Britain, and 12 Royal Navy men. The first wave of Argentines outnumbered the defenders by at least ten to one, and with every hour their weight of numbers grew more crushing. It was a baptism of fire for the commanding officer of Naval Party 8901, Major Mike Norman, who had assumed operational command of the Falklands only at 9am on April 1. At 3.30pm, he had been briefed to expect an invasion. The fight, when it came, was as fierce as it was short-lived. Norman deployed his meagre force resourcefully in an attempt to hold back the tide of troops, but it was hopeless. Holed up at the wooden-walled Government House with precious little protection from incoming fire, he and his men put up the bravest of fights, killing at least one Argentine and wounding three more, as they drove off the attackers, at least for now. After an uneasy stand-off, the islands' governor, Sir Rex Hunt, fearing a bloodbath that might extend to civilians took the only possible decision, bitter as it was; he ordered Norman and his men to lay down their arms. At 9.25am, the Falklands were under the control of Argentina for the first time since 1833. In Buenos Aires, the announcement was greeted with exultation and there was dancing in the streets; the junta had the triumph it needed.

The invasion sparked shock, disbelief and anger in Britain, fuelled by images of the Argentine flag being raised over Stanley and Royal Marines being paraded as prisoners. A public that knew next to nothing about the Falkland Islands to the extent of struggling to point them out on a map of the world was affronted that a hostile power had the temerity to invade a little piece of Britain, however remote and alien. Within the government, the mood was dark, even uncertain. The Prime Minister, Margaret Thatcher, would later recall that when she was told an invasion was imminent, 'I just say it was the worst moment of my life.' There would be ministerial resignations over whether more could have been done to prevent the invasion and soul-searching about the realistic prospects of recapturing such a distant outpost. Yet on 31 March, before the invaders had landed, the First Sea Lord, Admiral Sir Henry Leach, had told Thatcher that a naval task force capable of winning back the islands could be quickly assembled and sent to the South Atlantic. Late in the evening of the next day, the Prime Minister took the most momentous decision of her life up to that point, and ordered it to be made ready. In the meantime, intensive diplomatic efforts, aided by the US, got under way in the hope that Argentina could be persuaded to withdraw her troops.

Britain's anger over the crisis was voiced at an emergency debate in the House of Commons on Saturday the 3rd, when Thatcher told MPs that a task force was being readied to sail. In the Ministry of Defence and Admiralty, though, the practicalities of assembling it and getting it to sea presented headache after headache at a frenetic and exhausting round of meetings. The greatest problem was that the Navy – shrinking anyway as a result of defence cuts announced the year before – did not have the capacity to get all the troops, aircraft and military equipment necessary to the South Atlantic, let alone sustain the massive supply effort that such an operation required. The planners turned to the Merchant Navy, and the biggest mobilisation of British civilian shipping since World War Two got underway. It had been a long time since the requisitioning of ships had been required, but then it had been a long time since Britain had prepared for a possible war alone. The task force would eventually number well over 100 ships and more than half of them were merchant vessels. Tankers, freighters, roll-on-roll-off ferries, container ships, repair vessels, tugs – all would see service. This was the fleet that became known as STUFT – Ships Taken Up From Trade. It was an ugly acronym, and the source of many off-colour jokes about 'Getting STUFT'. The ships were either requisitioned or chartered, most of them rugged, unglamorous workhorses capable of operating in the swells and fogs of the South Atlantic. Negotiations with their owners were delicate, but had to be concluded quickly. There was nothing new for P&O in its ships taking part in military operations, and the company was proud of its service to the nation at times of emergency, which went back to the middle of the 19th century. Three-quarters of its fleet had been taken under government control during the Great War and a terrible price paid, with the loss of 989 lives and 89 ships. The Second World War exacted another cruel toll, with the loss of half the company's ships. Now P&O would be called on again to play a part, in what was by now was code-named Operation CORPORATE.

Very early in the planning process for the task force, it had been decided that if it came to fighting for the Falklands amid the islands' moors and mountains, it would fall to the Royal Marines to spearhead the assault. 3 Commando Brigade would be sailing south, its 40, 42 and 45 Commandos augmented by 3rd Battalion the Parachute Regiment, bolstered by two troops of armoured vehicles from the Blues and Royals. The brigade was not only ready for immediate amphibious operations; it was also expert in arctic warfare, thanks to training in Norway for a NATO role in the event of an attack by the Soviets, skills that could prove invaluable in the southern hemisphere where winter loomed. These were amongst Britain's toughest and finest troops, elite units with valiant histories, fierce pride and an intense rivalry between Marines and Paras over who was the best. There was no question that these were the ideal fighting men for the job; the difficulty lay in getting them there, as it quickly became apparent that the Navy's amphibious ships would struggle even to carry all the men, let alone the supplies they needed for combat. The answer to the problem was making her stately way into port.

At about the same time that Hunt called a halt to the fighting in Stanley, *Canberra* was mooring in Naples. It would be several hours yet before those aboard heard via the World Service that the Falklands were under occupation, and crew and passenger alike reacted with the same emotions as friends and families back home. For now, though, it promised to be a perfect last port of call; weather good, everything running smoothly, passengers in good form as they set off to see the sights or go shopping. The only thing out of the ordinary was an excursion that was anything but run-of-the-mill; a well-connected Roman Catholic priest had pulled strings and secured an audience with the Pope for a party of passengers and crew. All part of the service, another memory to cherish, another one for the album. And then there was the voyage conference; P&O's General Manager Fleet, John Turner, and his colleagues were due any time. It was Turner's first visit to the ship, and doubtless he would want to know everything possible about her.

He wasn't the only one. That afternoon at P&O headquarters in London, a phone call from the Ministry of Defence was picked up. Would senior managers be kind enough to attend a meeting within the hour? Many thanks. It was spelt out immediately that *Canberra* had been identified as a key component of the task force. This was an audacious piece of thinking by the military planners, to use one of the world's best-known cruise liners as a troop transport, but it would solve 3 Commando Brigade's problem as she could accommodate well over the number of passengers she usually carried. A long night in Whitehall lay ahead. The ministry had detailed questions and needed them answered quickly. They wanted to know *Canberra*'s maximum speed, her fuel capacity, the number of people she could carry, what tonnage of stores. Crucially, they also needed to know if she could be adapted for a role far different from cruising; was there any way helicopters could land on board? This would be no settled itinerary with regular ports of call; could she be refuelled at sea?

P&O had its own questions too, over requisitioning versus charter, insurance against loss, compensation for lost business. Getting answers from the government eventually dragged on for weeks, provoking a degree of rancour between the two sides. The meeting was still going on as its subject, lights ablaze as usual, bade farewell to Naples at about midnight, all aboard still unaware that the ship was under minute scrutiny. As she set course northwards for home, the P&O team in London were on the phones, summoning people into the office later that morning, Saturday 3 April. They were there early, poring over the plans of *Canberra*, working out answers to the detailed technical questions that the Ministry of Defence wanted answered, busy on the phones, and starting to liaise with the Royal Navy. A meeting to discuss adaptations to the ship to transform her into a troop carrier and helicopter platform was arranged in Southampton for the following afternoon. Naval constructors would be there, as well as a senior flying officer. But those planning the conversion of *Canberra* for possible war needed more than technical drawings; they needed hands-on experience of what she could do.

It was the most beautiful spring day in Worcester, and Michael Bradford was relaxing in his garden, listening to the news on the radio, which was dominated by the Falklands and the emergency debate in the Commons. He was on leave, and enjoying it. His leisurely morning was interrupted by the phone at 11am. It was P&O. Bradford was to report to Plymouth as soon as possible for a meeting about *Canberra*'s capabilities. He put some clothes together and drove south. Bradford – 'Sammy' to those with whom he worked – was an ideal choice to brief the Navy. At 50, he was one of P&O's most senior captains and knew *Canberra* as well as anybody, having joined her in the yard at Belfast and served on board for the next three years. As his career progressed, he had returned as deputy captain and relief captain. Most recently, he had been in command for the first half of the world tour now drawing to its close, departing at Sydney to go on leave. Especially usefully, he was also a captain in the Royal Naval Reserve, which gave him an insight into what the Navy was likely to require of the ship. Within hours, he was answering questions from Commodore Michael Clapp, the Commodore Amphibious Warfare, and his senior officers. It proved another lengthy meeting and one of its conclusions was that an eight-man advance military planning party should fly out to join *Canberra* for her final three days at sea, to carry out a detailed survey and plan for conversion not just into a troop transport, but a hospital ship capable of receiving casualties as well. Bradford would be one of the party, led by Major Robert Ward, Royal Marines Amphibious Operations Officer. Also included were Surgeon Commander Rick Jolly, and the Air Adjutant and Assistant Air Adjutant of 3 Para, Captain Bob Darby and Colour Sergeant Brian Faulkner. They were to fly from the Royal Naval Air Station at Yeovilton at noon the following day bound for Gibraltar, to where *Canberra* would be diverted to pick them up. The party was under orders to operate on a strictly need-to-know basis. Only the most senior officers aboard would be aware of who they were; no clue must be given to the rest of the crew or the passengers.

The last Saturday night of the world cruise was in full swing when the first of a series of cryptic telexes arrived from P&O that caused mystification. *Canberra*'s chief officer was the dark, quick-witted 38-year-old Martin Reed. 'We got this very guarded message that said, "Be prepared to change plans" and we were saying, "Tell us what you mean and we can be prepared for it,"' he said. Another message arrived, asking for the estimated time she would pass Gibraltar. By this point, the captain, Dennis Scott-Masson, had been alerted. The first radio officer, Graham Harding, found him wondering aloud what was going on. 'I took some of these telex messages up to him, and he said, "What's it all mean?"' Scott-Masson recalled, 'This was most unusual, because on a routine passage between two ports they don't ask us our ETA at waypoints, but we still had no clue what this was going to lead to.' *Canberra* would be off the Rock at 9pm the following day, and he replied to that effect. He found out what it all meant shortly afterwards. 'We got another message, secret to the Captain, saying the ship's going to be requisitioned, but he couldn't tell anybody,' said Reed. 'Obviously, he had to tell his senior officers and we were all sworn to secrecy, and he said, "And you," pointing at me, "will take the ship into Gibraltar. I'll be having my dinner." We weren't allowed to tell the passengers, but we'd have to change the sailing schedule and in that case they'd know something was up.' This was stunning news, so completely unexpected in the settled, well-ordered, tightly planned and scheduled world of *Canberra* that it left the officers who were told dumbfounded. 'I don't think there was much reaction, except amazement,' observed the purser, Maurice Rudderham. 'It's rather hard to adjust yourself to such a change in plans.'

A similar cloak-and-dagger air hung around the advance party as it flew out of Yeovilton aboard a Hercules C130 transport plane for the five-hour journey. None was in uniform. 'We didn't have any kit,' said Brian Faulkner. 'All we were told to take was civilian clothes, a change of clothing and our uniform, which we'd put on at a later stage. I actually didn't know where we were going, but on the aircraft I found out it was to Gibraltar. Once we'd landed, we were whisked off to The Rock Hotel, placed in rooms and told that we weren't to leave those rooms until we could all meet together and have a meal. At that stage of the game, I didn't know we were due to go down to the docks under cover of darkness, board a boat and sail out into the Mediterranean.' Ward, Bradford and Jolly did leave the hotel, for a briefing with a senior naval officer. As 9 o'clock approached, the party glided into the night aboard a P&O agent's boat. 'We set off out into the Med, and began to lose sight of Gibraltar,' said Faulkner. 'And then, right out there, we saw this huge floating palace. When we got alongside, everybody was looking over the side and then we were taken on board through one of the doors in the ship's side.' The decks were packed; men and women in evening wear craned for a view of the new arrivals, excitedly debating who they might be and why they were coming aboard.

The evening was already busier than usual for Reed as *Canberra* approached the rendezvous, bang on schedule. By then, he and the other senior officers had spent 24 hours chewing over what the requisitioning could mean for them. Reed was in full evening wear to compere the show, and the unintended irony of its finale meant he watched with a wry smile.

'It was the crew show that night, and I was running the bloody show.

I was producing it and directing it and introducing it. It was all sorts of things, you got stacks of crew coming forward to volunteer, and you whittle it down to something you think will work. Right at the end of it, and I'm not sure how it happened, they were dressed in blue duffel coats and tin hats which were still there from the old days, and gas masks with the end taken off so you could put the microphone in, and they were singing, "We don't want to join the army, we don't want to go to war". We'd set that up weeks before, it was just a total fluke, and I'm sitting there, thinking, "You poor bastards, you're just about to go to war". I went up to the bridge in top hat and tails, took the ship into Gibraltar, picked up the advance party and buggered off to do the second show.'

Canberra was buzzing with rumours about the new arrivals. The senior officers tried to damp them down, with limited success given the men's appearance and bearing. The unexpected appearance of Bradford, the only familiar face amongst the party, had caused a stir amongst the crew, who knew him well. 'Of course, we put the word out amongst the passengers that they were Board of Trade inspectors, Department of Transport or whatever,' said Reed. 'And that was fine, except they all had very short hair, tweed jackets, cavalry twills, and when you tried to talk to them they snapped to attention and called you "Sir".'

The passengers made no attempt to conceal their curiosity; nor did officers who were not in on the secret. 'We looked around, and people looked at us suspiciously because they hadn't seen us before,' said Faulkner. 'We were told that we weren't to mix with the civilian crew or give them any information about why we were there, but obviously they were suspicious because the ship makes an unscheduled stop and several guys get on board. Bob and myself were having a drink, and one of the ship's officers comes along to us, and we're having a chit-chat and he surmised that there was the possibility of a terrorist attack on the ship and we'd been put on board to counter it. We just shrugged our shoulders and smiled. The funny thing was, they had an entertainer on board, Tom O'Connor, and he made a joke that the ship's being taken over by the military and they're going south.' Inevitably, given that the news was full of the Falklands crisis, there were those on board who put two and two together, and came up with five. It was rumoured that *Canberra* would be used to evacuate the 1,800 Falklanders and leave the islands to their new occupiers. At least one of the crew, though, guessed correctly what was happening. The ship's medical department was at the heart of *Canberra*'s grapevine; people constantly dropped in for a coffee and a chat, and it was a hive of information and gossip. Angela Devine, an ebullient 36-year-old Liverpudlian nurse, heard a whisper about the requisitioning and shot off to tell her friend, ship's surgeon Peter Mayner. She barged in to find him in conference with the advance party. 'I went running down the alleyway to Peter's cabin and burst in, and said, "Peter, can you go to war?" and the whole room stood up. It was full of gentlemen who all stood up because a woman came in. I was absolutely mortified.'

The need for secrecy was obvious; it was still only two days after the invasion, and the extent of the Merchant Navy's contribution to the task force was yet to emerge publicly. The other imperative towards discretion was the nature of the negotiations between the Ministry of Defence and P&O, which had continued productively all weekend. P&O had not baulked at what was being asked of it, but in common with other shipping lines was determined to safeguard its own interests and that meant it wanted its vessels requisitioned rather than chartered. It was not just *Canberra* that the task force required from it; the roll-on-roll-off ferry *Elk* was needed to carry 3 Commando Brigade's equipment, including the light tanks of the Blues and Royals. Government powers effectively to commandeer ships would offer protection against the company being sued for breach of contract resulting from it being unable to fulfil its normal programme. This, though, required an Order in Council signed by the Queen, a step that had not been taken since the Suez crisis of 1956. The government agreed, and the order was put before the Monarch late on Sunday evening. The formal requisition notices for *Canberra* and *Elk* were hand-delivered to P&O early the following morning; at 3pm the House of Commons would be told of the powers the government had invoked. In the days that followed, two more of the company's ships, the liner *Uganda* and the ferry *Norland*, would also be requisitioned.

Whilst the formalities were being completed in London, the team aboard *Canberra* got down to business that night. 'The idea was for us to sort out the accommodation for the embarking troops and for Rick Jolly, who was in charge of the medical side, to sort out how it was going to be used as a hospital ship, and also how the casualties were brought down from one deck to another,' said Faulkner. The work proceeded briskly. 'Later that evening, after the second show, about one-thirty, two in the morning, we settled all the major details,' said Reed. 'We had everything roughly worked out by the time we went to bed that night, which was quite useful.' Matters had proceeded with equal urgency back in Britain during the course of the day. Every merchant ship sailing with the task force would have naval personnel on board, headed by a senior officer to work in collaboration with the civilian captain. For the smallest vessels, that meant one or two people; for *Canberra*, it meant dozens. Naval Party 1710, which was now being brought together, would board as soon as she arrived in port. *Canberra* was about to undergo a startling transformation, and the chorus line would find out what it was really like to go to war.

CHAPTER TWO

Ship of the Future

THE MEN WERE well wrapped up against the drizzle of a cold, overcast Belfast morning as they trooped in their thousands down to the waterfront, the studded soles of their boots clattering on the pavements. Their clothes denoted their status; caps and dark woollen jackets for those who got their hands dirty, bowlers and belted gabardines for those who told them what to do. These were the lucky ones, 10,000 with tickets to get into Harland and Wolff's Musgrave Yard on the morning of Wednesday 16 March, 1960; as many again clambered to whatever vantage point they could find outside to watch. In a city proprietorial of the ships it built, everyone wanted to see what she looked like now the scaffolding had gone. There she was; sleek and modern, a vessel for a vibrant new decade, so high that she had seemed to merge into the city's skyline over these past years. Men still at work downed tools at 12.15pm as the party of dignitaries climbed up to the podium at her bows, led by a slender figure, chic in fur collar: Dame Pattie Menzies, wife of the Australian Prime Minister Sir Robert Menzies. The police band struck up 'Waltzing Matilda' as she tied a sprig of white heather to the ribbon holding the bottle of wine brought with her on the voyage from home. At 12.30, it smashed against the bows and the ship was named *Canberra*. She refused to budge. Five seconds passed, then ten, as thousands held their breath. Almost imperceptibly, she began to edge down the slipway, gathering momentum, entering the channel with a crash to wild cheering as caps and bowlers were hurled into the air.

The Peninsular and Oriental Steam Navigation Company had made many innovations since its beginnings in 1837, and now it was doing so again. *Canberra* was tagged, 'The ship that shapes the future' in the press, and the company's chairman, Sir Donald Forsyth Anderson, had every confidence that she would do exactly that, cutting a week off the month-long voyage to Australia and offering the potential to break into the profitable Pacific cruise market. P&O's traditional trade route to Australia seemed secure, not least because of the number of emigrants leaving weary, near-bankrupt Britain in the years after the Second World War, tempted to new lives in a young country where hard work held out the prospect of prosperity, as well as better weather. These were the so-called 'Ten Pound Poms', ultimately almost a million of them in the 25 years after 1945, travelling on assisted passages paid for by the Australian government, keen to boost its population and economic growth, in return for that nominal contribution of £10. P&O had done well out of the programme, particularly in the lean post-war years, and by the mid-1950s saw no reason why it should not continue.

Anderson, born in 1906, was the product of his heritage; a direct descendant of P&O's founder, the sea and shipping were all to him, even in the face of ominous signs that the world he held so certain was changing. As *Canberra* was being readied for launch, the number of passengers crossing the Atlantic by liner was declining alarmingly and the numbers going by air increasing sharply. Anderson's heart remained with his beloved steamships; he insisted they had a future, admitting only the tiniest of doubts when he acknowledged to one interviewer, 'It will be ten years before I'm proved right or wrong.' His assessment proved prescient.

The journey to that rainy Belfast morning had taken four years. P&O issued its specifications for the new liner in the early part of 1956 to Britain's leading shipbuilders, who bid for the contract. The owners of Harland and Wolff enjoyed the happiest of Christmases that year; a few days before the yard shut down for the break, word came from P&O that it had been successful. This would be one of the greatest achievements of a company with the most distinguished of histories and a workforce whose skills had passed down through generations. The doomed *Titanic* had been built here; now they were to start work on a ship destined to become iconic not because she sank and lost lives, but displayed heroism and saved them. She would be the biggest merchant ship built in Britain for 20 years, 818ft 6ins in length, 45,720 gross tons, with a beam of 102ft, and a crew of 960. Her 538 first-class passengers and 1,650 tourist class could expect to sail for Australia at – for the time – an astonishingly swift 27½ knots. Her size and speed were enough to cause a stir in newspapers that still carried shipping columns; her cost, £17,021,000, provoked both amazement and national pride. Here was the boldest of statements that Britain was forging ahead into a new age of industrial excellence; only three years after a young Queen had been crowned, this was a period of growing confidence and ambition. P&O's super liner would be its flagship.

Heads must turn wherever in the world she went and passengers be seduced by her grace, beauty, style and comfort; she should, quite simply, be the ship everybody wanted to sail aboard and every rival line wished flew its flag. The task of creating the world's most distinctive liner fell to one of the most gifted young men in British shipping. John West was not yet out of his 20s, a teetotal, churchgoing former grammar school boy who after Durham University had gone into the shipyards of the Tyne before joining P&O. As Anderson was a product of his age, so too was West; forward-looking and determined to utilise every technological advance. The ship he designed was daring and dashing; a streamlined and soaring thoroughbred whose 14 decks rose to a bridge towering over the ocean, 108ft above her load line. He abandoned orthodox principles; her twin turbo-electric engines would be placed aft, rather than amidships, her funnels side-by-side instead of in line. That gave her a striking profile, as well as creating added space for airy, spacious passenger accommodation. Instead of steel, he utilised aluminium for her superstructure, cutting down weight and crowning her with a futuristically sculpted navigating bridge deck, its wings shapely and curving, officers' accommodation terraced below. She would be stately yet racy, and irresistibly glamorous. West's vision of what a modern liner could be proved enduring; for 20 years and more, she appeared new and fresh. By the time of her demise, she was mourned as a design classic lost.

Her interiors would be equally novel. Anderson, determined that his flagship had no equal in comfort and decor, followed the advice of his brother, Colin, who had introduced modernist design into Orient Line ships from the 1930s onwards, and appointed Sir Hugh Casson, director of architecture for the 1951 Festival of Britain and Professor of Interior Design at the Royal College of Art. Casson set down a series of principles for the team that worked with him, chief amongst which was, 'Every ship is an individual with a distinct personality'. He achieved his aim; no liner of the era was more stylish. Designer Barbara Oakley embraced the spaciousness West created. She came up with small, windowed courtyards around which cabins were grouped, allowing sunshine in, even though they had no direct view of the sea. White walls formed a backdrop to carpets, curtains and bedding in bright reds, tangerines and amethysts. Passengers could relax on furniture from Heals or Conran, surrounded by artwork by Edward Bawden and Julian Trevelyan. They would eat their meals off gunmetal grey crockery by Lady Casson with Mappin & Webb cutlery designed by Eric Clements, followed by coffee from pots by David Mellor.

There was ample time to refine such details. She was known only by her yard number, 1621, as her long, slow climb towards the Belfast skyline began on 23 September 1957, on slipway 14, with the laying of her first keel plates. P&O let six months pass before Anderson announced her name, cannily chosen to emphasise the closeness of his company to Australia. She would be *Canberra*, in honour of the capital, and he garnered good press there for the decision. The first indication the public had of how spectacular she would be came at the Brussels World's Fair in 1958, when an eight-foot scale model went on display, moving on to Olympia, in London, where schoolboys in caps and shorts prodded buttons and sections lit up to demonstrate the marvels of electric power in ships. There were three more years to wait until she was ready for the sea. It dawned foggy and cold on Saturday 29 April 1961, as the men of Harland and Wolff once again made their way to the waterfront, this time to wave farewell to the ship they had spent four years of their lives building. All the city wanted to see her off; the *Belfast Telegraph* recorded that roads became jammed as drivers pulled up wherever they could. A little before 10am, tugs eased her from the berth and she turned for the open sea. Under her own power for the first time, *Canberra* headed slowly into Belfast Lough, followed by a flotilla of small boats, their cheers still audible as she faded into the mist.

Her master was P&O's most experienced captain, Geoffrey Wild, who had served with the company since 1923. He had fussed and fretted over *Canberra* for the past year, and now, at last, would see how she performed as he put her through trials. Two problems became immediately apparent; West's design made her too heavy at the stern, which sat about six feet deeper than it should. Additional ballast was needed at the bows. The second was rather more alarming. 'She turned like a frigate, leaned right over,' recalled John Perry, the 23-year-old senior third officer. 'There were a few white faces on the bridge. You're really not meant to turn like that if you're a passenger ship.' Wild issued standing orders for turns, ensuring she behaved more sedately. The problems could be solved; he and his crew were thrilled by her. 'We had huge pride in her,' added Perry. 'This was the ship of the future, no question about it. She was awe-inspiring, the very size of the vessel, the modernity, she was unique.' Her home port was to be Southampton, because she was too big for P&O's usual terminal at Tilbury, and she came alongside 106 berth for the first time on 11 May. Two days later, the Duke of Edinburgh piloted his helicopter to the port to tour her. She was not quite ready for inspection. 'There was a frantic painting of the starboard side so she looked shipshape,' said Perry. 'Prince Philip, in typical fashion, kept galloping off on his own during the guided tour and then took off in his chopper and hovered over the port side, making it quite clear that he knew what was going on.' Six hundred invited passengers and the press came on board as trials continued, *Canberra* achieving a top speed of 29.27 knots. No liner sailed more smoothly; 14ft-long stabilisers resembling aircraft wings were capable of reducing a 29-degree roll down to a tolerable seven degrees. The shipping correspondent of *The Times* was impressed. 'Inside as well as out, she is a visually exciting ship, full of radically new ideas.' The decor was in keeping with the new decade. 'There is no mock-Tudor, neo-Georgian or bogus country club. The accent is on simplicity, cleanliness of line, with here and there splashes of colour and excitement, even shock. There is a marked contrast in style between first and tourist class; the former conveying a feeling of quiet and restfulness, the latter light and colour.' Some features, however, were a little too innovative. 'The widely-used plate glass doors and screens flattened the noses of some unwary passengers today; others got a wetting from decorative fountains in the tourist class lounge.' The fountains had been removed, and warning stickers placed on the plate glass by the time the first of her 2,238 passengers began boarding for *Canberra*'s maiden voyage. Those in first class had paid up to £550 for single tickets from Southampton to Sydney, and tourist class cost up to £235. Amongst the men and women boarding were 750 'Ten Pound Poms', on their way to new lives.

Her departure on Friday 2 June was one of the events of the year; front-page pictures, cinema newsreels, television and radio bulletins caught the cheering crowds who had gathered to wave off this glamorous symbol of modern Britain, the world's greatest liner sailing for Australia after five years of anticipation. They packed the dockside and the waterfront on the sunny afternoon, cheering themselves hoarse as balloons and paper streamers went up at 4.50pm, when the tugs moved her into the channel and she got under way. Across the port, ships sounded their sirens to wish her well, *Canberra*'s whistle blasting back her acknowledgment. Car horns added to the din as she made her way down Southampton Water, thousands at the shoreline, skipping out of work early or rushing down to Mayflower Park after school, to wave, cheer and see what must surely be a new era of dizzyingly fast travel by sea, a dazzling white thoroughbred on her way to the future.

No royal barge ever had a more triumphal procession than *Canberra* that summer, even though a problem with the freshwater manufacturing equipment delayed her arrival in Australia. She was a day overdue when she steamed into Sydney on 29 June, seemingly every vessel in the port on the water to greet her and thousands on the foreshore cheering her in. Don Chapman was the 25-year-old second radio officer. 'Britain could still take it for granted that we were special, and every port we went into, there was a huge welcome. We'd listen to the radio, and we'd be the first item of news in those ports; Australia had been waiting for us.' So was the Pacific; the welcome that awaited in Honolulu, where she and all aboard were garlanded with flowers, and in Vancouver, where light aircraft staged a flypast and the passengers could see every tall building packed with spectators. 'San Francisco was the biggest of all,' said Chapman. 'They set aside a day, called it "*Canberra* Day", they had bands all along the main streets and parades, there was a gun salute, and when we came into view they did what they had in the old days, sent a stagecoach galloping down from Coit Tower to *Canberra* to let the people know a ship was arriving.' The news that she was arriving brought the crowds back to Southampton on 4 September for her homecoming, even though it was a Monday morning. Work was needed; her funnels were soot-blackened and had to be extended to solve the problem. There was also a clash of aesthetics to be resolved; Casson's expansive vision had seen a children's area created aboard called the Pop Inn, complete with jukebox, tiger-striped faux-fur stools and internally-lit multi-coloured perspex tables. The backdrop to this early haven of psychedelia was pine-panelled walls, into which abstract patterns had been burned with a hot poker by a promising young artist called David Hockney. Children were encouraged to express themselves by adding to the patterns in whatever way they could. They did, sniggering. A P&O memo, stiff with offence, noted the panels had been, 'defaced by signatures in pencil, biro, ink, red lead and paint, and amongst the signatures there was a considerable selection of the most objectionable kind of public lavatory remark.' Casson, sensing that Hockney was a major talent, wrote to Anderson, urging that the panels be preserved. He was having none of it, replying, 'Hockney's immortal works have proved to be highly mortal.' The Pop Inn remained for now, but the panels were sanded down to obliterate the naughty words, as well as the pokerwork, and disappeared behind wipe-clean plastic.

For a time, it seemed that Anderson's instincts were correct, and *Canberra* had revived and renewed a golden age of ocean travel. Socialites and sultans were in first class, their entourages supervising the loading of steamer trunks onto her state-of-the-art electric conveyors taking luggage aboard. Heavy chests were also going up the ramps into tourist class; tools belonging to panel-beaters and plumbers, the means of earning their livings going with them, all included in the £10 fare. P&O used the airlines that threatened the old order of long-distance travel to preserve an atmosphere of indulgence, freighting in whatever was requested to satisfy whims. 'First class passengers could have anything they liked, even if it wasn't on the menu,' said Roger Lancaster, a 23-year-old radio officer. 'They could tell the head waiter a couple of days in advance what they wanted, and it would be arranged. I was at one table and they had Scottish woodcock, which was one of their favourites. No one ever said, "We haven't got that".' She carried sporting honour as well as national pride; the England cricket team under captain Ted Dexter joined at Aden, on its way to play the 1962/63 Ashes series, spending the next 11 days in black ties for dinner, followed by long evenings of louche badinage in the semi-circular Crow's Nest, forward of the bridge, with its 41 floor-to-ceiling windows overlooking the ocean. That summer, the newsreel before the main feature brought footage of her entering New York for the first time, fireboats with their plumes of spray escorting her into the Hudson River, small craft attending her like handmaidens, the helicopters of the police department flying in formation as an airborne honour guard. NBC transmitted a programme devoted to her; in the United States, as at home, she was news.

Not for much longer; the bright new decade of which she had been an emblem was overtaking her. Bookings showed a steady decline as the cost of air travel came down and routes opened around the world. Even though the numbers of assisted migrants held up as the 1960s progressed, they were not enough to keep tourist class full. Often enough, first class was half empty, too. Three weeks at sea to reach Australia seemed out of step with an age in which supersonic air travel was being contemplated and plans laid to send men to the Moon. Anderson's prediction that ten years would prove him right or wrong about the future of liners turned out to be correct; on Friday January 23 1970, the sort of crowds that had gathered to see *Canberra* away on her maiden voyage looked to the skies over Heathrow Airport as a huge, wide-bodied airliner made its approach. The Pan Am Boeing 747 from New York touched down safely, its 362 passengers getting off full of the excitement of knowing that they had just been part of history. The jumbo jet opened a new era of mass air travel over long haul routes; the ship of the future had been consigned to the past.

The years that followed were fraught. P&O acknowledged line voyages to Australia were no longer viable and brought them to an end, its difficulties aggravated by the oil crisis of the early 1970s that sharply increased *Canberra*'s costs. It announced that she would operate as a cruise liner, but even that presented problems; her 35-and-half foot draught made her too big to enter many ports. At the start of 1973, she sailed for America to begin a series of cruises from New York to the Caribbean. They were a failure, bookings for the first so poor that the second was cancelled; the remainder went ahead, but she was so depressingly empty of passengers that the cruise programme made a £500,000 loss. The nadir came that summer; on 1 June, P&O announced that it was considering scrapping *Canberra*. It was only 12 years since she had been feted around the world. A study was underway into reducing her draught to make her more suitable for cruising, but if that proved impossible, the company would look for a buyer, estimating scrap value at £600,000. As if to underline how far her fortunes had fallen, a little over a month later she ran aground in Grenada, remaining stuck for three days until tugs hauled her free.

Canberra was saved by Britain's growing appetite for foreign holidays, ironically enough fostered by the boom in affordable air travel. Package holidays, though, were suffering that turbulent summer; prices were yoyo-ing as the result of chaos on the international currency markets because of the oil crisis. P&O was to benefit; demand was growing for cruises from passengers who wanted to know exactly how much they would be paying. A month after *Canberra* was refloated from the shoals of Grenada, the company called another press conference; the older liner *Orsova* was being withdrawn from service, and she would take her place on the 1974 cruising programme. Class divisions on board would be abolished, all passengers being given access to the public rooms and swimming pools. She aimed for a more affluent market than the planeloads content with a cheap and cheerful fortnight in Torremolinos where they could get chips and Watney's bitter; fine dining, dressing for dinner, floorshows and cabaret were amongst the attractions. The elegance and comfort Casson and his designers had created for passengers of an earlier era met the expectations of her holidaymakers. Bookings were good for the start of her new career, a 1973 Christmas and New Year cruise to the Caribbean; they increased during the year that followed and through 1975. The year after that, an annual three-month world cruise was introduced to occupy her winters. If it was not 1961 all over again, it was heartening; the great white liner cheered wherever she went, her arrival an event, vessels in port sounding their sirens in salute. Her future was secure, not least because she attracted the affection and loyalty of passengers who returned year after year as the 1970s turned into the 1980s.

Canberra's brochure for the 1982 season tempted them back; pictures of cloudless skies, bronzed and smiling men and women playing quoits, silver-haired couples applauding the showgirls, beaming chefs presiding over tables laden with food. There was a cutaway diagram of the ship for newcomers, showing them where they could dine, drink, dance, watch a film, or sunbathe. There was so much to do on board that choosing between activities presented delightful dilemmas. The Mediterranean, Norway, the Holy Land, Mexico and the US beckoned, all in style. Her passengers that spring and summer guffawed at the unintentional irony of the brochures they found aboard. '*Canberra* is going places in 1982,' ran the blurb. 'Fascinating places that you might otherwise never have the chance of seeing again so easily.' There was another line that stuck with them in the weeks that followed: 'Every day, you'll face some of the most difficult decisions under the sun.'

CHAPTER THREE

No Women and No Foreigners

SHE FORGED northward through the swell of the Bay of Biscay at 22 knots under a gloomy sky, with the wind driving across her decks. Below, members of the advance planning party, yet to gain their sea legs, were suffering from seasickness as they pressed on with their tasks. It was hardly the weather for swimming, and so on deck Martin Reed had the Bonito Pool to himself as he took detailed measurements of its curves and angles in response to a request from the planners and engineers working on the changes to *Canberra*. 'I had to take taut wire measurements – take a wire from one side to the other and drop verticals from it and send the measurements back so that the engineers could get a profile. The wind over the deck was about forty miles an hour, blowing in all directions, and this piano wire was humming quietly.' All over *Canberra*, calculations were being made and options considered as the telex chattered out a never-ending series of instructions and questions; gradually a picture was emerging of the conversions that had been hammered out on that gruelling Sunday in Southampton. The Sun Deck would disappear under half-inch thick steel plate to form the main helicopter flight deck, the weight supported by the strongpoint that was the Bonito Pool, its 98 tons of water replaced by a mushroom-shaped lattice of girders. A smaller forward flight deck would sit on top of the Crow's Nest, the load being taken by scaffolding jacks that festooned the bar and timber supports at the forward end of The Stadium.

Both landing platforms were designed to bear Chinooks, the heaviest helicopters going with the task force. The steel to build them was already arriving on the quayside in Southampton so that work could start immediately she docked. Both ashore and onboard, a spirit of ingenuity and improvisation was emerging; answers to questions unasked and undreamed of until a couple of days earlier were being found. There had been no contingency plan for adapting this ship for carrying troops, still less for using her as a helicopter platform, simply because at no point in her 21 years at sea had the faintest possibility of either eventually arisen. Why should they? The Falklands crisis had come out of the blue, and so had the need for *Canberra* to play a part. Everything was being done from scratch, from the complicated design and engineering of flight decks to the questions over how thousands of soldiers would be accommodated and fed and casualties treated, if and when they arrived on board. As if to underline the urgency of the work, that Monday saw the sailing of the aircraft carriers HMS *Hermes* and HMS *Invincible* from Portsmouth. Submarines were already at sea, but this was a very public symbol that Britain meant business and the task force was on its way.

Some of the questions being addressed aboard *Canberra* appeared reasonably straightforward to answer. Accommodation was one of them. 'We were lucky, we had these convertible cabins,' said Reed. 'You had either two berths with facilities, or four beds without, so we changed all those into beds rather than loos.' Feeding and watering two-and-half thousand troops would be a challenge, and the responsibility for that lay with Maurice Rudderham. Luck was with *Canberra*. He was the ideal man for the job, having had extensive experience of serving on troopships during the Second World War and into the 1950s. At 57, he was one of the oldest officers, an avuncular figure with beetling eyebrows and a ready grin, and, best of all, in the discussions about the practicalities of looking after troops, the most insightful. He also had the keenest appreciation of the risks the ship faced, having been on board the hospital vessel *Tamba* when it was sunk off Sicily in 1943. Peter Mayner recalled how Rudderham brought a debate about whether *Canberra* would sail under the protection of the Red Cross emblazoned on her funnels to an abrupt halt. 'He said, "That wouldn't make any difference. I was bombed on a hospital ship with red crosses on the side during the war." That was very reassuring to us all.' The issue of whether *Canberra* should bear the Red Cross was quickly dismissed in any event; under the Geneva Convention her role as a troopship disqualified her from displaying the symbol.

Rudderham and the advance party quickly settled on the idea of the officers and senior non-commissioned officers eating in the Pacific Restaurant, where they would be served at table, and the other ranks using the Atlantic Restaurant on a cafeteria system. 'There were two entrances into the galley so you could have a flow of people picking up their meals and proceeding into the restaurant,' Rudderham said. 'So there was no real problem on the feeding side except for trays, so the word was put out to London to see if we could put our hands on 2,000 cafeteria trays. A quick look at the infantry and we were all right for knives and forks and spoons obviously.' That left the question of what to feed them and how to make supplies last.

Canberra was normally resupplied at its ports of call, with basic needs like fresh fruit and vegetables being supplemented by local specialities. In Europe, the bulk of the ship's provisions were delivered by lorries from Britain, which pursued the ship across the continent; a consignment had just been taken aboard at Naples. There would be no such well-rehearsed supply chain on the voyage ahead. What she needed she would have to carry, and be made to last. Feeding soldiers was a different proposition to delighting the eyes as well as the palates of paying passengers who expected the best and Rudderham knew that the food already in store would not fit the bill. 'The problem there was the smoked salmon and fillet steaks were not quite the thing we needed, we needed a lot of bulk food for cafeteria-type feeding for the troops.' On board and onshore, work started on drawing up a menu loosely based on the no-frills, filling meals provided aboard the *Uganda* on its educational cruises for schoolchildren. *Canberra*'s world cruise passengers had lunched on roast quarter of lamb or fresh crab; dinner brought blanquette of veal champignon or braised duck bigarade, with desserts of sumptuous gateaux or freshly-baked pineapple shortcake, meals prepared and presented to the exacting

30

standards of a luxury hotel by the galley. There would be no such fine dining for the foreseeable future, nor beautifully presented buffets presided over by chefs in perfectly pressed whites; troops needed solid, unfussy food that provided plenty of calories to sustain them through training. So it was to be cooked breakfasts of bacon or sausage with fried or scrambled eggs, lunches of baked hake, lamb stew or pork chops with cabbage, potato and mashed swede, dinners of roast beef and Yorkshire pudding, grilled liver or fried haddock, followed by sponge pudding and custard or fruit crumble.

Much thornier questions arose over how *Canberra* coped with casualties. She had her own sick bay on D deck, adequate for the needs of cruise passengers laid up for a day or two, or for as long as it took to organise a medical evacuation, but utterly unsuitable as a casualty receiving area, especially for large numbers. The most radical of rethinks was required; rooms devoted to relaxation, accustomed to chatter and laughter, needed to be transformed into operating theatres and wards where the intense concentration and terse, focussed dialogue of surgical teams saving lives and the ministrations of nurses to grievously wounded patients took place. One or more of the big public spaces close to the landing pads had to be completely transformed if men were to be flown aboard and treated. The answer was found on the Arena Deck. The Stadium, where passengers had applauded the crew show, was identified as a triage and resuscitation area, one side of it to serve as a four-table operating theatre and its stage taken up by an X-ray unit. The Bonito Club, venue for sophisticated cabaret, could be turned into a 50-bed intensive care ward and high-dependency unit, while the Island Room took the low-dependency patients. Walking wounded with relatively minor injuries could be dealt with in the Card Room. Bar fridges usually used for chilling champagne would store blood needed for transfusions. The grim realities of dealing with horrific blast and gunshot injuries, emergency surgery and maybe deaths, all the tragic consequences of conflict, the mopping up and repairing as well as possible of lives ripped apart in an instant, were discussed in the incongruous surroundings of a theatre and nightclub, as the spaces were walked and surveyed and considered by men who reflected that the carpets would have to come up because it was not hygienic to operate with them still down. Converting the rooms would take considerable time and effort, and continue for much of the voyage to the South Atlantic. There was another problem to be surmounted; getting casualties from the flight decks down to the hospital. *Canberra* had lifts, but they were useless for the job, being unable to take stretchers. Once again, though, the spirit of ingenuity and invention won through.

By now, the ship was gripped by constant speculation and debate. It was plain to both crew and passengers that the men who had boarded at Gibraltar were engaged on some vitally important task. Those who heard the World Service reports of the announcement in the House of Commons on Monday afternoon that the government was requisitioning ships could have made a shrewd guess about what was going on; they got a definitive answer the following evening. Scott-Masson summoned as many of his crew together as he could without giving the game away to the passengers and made the most extraordinary announcement of his – and their – careers.

'It was the night before Southampton that I was given the release to tell everybody what had happened and that the ship had been requisitioned by the Ministry of Defence and at that stage it was purely to take troops – we were even told which ones, it was 40 and 42 Commando and 3 Para down to some vicinity of the Falkland Islands – north of it, where we would transfer them to naval ships of some sort. Probably *Invincible* and *Hermes* were mentioned at the time, and I was asked to find out how many of my ship's company would volunteer to do this task. So in naval parlance I cleared the lower deck after dinner, which of course was very difficult on a passenger ship where you have all the people giving passenger service. So I got as many as I could into the forward restaurant – passenger restaurant – and announced that we had been requisitioned and what we were asked and expected to do, and I gave them 'til the following morning to report to their heads of departments those who would be prepared to go to the Falkland Islands or near the Falkland Islands in our capacity as a troop ship. And gratifyingly, next morning when the heads of departments reported to me, there was only one of my ship's company who didn't want to go, which was just remarkable, and he was an official conscientious objector – one of the junior officers – so you can say virtually 100 per cent volunteered.'

Gratifying it certainly was, but it was more, much more, than that. This was to be the first manifestation of a cheerful steadfastness amongst the crew that would endure throughout, even when they had their dark moments and needed the support of their friends in staving off fear. The public mood back at home was bullish, and in the closed environment of *Canberra* became distilled and intoxicating; the country had been insulted and it was jolly well not going to stand for it. The swift announcement of a task force and warships putting to sea had sharpened the appetite for a fight and fired the popular imagination; the notion of grubby, down-in-the-dumps, not-what-she-used-to-be Britain straightening her shoulders, dusting herself down and looking an aggressor in the eye fuelled a surge of patriotic fervour. All sorts of romantic and sentimental notions about standing alone against an enemy were abroad in a country no longer as sure of its identity as it once had been, and the ship was a microcosm of that; seizing on what seemed clear-cut right versus wrong provided clarity and purpose in an uncertain age. This was the chance to replay an heroic past all over again for generations longing for something to be proud of. Out of the blue, from the other side of the world and a land of which the public knew little beyond corned beef and curly-permed footballers to be wary of come the World Cup, emerged an identifiable adversary, hard-faced, grinning, triumphal as he paraded our lads with their hands clasped above their heads in surrender. That the country's leaders postured and preened in chocolate-soldier uniforms and chests full of gaudy decorations only helped in reinforcing their image as central casting villains for a people eager to unite and stand up to an aggressor who had terrorised fellow Brits and deserved a military boot up the arse in consequence. That the fight would be carried to the Falklands by ships also struck a chord with a public which liked to think they had an umbilical link to the sea, even if they came no closer to it than rolling up their trouser legs, taking their socks off and dipping their toes on a day trip to the coast.

The chance to be part of all this was irresistible, and the closeness of the crew, at all its different levels, played a key role; if one went, they all would. It was heady, exciting, gung-ho, and everybody wanted to be there. All were going to volunteer, from deck officers and engineers to bar stewards, hairdressers and entertainers. They would clamour to be aboard for this voyage. 'A certain amount of, "Let's go and get 'em", emerged among the crew,' said Don Cole, the 28-year-old second electrical officer. 'One guy had a T-shirt printed with "Falklands Task Force '82" on the front and "The Empire Strikes Back" on the reverse. There was a realisation after being told we would be asked to volunteer to make the trip: no one was forced to – we would have to sign on under a different set of rules that apply in a war scenario.' Cole knew more than enough to be caught up in the let's-get-'em school; his apprenticeship had been spent working on warships in the Vickers yard at Barrow-in-Furness, in Cumbria, and he was acutely aware of the risks, not least because he would be in the engine room, way, way down in the ship, where sound transmitted through the water boomed and echoed, and any impact would leave him far from aid. 'I had worked on many subs during my apprenticeship, and knew what submarines and torpedoes are capable of, and as I would be spending much of the time down below on the main switchboard, 32 feet below the waterline, I was a little worried to say the least.' Nevertheless, he did not hesitate to volunteer. 'I was single at the time, and it was a big adventure, so it wasn't a problem for me.'

For others, there was a professional imperative to volunteer. Susie West, the 30-year-old assistant surgeon, had joined *Canberra* for the world cruise on the clear understanding that there would be no job for her once it ended in April. Her role had been to look after the crew, but suddenly, unexpectedly, it seemed vital to her that she was aboard to help in whatever way she could: 'It seemed the obvious thing to me that I would actually be needed instead of just being part of the utilities of a cruise ship.' Angela Devine, too, was due to leave the ship, but felt drawn to stay: 'I wanted to go. What nurse wouldn't?'

Personal imperatives were at work too. Twenty-nine-year-old Sue Wood worked as assistant shop manager, and loved life on *Canberra*, which she had joined two years before. This had been the most memorable of world cruises – she and her boyfriend Graham, a barman, had decided to get married and tied the knot when the ship reached Hawaii. 'That was a big buzz around the ship, we had a party. They were asking for volunteers and Graham really wanted to go, and I thought if he wants to go, I ought to go with him.' In common with many, though, Wood never thought of the Falklands crisis leading to war and that the mobilisation of merchant shipping and the dispatch of a task force would fizzle into anti-climax: 'In all honesty, we thought we'd get to Land's End and it would all be over.' Her view was echoed at the highest level on board; Bradford would be staying as deputy captain. 'I think most people considered there would be a political settlement and we weren't really thinking about war at that time. I looked upon my voyage in *Canberra* as purely a cruise with a difference.' That sense of war being such a remote possibility that it could hardly be credited would persist in the minds of many on board for nearly a month to come, reinforced by ceaseless diplomatic activity – at least on the part of Britain and the US – to find a solution to the crisis.

But even as the crew talked themselves into going and their excitement mounted, the air of solidarity was shattered by a blunt instruction that was as bewildering as it was unsettling. Roughly half the ship's company were Asian, and even though they volunteered, they were told they would not be allowed to go. 'It certainly came as a big shock to us,' said Reed. 'We just got a message saying, "No foreign nationals", and it created huge problems; they were basically told to pack their bags and bugger off. We had an Indian deck crew, Pakistani engine crew and Goanese stewards; a bloody good crew.' This was a serious blow; the Asian seamen performed some of the most essential functions on the ship, and were highly valued both for their expertise and experience, as well as admired for their loyalty. Many had been with *Canberra* for years, and the various national groupings formed branches of the ship's family. Each ethnic group had its own quarters and galley where religious and dietary obligations were observed, and belonged to a long P&O tradition of employing substantial numbers of Asians that stretched back to the company's early voyages to the East.

There was also a hard-headed economic reason to use them in key roles in addition to their skills. In an era before pay discrimination on the grounds of race was declared unlawful, the Asian seamen were paid roughly a quarter of what their British counterparts received, about £80 a month compared to £74 a week. The National Union of Seamen had fought unsuccessfully for years for parity of pay, its most recent attempt being in 1978, but the inequality had remained. Now, though, the union flexed its muscles, and it would be those paid least who lost out. Word went round the ship that the governments whose nationals were aboard had requested they did not sail; the real reason lay closer to home. A terse memo to the P&O board noted: 'Asians (406) withdrawn from *Canberra* at NUS insistence, though deck and engine room crew had volunteered to remain.' In the union's view, the Falklands was a purely British crisis and only its nationals should sail. Its eye was on work for the pool of 3,000 unemployed British seamen, with the added incentive of what could potentially be a bumper payday denied the Asians.

Tuesday 6 April saw the government and the owners of requisitioned and chartered vessels agree normal pay plus 150 per cent danger money if the merchant ships went south of Ascension Island in the mid-Atlantic. The Asian crew would be housed in naval barracks when the ship reached Southampton before being flown back to their own countries at the government's expense, which was scant consolation. Scott-Masson said: 'They were not happy, because they were very worried that they were losing their jobs because there was no guarantee that the ship would return; and even if she did return, under what circumstances? And what would the future be? So yes, they were very upset, but had to accept.'

Events were moving at dizzying speed in the hours before Southampton, even as her passengers, still largely unaware that *Canberra* had been requisitioned, partied away the final night of their cruise of a lifetime. The strangeness of imagining what might well lie ahead in these public rooms full of laughter was not lost on those under no illusions about what retaking the Falklands would involve. Rick Jolly reflected: 'The dinner tables in the Pacific Restaurant sagged under multiple courses of an impeccable standard and there was a lively cabaret to follow. Looking around The Stadium nightclub with its plush fittings and thick carpet, it was very difficult to imagine bloodied operating tables and groaning wounded positioned there.' It was no less strange an evening for the Captain and his officers who had to maintain an unruffled facade of normality, undertaking the usual round of farewells and handshakes and chatter with passengers, even as they grappled with the linked issues of the loss of experienced crew, and who should stay on board. Scott-Masson said: 'Obviously, you did not want ladies' hairdressers, casino operators and various other fringe-type members of the ship's company who were necessary for paying passengers but would not be necessary for entertaining the troops – although the troops might have liked them. So there was a lot of discussion and we finally came up with a list of those we required, which in fact numbered roughly half of what we normally had as crew.' 'The crew took it very well,' said Reed. 'There was much hum-ing and hah-ing about who would go. The entertainment staff were not required, but they were saying, "We can stay and entertain the crew", and the waiters were all jostling for position – "Well, I've been here longer than so-and-so, so I should stay".'

One source of much of the hum-ing and hah-ing was over the female volunteers. The messages arriving on board had seemed clear. 'It was literally "no foreigners and no women"', said Reed. That enraged the women who had put themselves forward. Susie West recalled: 'I volunteered straight away to my senior doctor but the reply came back very quickly saying no, forget that, because women won't be allowed to go. It is going to be a military operation and they won't have any women. I was absolutely outraged. I couldn't believe that they could just say that.

I was a doctor and it didn't matter what sex I was.' The frantic pace of preparations to get *Canberra* converted and under way for the South Atlantic was plainly resulting in confusingly mixed messages; as West was being told she could not sail, P&O's chief medical officer was telephoning a 28-year-old nurse, Rosie Elsdon, who was on holiday, asking if she would be willing to serve. The mood amongst *Canberra*'s senior officers was that there should be no bar on women. The ship had substantial numbers of female crew, and there was no whiff of discrimination against them in normal circumstances. They were passionate about doing their bit, and the view that they should be allowed to was bolstered by an implied threat to kick up a stink in the press if they were excluded, according to Reed: 'They never actually threatened, but they let it be known that if we tried evicting them, there'd be a price to pay.' More importantly, they could play a vital part in the smooth running of *Canberra* on this extraordinary voyage.

The need for medical staff like West, Elsdon and Angela Devine – all of whose roles, at least initially, were to look after the crew – was obvious, but there would also be a huge range of administrative and practical tasks to be undertaken. Scott-Masson was told that the question of women sailing had gone to the government. 'I remember that even went up to Whitehall as to whether they would be allowed as they had volunteered, including these ladies' hairdressers and others. We had to make a decision, and finally it did come down from on high that, yes, women could go because anyway they fulfilled many important functions on the ship apart from the passenger ones. I mean my secretary for instance was a girl, and she was allowed to stay in the ship's company.' The ever-pragmatic Rudderham, with his long experience of trooping and the realities of getting large numbers of soldiers and their commanders on board and settled, instantly saw the value of the women who worked for him, not least those who staffed the Bureau, the ship's administrative heart. *Canberra* would be carrying very different passengers to those who usually came aboard, but organising their accommodation and smoothing the day-to-day running of the ship was akin to the normal requirements of cruising. He was also receptive to the ideas put forward by other staff so keen to stay that they were willing to take on very different roles. 'The Bureau staff could carry on doing administration and help with berthing. The ladies who had been doing bar service, well, that wasn't required, so they said "We could be like batmen and do cabin service for the officers", and that was agreed.'

Excitement at being part of a great adventure was one lure for those who volunteered, but so was a sense of duty. The willingness to serve her country burned brightly in Rosie Elsdon, from Cambridge, partly because the notion of doing so was deeply embedded in her family, and partly because she felt it was her destiny to go. She had joined P&O two years before, and was due to board *Canberra* for the first time in April, for four months of cruising in the Mediterranean, conveniently allowing her to meet friends in Italy. When the invitation came to sail with the task force, she did not hesitate.

I was very keen to go, partly because I come from a very service-orientated background: both my grandfathers were in the First World War and my parents were in the Air Force, my father was a Battle of Britain pilot, my brother was in the RAF, a Jaguar pilot at that time. I just felt thrilled at the opportunity to do my bit, even though I was a civilian. And I also felt somehow that it was right that I went, that it was somehow meant, which was quite important when we were under fire or heading into danger. I wasn't frightened of not coming home because I knew that whatever happened, it was the right thing. I was quite calm, although we had no inkling that we were actually going to get there. We thought like everyone else that we would just set sail and all the Argentinians would run away, and we didn't really think it was going to happen. When I was asked to go, my brother, who was in Germany with the Air Force, was horrified, he said, "I have trained all my life for this sort of thing and it's my little sister that goes to war".

She was to be one of 15 women selected to sail as part of a P&O crew whittled down from its usual 800 to 413. Everybody had a clearly defined role; all were considered essential to the running of the ship, from deck officers to engineers, from cooks to bedroom stewards, from carpenters to butchers, from shop staff to laundrymen. The government was at pains to play down the risks they faced; again and again it was emphasised that the merchant crews would be kept well clear of any possible fighting. *Canberra*'s fame and glamour made her the subject of intense interest, and the press was briefed that she was unlikely to come within 4,000 miles of the Falklands, the *Sun* reporting the day before she docked: 'The ship is expected to take troops to Ascension Island, where they will be switched to warships. It will not go into the battle zone, Whitehall sources said.'

The Wednesday dawned overcast as *Canberra* made her way into Southampton just as she had at homecoming after homecoming. As usual, everything ran like clockwork; she was bang on schedule, secured at 105 berth at 7.30am. There was an hour-and-a-half to go before the passengers disembarked, and it was time to let them in on the secret as they took their seats for breakfast. As he always did, Graham Harding joined those who had dined at his table during the cruise for a last meal, when Scott-Masson, his voice grave and his words measured, came on the loudspeakers to announce *Canberra*'s requisitioning. 'The response was quite electric,' said Harding. 'The hum of people talking became a roar, deafening conversations and excitement.' They wanted to shake the hands of crew, clap them on the backs, wish them well. 'When they left, they all left messages behind,' said Reed. 'Good luck, well done, bring it back in one piece.' There was even a touch of the last act of a stage whodunnit in the disappearance of the advance planning party to their cabins, where they shed sports jackets and slacks to re-emerge in uniforms. The announcement seemed like the trigger for *Canberra* to assume her new role; even as the passengers were preparing to leave, military and naval personnel were streaming on board. 'Before the passengers could even get off, there were lots of military-looking gentlemen coming up the gangways,' said Scott-Masson. 'And the passengers were all saying to them, "Have a go at them",

"Good on you".' By noon, the last passengers and their luggage had gone, and workmen from shipbuilders Vosper Thornycroft were coming aboard to begin the transformation from floating pleasure palace to troopship and helicopter landing platform.

It was only now that the ship was back home that those aboard realised the scale and scope of the operation that had been mounted in Southampton and beyond during those final few days before *Canberra* arrived. It was not just the planning of her conversion that had kept the lights burning long into the night; Sunday had seen the appointment of a Senior Naval Officer (SNO) who would work alongside Scott-Masson and head Naval Party 1710. He was Captain Christopher Burne, who recalled being summoned from his home in Somerset: 'I just happened to be between two jobs, so I was rung up and told to get going.' Get going he did, first being briefed in Plymouth and then heading to Southampton, where the naval party was swelling in numbers, eventually to more than 60.

The Falklands crisis had galvanised the Navy; every officer wanted to be part of the task force, even though they subscribed to the common view that it would all come to nothing. John Muxworthy, an energetic 39-year-old lieutenant commander, was no exception. 'For anybody in the military, this isn't being a hero. Nobody thought there was going to be a war, nobody thought anybody was going to get killed, it was just a gesture and they'd run away when we came. So it was an instinctive professional reaction that something's going on; it's active, it's operational, and I'd like to be in on it.' Like Burne, he was on leave between jobs, and telephoned his appointer, the officer who allocated postings. '"Hello, what do you want?", he said. "This Falklands thing – are you bringing any ships out?" He said, "Where are you?" I said, "I'm at home on leave, you should know that." "Ah yes, of course, right, get your bags packed, get yourself off to Southampton, you're now going to be the Supply and Liaison Officer onboard *Canberra*." And the conversation was about as long as that.'

After ringing back to make sure he had heard correctly, Muxworthy set off. He found the P&O offices in uproar. 'It was pandemonium, absolute bloody pandemonium. There were Royal Marine officers everywhere, there was Chris Burne – who I'd never met before – rushing about. There were people milling around, the phones were going non-stop, there'd been people sleeping there overnight, there were officers ringing up trying to get attached, there was a Royal Marines major rushing about being pompous. I met up with the P&O catering boss and we talked about food stores, how much food the ship should sail with, absolutely topped up, and we came out with some theoretical menus to ensure the food could last as long as possible.'

It was not just the naval and military personnel who were working flat out; so were P&O staff. The company was busy cancelling *Canberra*'s next four scheduled two-week cruises, up to 11 June, when she would have been due back from Vigo, and that meant sending out thousands of telegrams to disappointed passengers offering refunds, bookings on subsequent cruises or places on the new liner *Sea Princess*, which was due to sail on 13 May. That was for public consumption. Quietly, behind the scenes, P&O was thinking the unthinkable: what if the crisis did not fizzle out? What if *Canberra* was attacked and sunk? A day after the requisition notice was delivered to the company, it gave the government formal notification that it held the Department of Trade responsible for the cost of replacing her if she were lost. That possibility was almost too awful to contemplate, but nevertheless had to be considered, and in so doing, P&O turned its attention to how *Canberra* could be replaced. An amount of work had already been done; the loss of *Canberra* would be grievous, but an option for maintaining her niche in the luxury cruise market had also been identified. A memo drawn up for the board noted: 'It is difficult to assess a realistic value directly because (a) *Canberra* is not for sale; and (b) the market for large, complex, luxury passenger liners is virtually non-existent. She is an essential ship, fundamental to the future of P&O Cruises Ltd, and would have to be replaced immediately.' Her net worth to the company was estimated at £43m – later revised down to £35m – which was close to the cost of buying a ship P&O had already made enquiries about, sailing with the Norwegian American Line, a company struggling with financial problems. 'In practice, *Canberra* would probably not be rebuilt as she is.

And she would more likely be replaced – if she is lost – by purchase of an existing cruise liner similarly operating in the top segment of the market. One possibility (from the few realistic that exist) would be the nine-year-old *Vistafjord*, which from firm indications given to P&O by owners, could be available at $70 million (£39 million).'

Such deliberations had to remain strictly private. Outwardly, all was confidence. Scott-Masson was the ideal face of *Canberra*, and the reporters who interviewed him a few hours after she docked took away the impression of calm assurance underpinned by steely resolve that chimed with the mood of a country certain that upstart Argentine generals were no match for plucky old Britain. 'I shall take the ship wherever the Commander in-Chief of the Royal Navy decides to send me,' he told *The Times*. 'I have no fear whatsoever that anything might happen to my crew or my ship.' His ship was changing before his eyes. The newspapers noted that as Scott-Masson was speaking, she was being stripped of the trappings of luxury to which her passengers had long been accustomed. As men in naval uniform hurried on board, they were passing people carrying off potted palms and dryers from the hairdressing salon. Heavy curtains were being taken down, soft furnishings and breakable items removed. The *Canberra* would still be more comfortable than any troopship the men could have dreamed of, particularly those with experience of the 'Grey Funnel Line', as the naval transports were known. Still, compared to her normal state, she was spartan.

There was good reason for this beyond preserving expensive furnishings from possible damage. One of the greatest threats to *Canberra* keeping the naval planners awake at night was fire. This was not a warship where minimising the fire risk was part of the design and build; this was a floating hotel with the emphasis on opulence, full of wood and plastic that would burn all too easily. Vast quantities of flammable materials were part of the ship's fabric and could not be stripped out like cushions or curtains. Airy public rooms and spacious stairwells were blessings for passengers, but anathema to naval constructors, who saw them as areas through which a blaze could spread with alarming rapidity. Rigorous fire drills and precautions were a way of life on cruises, and would need to be even more exacting once the troops were on board and the ship was carrying more people than usual. Even with every precaution, though, *Canberra* would be nightmarishly vulnerable to fire if she was hit by a missile or bomb that touched off a blaze and trapped soldiers in their berths several decks down as the corridors filled with smoke; the consequences could be catastrophic. And then there was the glass, acres of it, vast picture windows allowing passengers to gaze out on the world floating by and *Canberra* to make her presence felt with a trademark blaze of lights at night. An explosion could send a lethal blizzard of glass shards through the upper decks – where the hospital would be.

An immense amount of work had to be done in what seemed an impossibly short time. *Canberra* was due to sail only two days hence, on the evening of Thursday 8 April. The weather had closed in, and a fine, steady rain soaked everybody to the skin as the dockside became crowded with stores and freight; food, ammunition, weaponry, medical supplies, additional fire-fighting equipment. The Sun Deck was filling up with big eight-foot storage containers known as chacons. Fork lift trucks buzzed in and out of the massive cargo sheds that opened onto the wharf with goods on pallets that were going up conveyors into the ship through the sea doors. There was a touch of black humour as the loading continued; boxes of corned beef marked 'Product of Argentina' went on to catcalls and laughter.

The soundtrack to it all came from 60 feet above, on deck, where the flight pads were being built, continuing hour after hour as daylight faded and night drew on; the cutting of metal, the showers of sparks from the welding torches, the groaning and creaking of huge sections of steel plating, the clanging and scraping of girders being bolted together into a lattice in the empty Bonito Pool, hammering, the shouts of the Vospers men, who although working flat-out, were falling behind schedule, hampered by the worsening weather. The wind had strengthened in the hours after *Canberra*'s arrival, causing problems for the floating crane brought in to lift aboard pre-fabricated 15-ton panels from barges that delivered them to the ship's side. The crane was lowering as well as lifting; large sections of the upperworks were being cut away. Guard rails and windbreaks went; anything that could obstruct a helicopter's approach was ruthlessly discarded and ended up on the dockside in a tangled heap. 'We had to keep an eye on that,' said Reed. 'We were recovering things like lifebelts and bringing them back.'

But the sense of purpose and spirit of co-operation between all sides was smoothing over difficulties. 'It was very good, people would listen to you,' added Reed. 'They'd say, "Can we do this?" and I'd say "Yes" and if I said, "No" they'd say, "Right, fine, we'll find some other way of doing it".' *Canberra* was undergoing a radical transformation, yet retained her grandeur. John Turner, whose first visit to the ship had coincided with her requisitioning, marvelled at that: 'She never lost her shape, that shape which is very recognisable and quite well ahead of her time, but it was certainly odd to see what was happening to some of the finer areas of the ship, particularly the Crow's Nest, to see that full of scaffolding and struts was a bit strange.'

The spirit of ingenuity that had sprung up in the few days since requisitioning would now equip *Canberra* to stay at sea indefinitely – and enable her to get wounded men into the hospital with a minimum of delay if she was called on to do so – thanks to two innovations that both had a touch of Heath Robinson about them. The first addressed one of the fundamental questions that had been asked of Michael Bradford when he had been summoned to Southampton – could she be refuelled at sea? This would be a first for a cruise ship. *Canberra* normally refuelled at her regular ports of call, and her bunkering system for taking on oil could not be used while she was under way. 'It was too low down in the ship and too dangerous to use in rough seas,' said Don Cole. 'So they had to come up with an answer, and they came up with the rather clever idea of using one of the goods lifts that ran from the stores quite low down up to the galley area.' Cole and fellow electrical officers took the lift out of commission. A lifeboat was taken off the starboard side and pipes installed through the bulkhead where it had been and down through the lift shaft into the ship's main bunkering pipe. Above the Promenade Deck, plates were welded to *Canberra*'s side that would support fuel lines hauled across from tankers, which could then feed directly into the newly-installed piping. A test showed that the system worked, but it would be slow. In port, *Canberra* could take on up to 1,800 tons of fuel an hour; at sea, she would take only 100 tons an hour, which would mean sailing close alongside a tanker for hours on end as it was pumped aboard. 'Imagine the concentration required for shipkeeping by the navigators to keep the ships so close for so long,' said Scott-Masson. 'We had to learn a lot, because I think it's probably unique that any passenger ship had ever been refuelled at sea by a tanker.'

If the adaptations to take on fuel were ingenious, the means of getting casualties from the flight deck to the hospital was inspired. There had been much head-scratching, and even more worry, about how to bring potentially critically injured men to the help they needed. There was nothing high-tech in the answer that a group of the Vospers men, plus a naval medic and a Royal Marine carpenter came up with. In fact, it would not have looked out of place aboard one of Nelson's ships, involving as it did a dock porter's trolley, a ramp and a length of rope. A bulkhead was cut out and a ramp of steel and plywood constructed from the flight deck to The Stadium at a 45-degree angle. The rear of the trolley rested against the slope supported by a front assembly that kept it horizontal as it was hauled up and down by the rope in the manner of a funicular railway. A casualty stretchered onto the trolley would remain flat as he was hauled smoothly down from deck to receiving area in a matter of seconds.

She was nearing readiness, almost prepared for the dangers and uncertainty that lay ahead. The military were by now firmly ensconced on board; the units she would carry were setting up their administrative offices where a day or two before all had been leisure. For Naval Party 1710, that meant the unlikely setting of Steiner's hairdressing salon. One of the three shops was stripped of its expensive perfumes and even more expensive jewellery to become the military force commander's office; 40 and 42 Commando found themselves in the photographic shop and the annexe to the Meridian Room respectively, and in the Writing Room, 3 Para's orders of the day supplanted letters and postcards home. She was braced for the arrival of the men whose daily lives would be run from each of these offices; outside all of them, the corridors rang to the sound of hammering as hundreds of yards of hardboard were laid over the carpets to save them from the soldiers' boots. *Canberra* was about to welcome her most unusual passengers.

CHAPTER FOUR

Give the Argies Some Bargie

THE FIGHTING men bound for *Canberra* were spread far and wide. Easter leave had begun and the first priority was to get them back to their bases. Contacting the troops was not so very different to how it had been in the run-up to the Second World War; notice boards were posted at railway stations ordering men to contact their units immediately. One young Para heading for Scotland to see his parents caught a glimpse of the order and brought an express train screeching to a halt as it hurtled through Newcastle station by hauling on the emergency cord. Those who could be contacted by telephone were, as officers and NCOs of 40 and 42 Commando and 3 Para set about making scores of calls. The families of others were surprised to find police officers knocking on their doors with the message that their son should contact his superiors without delay, the addresses of those proving troublesome to track down having been passed to their local stations. The shrewdest amongst them guessed what might be happening as they heard the announcement of the task force on the news and got in touch without being summoned.

For their commanders, the call came early. It was 4am on the Friday – before the Argentine invaders went charging ashore – when the bedside telephone rang at the Dartmoor home of the commanding officer of 42 Commando, 46-year-old Lieutenant Colonel Nick Vaux. In common with most of his men, Vaux had just begun three weeks' leave after winter training in Norway and was booked on a flight to the United States for a holiday with friends there, with whom he had arranged to meet that evening. Instead of taking him to the airport as scheduled, Vaux's staff car returned him to Bickleigh Camp in Devon.

Later that same day, the CO of 3 Para, 39-year-old Lieutenant Colonel Hew Pike, just embarked on a weekend in Wales with his family, was called by his second-in-command and briefed. He raced back to the battalion's headquarters at Tidworth, in Hampshire, where, as in Devon, a whirl of activity was already under way. Even though on leave, 3 Para was designated as a spearhead battalion, on standby for immediate deployment anywhere in the world, which Pike had guessed might be to Northern Ireland, where tension and sectarian violence were on the increase. 'Knowing they're on standby and being a parachute battalion, they tend to keep their ear to the ground wherever they are, so we did post notices at stations to get them to come back,' he said. 'One guy came back on the Saturday morning from the Isle of Wight, where he was getting married that afternoon. He was going to miss his wedding, so we turned him round, got him married and told him to report back on the Monday morning.' All the commanding officers faced a clamour of requests to be included; just as naval personnel were calling everyone they could think of to try and get aboard a ship, so it was with Paras and Marines. Nobody wanted to be left out, and there was bitter disappointment for those who were. One of Pike's company commanders was American, and his request for permission to go went to the Chief of Staff of the American Army in the Pentagon – ironically, a sometime golfing partner of General Galtieri – before being finally refused by the US State Department.

On the Sunday, when the final arrangements for requisitioning *Canberra* were put in place, Vaux, Pike and the commanding officer of 40 Commando, Lieutenant Colonel Malcolm Hunt, attended a briefing in Devonport with the commander of 3 Brigade, Brigadier Julian Thompson, at which they began to grapple with the logistics of fighting a campaign in the South Atlantic, and started to learn about the Falklands. There was much to learn. In common with the rest of Britain, many within the three units knew nothing about this distant outpost, even senior officers. 'I had absolutely no idea where the Falklands was, none at all; it was extraordinary how ignorant one was,' said Major Roger Patton, the

40-year-old second-in-command of 3 Para. 'We sort of thought when it first came up it was some island off Scotland because it sounded like the Shetlands.'

His vagueness over the geography was shared all the way down to the most junior ranks. At just 17, Mick Southall, a private in 3 Para's B Company, had finished his training only three weeks before. 'Everyone was looking up at Scotland, and wondering how the Argentinians had got up there,' he said. 'Honestly, everyone was saying, "Are the Falklands in Scotland?"' Others, though, knew better. Chris Sheppard, a 24-year-old Marine in 42 Commando, had served a year on the islands as part of the small garrison. 'The good thing was that the section commander had also been there, so we were more than amused to be going back to that place because we knew it quite well and we didn't particularly like it. I immediately knew we'd be going back there to get it because I'd been to Argentina; I knew their mentality, they weren't going to leave and I knew Thatcher wasn't going to let this go by, so I was foaming at the mouth like a mad dog. I wanted to get down there and kill someone, basically.'

Such a gung-ho attitude was absent from the commanding officers' deliberations. They were under no illusions about the scale and hazards of the task ahead if diplomacy came to nothing. 'I was conscious that this was a real emergency,' said Pike. 'We're up against a potential enemy with a proper air force, a proper navy, an army that includes tanks and artillery – in fact, on paper, quite a formidable opposition. By the end of that weekend, we were really in the thick of it and learning about the Falkland Islands and the background to the whole thing, all the stuff we really didn't know anything about at all. But it was, of course, extremely exciting and we were thrilled to be involved in it.'

Surprise followed surprise as events unfolded over the weekend; all three commanding officers were taken aback to be told that their units would be sailing south aboard *Canberra*. 'It was totally unexpected, and came at very short notice,' said Vaux. 'To our astonishment we're told we're off to Southampton to embark in a luxury liner, and as we're going through that process we learned that she was in Gibraltar. I'd sent a young lieutenant, Tony Hornby, as part of the advance party and when we met up, he said to me, "This is a magic ship; these people are really here to help us, they're being so flexible." That was unexpectedly reassuring and a very cheerful revelation.' If the three units knew little about the Falklands, they knew even less about *Canberra* and the world she occupied. Upmarket cruising with its fine dining, dressing for dinner and well-heeled, often elderly, passengers was as alien to the young soldiers, many of whom were still in their teens, as a different universe. 'When we were told we were going on SS *Canberra*, nobody knew what that was,' said Guy 'Bungy' Williams, serving with 42 Commando. 'We had no idea it was a liner. I was in K Company, and most of us were very young, mostly 18. I'd had my 18th birthday in the March.'

The youth of substantial numbers of the Marines and Paras was as much of a surprise to many of the P&O crew as the ship was to the troops; these passengers appeared especially fresh-faced in contrast to the blue-rinse brigade who customarily cruised on her. Those not yet 18 would not have been allowed to serve in Northern Ireland, but could be deployed to fight, kill, or potentially be killed or maimed in the South Atlantic – provided their parents gave permission. 'I had to ring my mum and ask if it was OK to go,' said Southall. 'Bless her, she said, "Be careful." She didn't say, "Don't do anything silly," but she did say, "Don't make any mistakes".' How young so many of these soldiers were was not lost on their officers and NCOs either. At 27, with 12 years' service under his belt, Laurie Bland, a Corporal in 3 Para, classed himself as mature and experienced. 'You've got your section, seven guys, to look after and one of them was only 17. I've got a lad there who can't go in a pub, can't go in a bookies, can't vote, but he can go 8,000 miles away and do his best for his country. By virtue of taking those kids there, I'm beholden to their mums and dads to bring them back.'

The teenage troops who sought their parents' permission to sail south with the task force used the opportunity to say their farewells. Their older comrades grabbed whatever chance they could to speak to or see loved ones, amid the hectic preparations. For Laurie Bland, a father of two daughters, Lisa and Kirsty, aged one and four, that meant a hurried trip to see them and his wife, Sharon, in Aldershot: 'It was my daughter's first birthday, and we had a little party for her, and she took her first steps as well, which was quite poignant, and my eldest daughter started school at the same time. You think that if 3 Para's ready, the world's ready, but *Canberra* wasn't ready, so there was a bit of a delay. I went anyway; you can't keep saying goodbyes, just get it over with.'

Each did his best to reassure those closest to him. Steve Brabham, a 28-year-old sergeant in 3 Para, played down what might happen to soothe the worries of his fiancée, Jacqueline. 'I was due to get married on the 28th of August, so I said, "It's alright love, I'm only going for a holiday cruise, about a month and we'll be back, don't worry about the wedding." Anyway bless her, she went through and continued with all the arrangements, and she was in a real state, it was a testing time.'

In whatever way they were expressed, and at all levels, the farewells were profoundly moving for both the soldiers and those who loved them. A few days afterwards, Hew Pike set down in a letter to his wife, Jean, how the car taking him to Southampton turned the wrong way for him to give a last wave to her and two of their children, William, 12, and Arabella, 14, as they stood at the landing window of their house: 'I'm sorry the car turned the wrong way. Probably just as well! I'm sorry too that my goodbyes were rather short but it really would have been too tearful otherwise, I feel. Poor little William was almost in tears and you certainly were, and no doubt Beezee [Arabella] would have joined in! Anyway, God bless you all.'

Underpinning everything was ceaseless activity; lorries rumbled through the gates of the bases hour after hour, delivering stores and equipment. Normal procurement procedures were discarded; items that customarily took weeks to arrive appeared overnight, and the loading of stores began onto four-ton lorries that were dispatched to Southampton. There were problems to be sorted out; it took Pike days of arguing to win 3 Para then state-of-the-art Clansman radios to replace antiquated equipment. In Devon, 42 Commando's arctic kit had not been fully unpacked since the unit's return from Norway, which was causing headaches. Nevertheless, the Marines and Paras were ready to go.

They were, unexpectedly, to be joined by a group of men who would win a uniquely affectionate place in the hearts of both civilians and military personnel aboard *Canberra*. The designated role of the 37 members of the Royal Marines Band of Commando Forces, under the command of their director of music, 37-year-old Captain John Ware, had been to guard the home bases while 40 and 42 Commando sailed south. Now though, Ware was told that the band would be sailing with them, attached to the medical squadron as paramedics and stretcher bearers.

Military bands had a long and proud history of going to war where, in addition to boosting morale with concerts, the musicians provided invaluable support to the fighting men. So it would be again. The decision to send the band to the Falklands was taken by Thompson and Major-General Jeremy Moore, commander of Commando Forces. For public consumption, though, the deployment of the band had to be discreet. 'They had both said that they wanted us to take our instruments because they were very aware of what the value of having a group of musicians making music around could be,' said Ware. 'But the stipulation was that we were not allowed to carry all this equipment over the gangway. All the band equipment, instruments, music stands, music, had to be stowed in a chacon. The main reason for that, of course, was everybody understood that there could be some adverse publicity if the media got hold of the fact that there were a load of Marines walking along the gangway of the *Canberra* to go to war carrying trombones and that sort of thing. So, to that extent we had to be a little secretive about it.'

Embarkation might be kept low-key, but before that the band had the chance to show its mettle by playing for a farewell parade that Vaux had decided on to salute Moore, soon to retire, and his long and distinguished association with 42 Commando. The General addressed the troops, and then there was a moment when Vaux allowed himself a touch of flamboyance in giving the final order: '42 Commando, to the South Atlantic – Quick March.' The order attracted a blaze of publicity in the press and on television; if, in Southampton, Scott-Masson had radiated assurance, so here too all was confidence and purposefulness as the commando marched crisply away. In Devon and Hampshire, men boarded coaches bound for the port, where embarkation was due to begin at midday on Thursday 8 April. Hunt, Pike and Vaux set off in their staff cars. On board *Canberra*, they would be under the authority of Colonel Tom Seccombe, brought in at the last moment as deputy commander of 3 Brigade. He was a highly experienced soldier who would be in overall command of all the military personnel on board, and could also provide leadership of the brigade should anything happen to Thompson and his staff, who were aboard HMS *Fearless*. There was another reason for his presence, as Thompson wrote later: 'His sense of humour and abundant common sense were to be a priceless asset during the voyage south, controlling the three strong-willed commanding officers embarked in *Canberra*, who for days on end were not under the eye of their Brigade Commander.'

A group of civilians unconnected to either the military or P&O was also heading for Southampton to join the ship. After days of lobbying from Fleet Street, the Royal Navy had reluctantly agreed to make space for 13 journalists, shepherded by two minders from the Ministry of Defence press office. Reporters were already at sea with the HMS *Hermes* battle group, but permission for them to go had been granted only grudgingly. The Navy was no keener on having journalists aboard *Canberra* but relented in the face of pressure. They came from major national newspapers, the *Daily Telegraph*, *Daily Mirror*, *The Observer*, *The Sunday Times*, and the *Evening Standard*, as well as the BBC, ITN and Independent Radio News, the *Glasgow Herald* and the *Express and Star*, Wolverhampton, representing the regional press in England and Wales. Dispatches would be pooled for use by all newspapers and broadcasters. Their deployment had the same air of urgency and improvisation that characterised the rest of the operation to get *Canberra* to sea as quickly as possible.

John Shirley was *The Sunday Times* reporter assigned to go, but did not know for certain that he had a place on the ship until a colleague placed a note on his desk bearing the message, 'Pack your knickers'. Even though excited about going, he believed, in common with so many others, that the Falklands crisis would blow over. Besides, he had a personal imperative to join the ship. 'I had been having an affair with the secretary on the Insight team, which had just broken up, and I said, "Great, three weeks, that's just fantastic." Three weeks and it will get settled. I'll sail down to Africa, write a couple of stories, by the time I get back, she will have got over it, and I will have got over it, so I was mad keen to go.' There were hoops to be jumped through to satisfy officialdom, and they revealed the bizarre nature of the operation under way, as well as how long it had been since the Navy had mounted anything on this scale. The reporters were ordered to the Ministry of Defence to sign the Official Secrets Act and be issued with accreditation papers. 'It was absurd,' said Shirley. 'All these accreditation papers are in English and Arabic. All these things had been printed for Suez, they hadn't done this sort of stuff since 1956 – nonsense, complete nonsense.

Kim Sabido, from Independent Radio News, was also taken aback by the archaic nature of the documentation: 'There was this little green book with advice for war correspondents, and it was so old it was unbelievable. They didn't have any template to run things off apart from Suez; it was all being done on the hoof and it was so surreal, you couldn't take in all that was happening.'

The surreal air persisted when the correspondents, armed with their Arabic credentials, arrived in Southampton. 'It was weird,' said Sabido. 'We were all milling about at the port trying to find somebody who knew what was going on, talking to the other reporters, you've got your suitcase that you've just managed to get shut and your two pairs of shoes and you're talking to the MoD people.' Eventually, only a few hours before *Canberra* sailed and after a deal of uncertainty over who would be going, the journalists were gathered in the bar of an hotel, where they were addressed by Christopher Burne, the ship's Senior Naval Officer. His relationship with them would, at least initially, be strained but for now he was keeping whatever reservations he had about having reporters on board under wraps. The late Jeremy Hands, of ITN, wrote of him, 'Six foot plus, brimming with confidence and authority, this Captain of the Queen's Navy was an awesome sight.' Burne was brisk in what he had to say, noted Hands. 'You're all coming with us. I insisted on it, and despite opposition from other quarters they let me have my way on this point at least. So I'm delighted to have you with me. OK? Super. OK, some of you will be in the Asian quarters, alright? But at least we'll get you there. OK?'

So much for the accredited correspondents. Resourceful interlopers desperate for a place resorted to subterfuge, counting on the frenetic atmosphere to cover them slipping aboard. John Muxworthy recalled, 'We actually had people trying to smuggle themselves on board. One bloke who came along picked the wrong person, because I was doing liaison with the press as well. This chap came up and said, "Excuse me, I'm from the daily something-or-other, where's my cabin?" So I said, "Ah yes, hang on a moment, I don't seem to have you on my list. Where's your letter of authority?" "Oh it's all been arranged by telephone." So I told him to wait there a moment and I got the master at arms to stay with him, and about ten minutes later when we verified he didn't have permission, he was almost frogmarched off the ship.'

The pace of work aboard *Canberra* was, if anything, quickening as the scheduled embarkation time for the first troops approached. It was becoming plain that the flight decks were unlikely to be completed in time for a scheduled sailing of 8pm on the Thursday, and it looked increasingly likely that her departure would be delayed for 24 hours. Technical problems were being grappled with for hours on end, amongst them the installation of satellite communication equipment. 'It was very new technology then,' said Graham Harding. 'They got one wired in, and the bloody thing wouldn't work. I couldn't get any life out of it, so they had to pinch a demonstration model out of the agents in London and get it down by truck. They slammed it in and that one worked.' Issues and new challenges arose constantly; it occurred to the Naval party that *Canberra*'s trademark blaze of lights would have to be blacked out if she entered hostile waters or she would be a prime target for submarines, and so there was a scramble to get bolts of canvas aboard to cover windows along with masking tape to hold it in place. Electrical officers already busy as part of the conversion were set to isolating circuits that could turn off whole banks of lights at the flick of a switch.

The practicalities of feeding the embarked forces were a constant preoccupation; the Asian crew barred from sailing had included half the cooks and those who did preparation work in the galley. Eleven Naval cooks joined the ship to help, but *Canberra* would still have far fewer people than usual turning out meals – albeit to a much less luxurious standard – and getting on for twice as many mouths to feed than she was accustomed to. Sustaining the troops meant stores were still pouring on board, and every spare square foot was being taken. 'We gradually filled up,' said Maurice Rudderham. 'We filled all the store rooms with large quantities of long life milk. We just didn't have enough room. We had all the vestibules full of cartons of milk, plenty of sugar, flour, the basics we had to make sure we had.' *Canberra*'s role as a troopship had gripped the popular imagination to such an extent that in addition to the supplies coming aboard, offers of extra food and drink were being made from all directions. Supermarket chains donated chocolate and sweets, breweries offered cans of beer. Another offer, too, was graciously accepted: top-shelf soft-porn magazines from high street newsagent W H Smith, the centrefolds of which brightened the cabins of young soldiers in the weeks ahead.

Military supplies continued coming aboard relentlessly, and resulted in *Canberra* being massively overloaded by well over 10,000 tons when she set sail. But such was the urgency to get her under way, and her vital role as a troopship, that concerns over the effect this could have on her at sea were waved aside by government officials. The dockside cranes were swinging chacon after chacon onto the deck, and every hour seemed to bring new requests to get even more on board. 'They'd come up to you, "Can you find room for another 2,000 cases of compo rations?"' said Martin Reed. '"Yes, probably, when do you need it, how much will it weigh? Don't know either. Well, probably won't use it for some time, which is OK, that means we can put it relatively low in the ship".'

But as additional consignments kept coming in, and the tonnage mounted, Reed became increasingly concerned that *Canberra* was over-loaded, which could seriously affect her stability at sea. He was right; the company providing P&O's technical support confirmed that she was 13 inches lower in the water than she should be, way over her maximum legal load limit. 'These requests for extras kept adding up, and to be 13 inches over our mark was a hell of a lot,' said Reed. 'It's something like 800 tons an inch. So we got hold of the Department of Trade inspectors and they just came down and painted a new line on the ship's side and we got a new loading certificate saying it's all fine.' And that was before the troops arrived with their personal kit and weapons; *Canberra* would set sail with approximately 3,000 people on board, roughly twice as many as she usually carried, which of course in itself presented Reed with difficulties. 'The problem was all the kit they had, we had to work out were they going to dump it in the cabins or somewhere else; and if they did that, where were they going to put it?'

Amongst those already aboard were 129 crew new to the ship, drawn from the pool of unemployed seamen brought in to replace the Asians. 'They came from everywhere,' said Reed. 'Ex-ferrymen, ex-cargo ship, ex-everything you could think of, except passenger ship. It took quite a long time to knock everything together. I was very lucky, got a bloody good bosun, and one of his best mates was handy as well, so right away, I was OK, but some of the crew who turned up were rather strange.' Indeed they were, not least one epic drunkard who eventually had to be confined to his cabin. He and a handful of others who were simply not up to their jobs would be offloaded at Ascension Island and sent back to Britain. 'Deck seamen were pretty straightforward, you've just got to teach them the oddities of the ship,' added Reed. 'Engineering was more difficult.' The first engineering officer, Norman Pound, said, 'Most of them were OK, but the odd one wasn't. Fortunately, there was enough engineering officer expertise to run the ship. If push had come to shove, with assistance from about a dozen, we could have sailed with anybody.'

The troops were arriving at Southampton and for 3 Para there would be an infuriating exchange of messages with the ship as the men waited at a Territorial Army base for their turn to embark. 'We got this message that we were to take our boots off, because boots could not be worn, and men were to get into sports shoes,' recalled Lawrie Ashbridge, the Regimental Sergeant Major. Even with acres of hardboard laid to protect *Canberra*'s carpets, it was apparent there were those aboard who still fretted over the impact of military feet. This did not go down well with the Paras, and a suitably robust response went back. 'It was "Up your pipe, pal",' said Ashbridge. 'Then another message countermanding that, "All right, you don't have to take your boots off". Alright, it was a cruise ship, and they were thinking, "Typical soldier, going to be coming on here in their boots," and yes we are, and we're not taking them off, either. Can you imagine the press covering it and seeing us all in daft footwear?'

The Marines began boarding first, and lost no time in engaging in some poker-faced gamesmanship at the expense of their rivals in the Paras. 'They bagged all of the good accommodation, and saved the lower decks for the Paras,' said Muxworthy. 'When the Paras came on board, they explained that they had saved this accommodation because the Paras were not used to being at sea and the lower decks were much more stable than the upper decks, so there were the Royals in huge luxury cabins which were rather better than those the Paras had.' The groundwork for this plausible con trick had, at least in part, been laid by the bright young lieutenant that Vaux sent to join the advance party in Gibraltar, Tony Hornby. 'He was one of those people who was naturally numerate and Hornby absolutely dazzled the rest of the team about how many cabins 42 Commando needed,' said Vaux. 'When we were all embarked, we realised that we'd got about a quarter more accommodation than everybody else, and my lot told me this and I thought "That's great." People started muttering about it and one was able to say, "Well, come on, we're all settled in now," but eventually it became a major issue and it was all thrashed out very amicably in a series of meetings.'

By early Thursday afternoon, the clamour of the dockside with cranes busy, the Vosper Thornycroft men still labouring flat out on the flight decks and a human chain passing stores from hand to hand as they piled into the ship was added to by throngs of soldiers loaded down with kit and weapons, making their way laboriously up the gangplanks. As NCOs barked orders to marshal the troops, embarkation was orderly but slow, because of the sheer weight each man carried. Robert Fox of the BBC wrote, 'They seemed like giant snails carrying mountains of equipment on their backs, water bottles, shovels, pickaxes, sleeping bags and scruffy rolls of foam rubber, their vital under-matting, were slung every which way across the bergens, or rucksacks.' The sight of the great white liner that was to take them into the unknown made an indelible impression on all who boarded her, from the most experienced to the least. Vaux said, 'What a wonderful, elegant, pristine ship it was, in comparison to what we were used to going to sea in. This was just amazing.' 'It was this strange dream of us going to war in this boat,' recalled Roger Patton. The teenage Mick Southall was over-awed by the sheer scale of *Canberra*. 'The first thing that struck me was the size of the two funnels at the back. I thought, "God, it's absolutely huge." It was just massive and incredibly difficult to get round at first.' To help with that, there were signs and diagrams everywhere, arrows that pointed the way and men posted on staircases to direct troops to their cabins. There were also darkly humorous 'welcome on board' signs all over the ship, which read, 'P&O Sunshine Cruises welcomes 40-42 Commando, Third Paras, across the Atlantic with dry feet, courtesy of the *Canberra*'.

The men needed every pointer the crew could give them. *Canberra* was a maze of passageways, stairways, vestibules and public rooms that opened onto decks. This was like no troopship they had ever seen, let alone imagined, as they absorbed names and locations. The Crow's Nest, at the top of the ship, had floor-to-ceiling picture windows commanding a view over the fo'c'sle, swivelling bucket chairs, decorative black-and-white buoys port and starboard, semi-circular bar, and a marble spiral staircase that led down three decks to the Meridian Room on B Deck, all genteel pink furniture and ornate light fittings, a piano to accompany civilised conversation still in place. The William Fawcett Room aft on the same deck, a bright and airy old-fashioned palm court, was the other large room.

The Stadium, stripped of its velvet drapes and seating, remained recognisable as a theatre even though medical supplies and equipment were piling up; the Alice Springs Bar, with its wipe-clean furniture still resembled a poolside lounge. Food, always on the minds of troops, led them to the restaurants on E Deck; the Pacific, where officers would eat, elegant and low-ceilinged; the Atlantic, set aside for the men, spacious and more functional. The cinema, wood-panelled with comfortable red seating, caused a stir of excitement; whatever the voyage held, they would at least be entertained, even if finding their way back to their cabins after a film led them into wrong turns for days to come.

It was not only the troops who found boarding *Canberra* somewhat disorientating. So did Rosie Elsdon, who arrived in the midst of embarkation.

'It was chaos. It was a real shock when we arrived in Southampton because normally you see all the passengers waiting, you see all the food going on, but that day there were soldiers everywhere, and they were all carrying their bergens and their guns. I don't think I'd seen a gun before, and it was quite scary seeing all those soldiers ready for action. I didn't know my way round the ship because I'd never been on board before, and they kept asking me the way, because I was in uniform, and I said, "I'm sorry, I don't know any more than you do" and it was so confusing. There were so many different uniforms, so many different dots and stripes and colours. A friend of mine who was in the Army came down that day, and he wrote out a picture of all the different ranks and bits and pieces to help me, which was very useful.'

She had hardly got on board before being unsettled still further by a blunt reminder of what might lie ahead. 'One of the first things was this green form being thrust into my hand saying "Will you write a will" and at 28 I'd never thought about writing a will, so that made me gulp, and I thought, "Oh gosh!"'

The decision was taken to delay sailing until the following day, principally because the Vospers team was awaiting another delivery of steel for the flight decks. Once again, they would work through the night. It was now that the troops heard from Scott-Masson over the loudspeakers for the first time, as he welcomed them on board with an address touched by humour.

'This is an unusual role for this ship and we hope you will be as happy as the passengers that we normally carry – but of course with the added advantage that you are not paying for it. The P&O has a long history of association with Her Majesty's Services and we are delighted to welcome on board the Third Battalion, the Parachute Regiment, 40-42 Commando and all the embarked services personnel. We believe this voyage to the sunshine cruising area, for which we are well adapted, will provide a unique experience for those on board. Nobody knows exactly what the future holds for us, but I have no doubt that working together we shall accomplish everything that is asked of us and, believe me, you have the full support of all the ship's company which I command. It has been most encouraging to receive an enormous amount of good wishes for the unusual deployment that we are about to embark on.'

There were wry smiles at the South Atlantic being termed 'the sunshine cruising area' but it helped to break the ice with his new passengers. It was his ship, and his way of starting to establish a working relationship with the men commanding the troops was a round of hospitality akin to the routine of cruising. 'That evening, Dennis Scott-Masson gave a very elegant reception for the commanding officers up on the bridge,' Vaux recalled. 'I admired that, when you think of all the pressure and problems and worries that he had. The whole attitude from him, and everybody all the way downwards was to be as helpful as possible.' It made perfect sense to host them for drinks; the senior P&O crew could start getting to know their military counterparts, try to find common ground. In their turn, the military officers could begin to take the measure of the men running the ship. Two days later, Scott-Masson would follow up the reception by hosting a dinner.

It was time for the P&O crew to say their farewells, just as the soldiers had a day or two before. The company was already putting in place arrangements to issue a weekly newsletter to the families of those aboard, and now it set about issuing passes for the port, not always with the greatest sensitivity for individual feelings. 'I was told that if you were married and had a family, they could come and see you in Southampton before the ship sailed off,' said Susie West. 'But if you were single then nobody could come. And I was absolutely furious; I had been away for three-and-a-half months and I actually just wanted to see my mother and my family. I felt I was being discriminated against hugely just because I didn't have a husband. I kicked up a fuss and eventually she was allowed on board.' Preparing for the visit focussed West's mind on the risks she was running, as she gathered together her souvenirs of the world cruise to hand over to her mother. 'I had bought some beautiful leather boots in Naples and I thought I can't take those with me, so I'll send them home and if I get killed in action one of my sisters can wear these gorgeous boots.'

Families were wondering aloud about keeping in touch and possible censorship of letters. Rosie Elsdon and her parents came up with an ingenious solution.

'My parents and I had this code, although we didn't think I'd really get down to the Falklands, we knew that if I did, I wouldn't be able to say where I was. Strawberry meant that I was at Ascension Island, blackberry meant I was in the Falklands and gooseberry meant South Georgia. I would put that somewhere in the postcard or the telegram, so that from that word, they would know where I was, and I did use it. I'd say "The blackberries are growing well," or something like that. And then just before we sailed, my father gave me his St Christopher, which he'd had in his pocket all through the Battle of Britain, and he gave it to me with tears in his eyes. This St

Christopher had always brought him back from his sorties. It hadn't always brought him back in one piece – he was shot down and injured quite badly – but he always survived and he gave me that St Christopher to say, "Come back safely".'

Good Friday, 9 April, dawned cold, windy and dull. The daylight hours were once more filled with non-stop activity as yet more stores arrived, and the Vospers men kept up a punishing pace. The midships flight deck was almost complete, but there was a long way to go forward of the bridge. They would have to be finished at sea, no easy task for the 26 workmen who agreed to sail, especially if the weather was rough. The eyes of all Britain were on *Canberra*, television and radio broadcasts full of the imminent departure. As the day wore on, the bank holiday traffic around Southampton grew ever heavier as the loved ones of those aboard headed for the docks to see her off, and well-wishers found whatever vantage point they could to watch her leave. They crowded into Mayflower Park, stretching down to the water's edge, which by late afternoon was packed to capacity with thousands, shoulder to shoulder. Many more lined the Hythe shoreline or found spaces on Town Quay. Almost unnoticed, the ferry *Elk*, berthed not far away, laden with 3 Brigade's hardware, got under way for the voyage south. Her orders were to keep close company with *Canberra* and a warm kinship would develop between those aboard the two ships.

The star of the show was the focus of a wave of patriotic fervour; the public imagination had been caught by the idea of this elegant liner setting sail to help right a wrong. It had been less than three days since she had arrived home to discharge her suntanned, well-fed passengers in the bright colours of holiday clothes, their place now taken by lean, hard-faced, determined troops in khaki champing at the bit for the chance to fight for their country. The memory of the pool around which cocktails had been served only a few sunsets ago seemed to belong to another age, no clue of it visible beneath the sheets of dull steel plating braced for the load of military helicopters.

The news bulletins ticked off the hours and the signs that she was being readied to sail; the clang of the doors on her side being closed up, the crane that lifted huge tonnages of stores and steel aboard towed away, the bustling arrival on the dockside of two military bands, one from the Parachute Regiment, the other from the Royal Marines, to play her off. They struck up as the light began to fade, locked in rivalry as to which could stir the crowd most deeply with music embedded in the national psyche, and on this evening of all evenings guaranteed to bring a lump to the throat of all who heard it – 'Rule Britannia', 'Land of Hope and Glory', the Royal Navy march 'Heart of Oak', and the regimental marches of the Royal Marines and the Parachute Regiment respectively, 'A Life on the Ocean Wave' and 'Ride of the Valkyries', each cheered to the darkening sky, the roars of the crowd vying with those from the ship as they competed and communed as closely as the bands.

From everywhere banners swirled, heartfelt and punning alike; COME BACK SAFE AND SOON, GIVE THE ARGIES SOME BARGIE, most often simply GOOD LUCK. Woven through the music, and often enough through tears as well, declarations of love were shouted to those now gathering at the ship's rail. From out of the twilight, three tugs festooned with good luck messages chugged towards *Canberra* and came alongside. At 8.13pm, her last line was clear, and she eased out into the Channel as the bands played 'We Are Sailing'. It was a moment of intense emotions, of excitement, trepidation, even incredulity that this was really happening; try as they might, many of the soldiers and P&O crew at the rail could not hold back their own tears, and they flowed as freely amongst those waving and shouting out a last 'I love you' from the shore as the ship got underway.

There had been no scene like this in Britain since the end of Empire, a troopship setting course for conflict in some distant land, and it unleashed a great wave of nostalgic sentiment. However peculiar and anachronistic it seemed to be embarking on a 19th-century style colonial war over a place few knew much about towards the end of the 20th century, there was in these moments an upsurge of pride that sent shivers down the spines of the people who had gathered to see this, or watched on television. This stately liner, her brilliantly white paintwork a beacon for a just cause and the men in uniform waving and shouting their farewells was the embodiment of the best the country had. Nick Vaux, on the bridge wing, drink in hand, soaked up the extraordinary atmosphere. 'It was the first time that one appreciated that the nation was really quite psyched into this, all those people. But one was still quite bewildered by the whole thing.'

There would be no blackout for now; *Canberra* was in her pomp, proudly displaying herself, her lights reflecting on the water. She sounded her whistle as she passed Royal Pier and the troops on deck snapped to attention; the sonorous boom of it in the darkness touched off cheering and waving from the crowds muffled against the chill night air in the park and on the foreshore, who had waited hours to be part of this moment, hoisting children to their shoulders for the sight of it, just for the memory. A cacophony of car horns answered her as drivers flashed their headlights and emergency vehicles switched on their blue flashing lights in salute. Up above, on a hillside far from the water, the residents of a block of flats had synchronised their lights to flash out 'Good Luck'. In all her years of departing Southampton, there had never been a send-off remotely to rival this.

'It was very strange that night, very, very moving,' recalled Martin Reed. 'All the way along the coast you had people flashing their lights. But when you looked alongside, instead of seeing the blue rinse brigade, you've got all these young troops and there was a lot of apprehension that some of them wouldn't be coming back.' The soldiers who had waved and blown kisses and shouted that they would be home soon knew that only too well; for every one that was exhilarated, another was pensive. All too soon, the cheers were left behind, and the lights of home fell astern. As those ashore strained for a last glimpse, the white of *Canberra* faded into ghostliness, melting away as the night enveloped her. Aboard, the men began to drift away from the rails to wonder what awaited half a world away. For 27 of them, it would be lives cut cruelly short.

CHAPTER FIVE

Four Times Round Equals a Mile

THUD, THUD, thud, thud – the soundtrack to life on board *Canberra* was the relentless drumming of feet pounding on the Promenade Deck. Circuit followed gruelling circuit for the Marines and Paras who discovered to their delight that *Canberra* was the perfect floating running track, equipped with a measured mile around which they could stretch themselves for hour after hour. Where cruise passengers had strolled the most gentle of miles with a smile to walk off yet another lavish lunch or sharpen the appetite for dinner, now the deck was filled with soldiers pouring sweat and grimacing with effort as their PT instructors pushed them on and on, up to and beyond their limits. Hearts racing, straining for breath, again and again they circled, from the sun coming up until dusk fell. The ever-present thunder of squads of men circling the deck worked its way into the consciousness of everyone, civilian and military alike, anywhere nearby; they felt the never-ending clump-clump-clump through the soles of their own feet, heard each group approach panting like steam locomotives, then pass, the sound of them fading only to be replaced by the next. 'You could hear the beat of the boots going around and around the deck, every day, all during light hours,' said Brian Faulkner. It could be infinitely more unsettling than that; companies yomping or tabbing around the deck in full marching order delivered such a ferocious impact to the disintegrating deck that it set the superstructure of 45,000 tons of steel and aluminium vibrating, recalled Maurice Rudderham. 'We were up in the captain's office having a conference, and we couldn't think what it was, as the ship was waving slightly with the weight of these men going round in step; so they were told they could only go round . . . not in time, or not in step all the time.'

At first, they ran in sports kit, but as *Canberra* headed south, the drumming grew heavier, yet more percussive, ever more purposeful, as trainers, shorts and T-shirts were discarded in favour of boots, battledress and bergens, the men and their officers steeling themselves for whatever awaited, honing their level of fitness to shorten the odds against them if it came to a struggle against the demands of a hostile landscape as well as the unpredictable threat of the enemy.

It had been a bold and inspired stroke to requisition *Canberra* as a transport; now, as she sailed from Southampton, the benefits she could bestow on the men of 3 Brigade became clear to all exploring this most incongruous of troopships as dawn broke on her first day at sea, and she headed south-west towards the Bay of Biscay once more through grey, windy weather and a swell powerful enough to remind those unused to ships that their sea legs would not be won without some discomfort. *Canberra*'s gifts to the embarked force had been plain from the moment the advance party boarded in Gibraltar; there was not only the space to accommodate a fighting force, there was the room for it to train and maintain fitness over the course of a long voyage as well.

Men cooped up aboard overcrowded naval ships sailing south worked hard at keeping themselves in peak condition, but were handicapped by cramped conditions. They joked bitterly that their only exercise was 'the guard rail dash' – a two-pace advance to the rail and back. Not here; the scale of a liner with a circuit designed for gentle promenading – and for so many years filled by passengers who did just that, taking the air as they strolled – was serendipitous for troops who would find themselves on forced marches in some of the harshest conditions ever encountered in modern warfare. In the weeks ahead, ploughing on though filthy and freezing, officers and men alike gave thanks for the edge that endless circuits of the Promenade Deck had maintained. That the laps added up to a recognisable sum helped as a yardstick for training and were seized on enthusiastically. 'I was very good at giving out information in those days,' said Martin Reed. 'And I told them that four times round the Promenade Deck was a mile. Oh God, that was it. Off they went and they ran from day one until they got off, 4,000-odd man-miles a day.'

The deck was an ideal running track, available in all weathers. The concern over boots that had ruffled the Paras' feathers before embarking resurfaced, but was resolved quickly and amicably as military and merchant marine settled into a spirit of co-operation. 'We were concerned about the heavy boots and the effect on the decks, we mentioned that right at the beginning,' said Reed. 'They said, "That's fine, they can use trainers, but they might have to use their boots sometimes."' The poor old Promenade Deck suffered grievously under the impact of the troops' unending training, but whether in sports shoes or boots, it was a boon for soldiers who had braced themselves for confinement aboard ship. Marines who had previously sailed in the spartan conditions of naval vessels could hardly believe their luck at having the space to train, and for the Paras, less familiar with life at sea, *Canberra* provided the happiest of introductions. For all, the chance to get the blood pounding on a long run, albeit on a monotonous circuit, sharpened minds as well as bodies. 'It was to blow the cobwebs out of people's heads and get their minds on what they were going to be doing,' said Mick Southall. 'I got to know that deck very well. I did the half marathon, 52 times round, 13 miles, it took a good hour-and-a-half at least, but because I'd only just come out of basic training, I was incredibly fit and so young that the running round all day didn't bother me at all.'

He wasn't the only one; there were both officers and men who were enthusiastic runners anyway, amongst them several who had been training for that summer's London Marathon, and even once PT sessions were over, dedicated individuals could still be found putting in yet more circuits, just in case the Falklands crisis blew over and they found themselves back in time to take to the capital's streets. 'I was going for a six-mile run every day, just like on the road, and that was great both for morale and physical fitness,' said Chris Sheppard. Everybody felt the benefits of those endless laps, however exhausting they were. 'We were fitter when we got off than when we got on,' said Laurie Bland. 'It was very competitive, very gruelling, started with shorts and trainers, then with webbing on, then bergens and weapons.'

If it seemed odd to be running around the deck of a cruise liner, the sense of unreality was heightened by the polite solicitousness of P&O crew who treated their new passengers with the same thoughtfulness they customarily showed those on cruises. Men slumping down to catch their breath after a punishing run were surprised and delighted to be served refreshments by immaculately turned-out waiters. It was a surreal juxtaposition; sweat-stained soldiers with dark wet patches around the armpits and on their chests and backs, swearing at the effort they had put in with whatever wind they had left, and waiters in natty red-and-yellow waistcoats, bow ties, not a hair out of place and neat little plastic badges that bore their names, smiling, friendly, chatting with the same easy charm that the blue-rinses loved. 'We were knackered, we'd just sit in this rest area after we'd been pounding the deck,' said Steve Brabham, 'And out this chap would come with tea and coffee, fantastic chap, and he seemed to know exactly what to do at the right time.' Such service was unfamiliar to the troops, and their gratitude for its kindness helped to establish a mutual bond of affection and respect between the embarked forces and their civilian hosts.

Huge though *Canberra* was, the logistics of keeping a couple of thousand troops on the run round the Promenade Deck took some sorting out, and officers applied themselves to the task as soon as they had dumped their kit in the cabins. 'There was a jigsaw puzzle of movement around the ship, because obviously you couldn't all run round the *Canberra*'s deck at the same time,' recalled Hew Pike. 'You had periods allocated for PT for each battalion or commando and similarly for weapon training and medical training and for briefings and all the rest of it. So there was a very complicated programme. We needed to run a very intensive training programme, to keep people busy but also to focus on the things we needed to focus on, the fighting. We all had to presume from the start that there would be fighting.' Tweaks quickly became necessary to the PT programme. 'There was a daily order, and it said, "As from twelve hundred today, the running on the Promenade Deck will be counter-clockwise" because everyone was getting dizzy going round the same way,' said Reed.

Dizziness was not the only unsettling issue to deal with as officers and men alike caught their breath after the heady, hectic days of deployment. The ship itself, its vastness, its peacetime routines, its crew's remoteness from the everyday realities of military life, had to be addressed; the embarked force needed to get off to the most purposeful of starts. 'It was disorientating, in that people like me and the rest of the Royal Marines were accustomed to going on warships, with all the restrictions and cramped conditions and regulations, and here we were in this spacious, elegant ship, where those things were almost irrelevant,' said Nick Vaux. 'Ironically, it was the embarked force that very quickly imposed its own discipline on itself, because we recognised we had to. It was us that said, "OK, this is for senior NCOs, that's for officers, this is all out of bounds". At meetings with people like Martin Reed, he was saying, "Well, you don't have to do that", and we were saying, "No, no, we know that if we don't do this now, it'll all get out of hand." So a partnership grew up spontaneously right from the beginning. Pretty quickly, you saw the whole thing changing, and we changed it as well to make it more functional for training.' Not the least disorientating element for Vaux and his fellow commanding officers was their accommodation. 'It was luxurious,' said Pike. 'It was huge and I used to have my daily conference groups with all my sergeants in my cabin, so it was very useful. I didn't feel too guilty about it because it was such a useful space, and I'm sure the other COs found the same.' Vaux certainly did. 'I had this amazing stateroom, and that meant I could have orders groups and even little soirées with people, which took the tension off and helped to build up relationships.'

The men were no less pleased with their cabins, four-berths for the ranks, two-berths for NCOs – even if finding their way to them was initially bewildering. 'I don't know how many times I got lost,' said Southall. 'I went a different way back to my cabin every night.' 'It was like a moving city,' said Kim Sabido. 'Going from one deck to another you realised how massive it was, you got a feeling for the length, breadth, depth. It wasn't intimidating, but it was awesome, and I couldn't imagine them turning it from a cruise ship to a war ship.'

For the senior NCOs, *Canberra*'s scale, her bewildering labyrinth of corridors and staircases, presented a headache in keeping track of the men, according to Lawrie Ashbridge.

'It was the size of the thing. I had to get out and find where everybody was. It wasn't like getting the battalion on parade where I could see everybody in front of me; now I couldn't see anything except this cabin I was in. Some of them that were in four-men cabins were chuffed to bits. Just a few months before we went, on the last operation in Northern Ireland, they were living in crap. I put my head on like a Tom, a private soldier, and thought, "This is a great way to go to war", and their next idea is, "How do we entertain ourselves here?" That became who drinks where, how many cans and so on. I'd been a private soldier; I knew them, I thought like them. "I could get myself lost on this boat for weeks and nobody would ever know, I could be rat-arsed for a week and nobody would ever know" and we had to quickly orientate the minds of the soldiers to, "Hey, this is war, pal". I had to get through to them the enormity of what could happen, not when we got to war, but getting to war on a ship. In the back of my mind it was always there that we were going to get up one morning and someone's gone over the side.'

Not everybody was as enamoured of their accommodation as the COs in their staterooms, or the men who quickly made themselves comfortable. The pressmen found themselves in the Goanese quarters, way down on G Deck, which reinforced their belief that the Navy in general, and Captain Burne in particular, had them aboard under sufferance. 'One of the first things we did was to try to get out of these bloody cabins,' recalled John Shirley. 'We were somewhere in the bowels of the ship and pissed off at being dumped in the basement.' According to John Muxworthy, though, there was no mischievousness, let alone malice, in the allocation of cabins. 'They didn't arrive until pretty late, by which time all the big cabins had gone, so all we could do was stick them in tiny corners.' Protests brought a move up a few decks, but into cramped four-berth cabins

The question of the journalists' accommodation was to remain a touchy subject for days to come; a quiet intervention by Nick Vaux helped to secure more spacious two-man berths, and so did some old-fashioned bribery. 'What the buggers had done was they'd gone around and found a super cabin and bribed the Royal Marines to go in there,' said Muxworthy. It was a little more nuanced than that; the Marines who had pulled a fast one on the Paras when the troops were embarking made it clear they could also pull strings. 'It was all a bit of a lark,' said Shirley. 'There was a lieutenant, quite sparky, who was quite friendly with me and he offered to let us do a swap with his cabin in exchange for money, and in the end we didn't take his cabin. I think he probably used the fee we gave him to buy someone else's cabin.' And doubtless he made a profit in the process.

Others were more straightforward in going about improving their lot. The men of the Naval Party took their time in weighing up what the ship could offer, and then approached Reed. 'The Chief Petty Officer came up to me and said, "All your deck cabins for the Indians and Pakistanis, are you going to use them?" I said, "No, it's inferior accommodation." "We've just come off a frigate sir; that would not be inferior accom-modation!" I thought, Ah! "Would you like them?" And he said, "We would kill for it," so we gave them all that space. It had two galleys, so they could have a day and a night galley, and all the accommodation they wanted; they could have storage space. I said, "It's not tip-top accom -modation," and he said, "We can clean, sir" and off they went and did just that. They cleaned the whole place out until it was sparkling and made it their own accommodation, which was brilliant.'

Settling into *Canberra* after her rousing send-off was novel and even disconcerting for military and civilian alike. For the troops, there was exploring to be done, and for the P&O crew, there was a whole new way of life to get used to, an entirely new vocabulary to learn, all the jargon of Marines and Paras to become familiar with. Marines were 'Bootnecks' or 'Booties' and Paras 'Toms'; the green berets referred to marching in fighting order as 'yomping', the red berets as 'tabbing'. If a Marine acquired an item of kit without the knowledge or permission of its rightful owner, they called it 'proffing'; to the Paras, the same exercise was 'blagging'. All matters Naval were 'pussers' to the Marines, and the RAF 'crabs'. Breakfast, lunch or dinner was 'scran' or 'scoff', and the chocolates and sweets which both Marines and Paras devoured were 'nutty'. Your mate was your 'oppo' and your most admiring term of approval 'wazzer'. It wasn't just the soldiers who had their own language; so did the Navy, which talked about 'rassing', which meant replenishment at sea, or 'vertrep', which meant vertical replenishment, stores coming aboard by helicopter, often enough watched by 'goofers' or bystanders with nothing useful to do.

This – initially bewildering – slang swirled around the ship, and the bars that had been allocated to the various units before sailing. Each had its own, which was out of bounds to other units, not least to prevent any rivalry between Marines and Paras resulting in fighting. So 40 Commando was in the William Fawcett Room, 42 in the Peacock Room and 3 Para in the Alice Springs Bar. All were banned from the P&O crew bar, known as the Pig and Whistle. The ranks and junior NCOs were limited to two cans of beer a day, a restriction that did not apply to senior NCOs and officers. There was no segregation of officers, who drank together amid the scaffolding jacks of the Crow's Nest, though there was a polite tussle over whether the bar should be referred to as the 'officers mess', which was the Army term, or the 'wardroom', which was the Navy's. The Army won. P&O officers also drank in the Crow's Nest, as did the journalists, who had the honorary rank of captain, and evenings in there helped forge bonds of trust, respect and friendship between those preparing themselves to fight a war and those responsible for getting them there.

Neither side knew quite what to expect of the other at first. One of the key members of the surgical support team attached to 3 Brigade was the consultant in psychiatry at the Royal Hospital Haslar, the Naval hospital in Gosport, Surgeon Commander Morgan O'Connell, who had some firm and unflattering opinions on the merchant marine. 'When I joined *Canberra*, I had a very preconceived idea of the Merchant Navy – alcoholic, homosexual drug addicts. But in turn, they had a preconceived idea of us; as far as they were concerned the Marines and Paras are trained to kill, so if you look cross-ways at them, you're dead. So we had a lot of learning to do across the two communities.'

Vaux, who had already been impressed by Scott-Masson's determination to do all he could to be helpful, was relieved to find that a spirit of co-operation was shared by all. 'People came with the recognition they'd have to adapt. It couldn't just be one-sided. The worst way it could have started was if they'd all been resentful, "Bloody hell, we were just going to go off on another cruise, embarking all these passengers who'd give us large tips" and there was none of it, no sign that they didn't want to do the job.' The understanding that quickly developed was aided by the RNR experience of *Canberra*'s senior officers; besides Scott-Masson and Bradford, Reed and the first officer, Philip Pickford, also served in the reserve.

Even so, barriers needed to be broken down and understanding forged, and a glass or two in the Crow's Nest played a part, as did finding a topic of conversation other than war that enabled individuals to edge towards each other on common ground. 'It was a little bit tense at first,' recalled Don Cole. 'Some of the army guys tended to stick in their own little groups, but I got chummy with a couple of Marine officers. We just seemed to hit it off, started talking about what we were all into and ended up talking about football or something completely different, just to take the heat off.'

One group that formed tight-knit relationships from the very start was the medical team. Rick Jolly and Peter Mayner had got on exceptionally well when Jolly joined *Canberra* at Gibraltar. Before she sailed from Southampton, they decided to form the *Canberra* Medical Society, part social grouping, and part intended to disseminate knowledge, inviting speakers such as commanding officers to talk about their areas of expertise.

Mayner was its chairman and Jolly its secretary. 'I was deemed to be the treasurer, which was a bit of a joke really because no money ever parted hands,' said Susie West. 'I think we all thought it was our idea, not that it ever mattered, but as doctors we had quite a focus.'

The focus on readying *Canberra* for action began as soon as she had left the cheers of Southampton behind. The 3 Para battalion log for her first full day at sea, Saturday April 10, noted: 'The "darken ship" procedure went well last night. Ensure that all curtains in rooms are closed at sunset and reopened at sunrise. Lights in offices to be switched off during dark hours. Cardboard cut-outs are being made to block windows to public rooms.' *Canberra* had rendezvoused with *Elk* and the Royal Fleet Auxiliary tanker *Plumleaf.* She was proceeding at what was, for her, a very stately 18 knots, her speed limited by what *Elk* could do.

There was other company, too. 'We were trailed by a Soviet spy ship,' said Philip Pickford. 'It was almost waiting out in the Channel for us, not a very big ship, about the size of a minesweeper, but bristling with antennae and listening in to all our transmissions, so we had to maintain radio silence at certain times to make sure they didn't hear any of the strategic or tactical signals.' The spy ship was quickly identified by the Navy; it usually positioned itself off the northern coast of Ireland and monitored the movements of British submarines based in Scotland. It became a familiar presence all the way down to Ascension Island, occasionally coming close enough for those aboard *Canberra* to see telephoto lenses and binoculars trained on them, and acting as a reminder that the Soviet Bloc was taking the keenest interest in the curious drama unfolding between Britain and Argentina.

For now, what it was seeing was the continuing transformation of a cruise liner into a ship fit for a military operation. The Vospers workmen were still busy on the forward flight deck, but work was nearing completion on the main landing pad over the Bonito Pool. Not long before midday on the Saturday, the approaching clatter of two Sea King helicopters from RAF Culdrose, in Cornwall, brought spectators out to see a new chapter in *Canberra*'s story being written. The cross-winds that

Reed had experienced while taking measurements of the Bonito Pool in preparation for its conversion were making themselves felt once again as the pilots criss-crossed the deck, taking their time before hovering to winch down supplies and take up mail. Then it was the moment of truth; gingerly, slowly, the Sea Kings descended, the down-draught of their rotors whipping at the hair and clothing of everybody watching. The steel plating groaned and creaked under their weight and shifted a quarter-of-an-inch back and forth. No matter; the designers and the Vospers team had come through with flying colours. The first test of *Canberra*'s conversion had been passed.

Within 24 hours, the midships flight deck would be declared fully operational; the forward flight deck would be ready within a week, even though worsening weather and rising winds would make the workmen's task exceptionally difficult and at times hazardous as gales swept the ship. The spirit of improvisation showed itself once again. There was no anti-skid paint aboard, so Reed mixed sand into ordinary green paint to give the flight pad as much grip for the pilots as possible. The troops were improvising too. 'One colour sergeant came up and said, "You got any sand on board, sir?"' recalled Reed. 'Yes, I have, I'm going to use it on the flight deck to make sure it's non-slip. "Can you spare any?" They wanted to build a sand table, and that's what they did, underneath the flight deck, amongst all the girders, they mocked up the islands in sand and worked out what they were going to do.' The ingenuity amongst the girders was not limited to three-dimensional modelling; in short order, the mushroom of steel sitting in the Bonito Pool was used to suspend climbing ropes, up and down which Marines and Paras swarmed.

Fitness was everything, but the thud, thud, thud of running soldiers was taking its toll on only the second full day at sea, Easter Sunday. 'The Promenade Deck is already beginning to suffer,' noted the 3 Para log. 'The poor old composition decking, which was always the bane of my life anyway, really suffered,' said Reed. 'It's about two-and-a-half inches thick, and if the bonding moves at all, it starts to crack, water gets underneath and suddenly you've got all these feet banging away.' It was a strange, unfamiliar Easter Sunday for those aboard; church was full, the hymns sung enthusiastically to the accompaniment of the Royal Marines Band, the lesson read by Scott-Masson, and then back to the laps of the deck. Life was already settling into a routine of training, meals, relaxation and then bed. Hew Pike wrote to his wife that evening.

Today was noticeably warmer, but it is now quite rough – but so far, no pills and not seasick! We are doing running (30 mins) and 30 minutes' circuit training – exercises, sit-ups, fireman's lifts, press-ups, and so on, each day. Because there is so little space for fifteen hundred men to train in, the whole thing has to be very carefully programmed. And of course we are doing a lot of other training as well. The P&O cooks, waiters, maids and stewards are still on board, so life is pretty comfortable. The food is excellent. The soldiers are not too cramped and there are lots of washing machines and irons. Colonel Tom Seccombe (Royal Marines) is the Military Force Commander on *Canberra* and Deputy Brigade Commander, he is an excellent chap, very relaxed and with a good sense of humour. We had a lot of telegrams from parents and families of soldiers, and quite a few from military people. Some of the waves are almost reaching my cabin window now. Last night, after dinner with the Captain I joined a 'Doctors Party' – the '*Canberra* Medical Society' has been formed by all the doctors and surgeons on board.

The weather improved as each day passed, and with it the pace of training grew ever more intense. Robert Fox wrote: 'Some of the workouts seemed excessive, judging by the number of serious ankle and shoulder sprains the physiotherapists had to deal with. Down in the sick bay, I saw something I never expected to see in my life – shoulders and legs literally locked by muscle fatigue.' The warmer weather brought the men out onto the newly completed flight deck for punishing PT sessions. The drumming of running feet now underscored the rhythmic chanting of 'Now it's hurting – yes it is' as groups of men, their faces contorted with effort, hefted heavy wooden beams above their heads over and over again to build upper-body strength. The air was filled with the thuds of bodies crashing to the deck and the grunts and gasps of exertion as soldiers practised unarmed combat on each other. Every space was filled; those awaiting their turn in the open air of the flight deck braced their feet under *Canberra*'s guard-rails and forced themselves through endless sit-ups. In the foyers of the decks, groups of men put themselves through shuttling – bursts of high-speed running in a confined space – to the chant of 'A shuttle a day keeps an Argie away'. Determination was written on every face, every grimace of pain worth it for the incremental increase in fitness it brought. They looked strong, hard, lean, fearsome, the aggressive aspect of many accentuated by the skinhead haircuts they had before sailing.

The atmosphere amongst the troops as they trained could be raucous; black humour was in the air and it was not for the faint-hearted. Sunshine brought out some T-shirts emblazoned with inventive slogans for the training sessions, Jeremy Hands noting amongst them 'Falk off, Galtieri' and, inevitably, plays on the words of Andrew Lloyd Webber and Tim Rice's huge hit song from the musical *Evita*, 'Don't Cry For Me Argentina', which translated as 'Start Crying for Us Argentina, We're Coming to Bomb the Shit Out of You'. The tattoos revealed when the troops worked up a sweat and the T-shirts came off were in a similarly broad vein. Hands wrote, 'There were the tough guy types, promising "Death Before Dishonour" with decorations of daggers and snakes. Comedians had "Cut here" around their necks, and there was at least one "Go and F**k Yourself" tattooed on the outside of the little finger of the right hand which only showed when saluting.' That black sense of humour was tickled pink in those first few days by one of the denser acts of the British Forces Post Office, which announced that the designated postal address for *Canberra* was BFPO 666. Not a hint of irony, still less that anybody with clout at the BFPO had any knowledge of scripture, or ever saw the horror film *The Omen*, was to be found in branding the elegant ship and her aching passengers with 666 – the mark of the Devil. Despite the hilarity at 'Satan's postmark' on board, nobody at P&O back in Britain appeared to get it either, blithely informing relatives of the crew that they should use the number to write to their loved ones. Three more weekly newsletters would be sent to families before somebody woke up and a new postal address was given out, with the firm instruction, 'The previous number 666 should not be used'.

There were laughs to be had without the help of the BFPO. Poker-faced mickey-taking, mostly at the expense of the Navy, began as soon as the lines were cast off at Southampton. Instructions issued constantly from the loudspeakers, and the traditional Navy pipe of 'Do you hear there?' prompted sniggers especially amongst the Paras. 'The blokes cottoned on straight away,' said Laurie Bland. 'For days afterwards, all the lads were saying "Do you hear there?" just to embarrass the Naval types and the Marines as a piss-take.' The Navy's sunset pipe, when all on the upper deck should face aft and salute, fared no better. Hands wrote, 'The exercise was cancelled after the second evening when the Naval party realised that they could never stop the moving little ceremony being interrupted each time by 2,500 voices shouting in unison "Bollocks!"'

Nor were the P&O crew immune from having a rise taken out of them, as when soldiers were posted as lookouts on the bridge. 'It was always a guinea a minute to go up and speak to the civilian crew and Naval party,' said Lawrie Ashbridge. 'The first time we did it, I spoke to the watch officer and said, "How's our guys doing?" and it was, "My God, if they see the least thing, if a wave looks a bit wrong, they tell us. If they keep this up, nothing will get anywhere near us." Typical airborne soldiers, they were playing this ship's crew, and they never knew it. They were making a mockery of them in a quiet way. It was keeping themselves occupied.' The crew, though, were more than capable of keeping a straight face while winding up their passengers, as the young Mick Southall discovered on guard duty when he fell into conversation with the helmsman taking *Canberra* through the dead of night. 'I said, "That's really interesting, can I have a look?" and he says "Yeah, yeah, have a look" and I was holding this sort of figure-of-eight wheel, and he says, "You move it this way, you move it that way" and then he says, "Hang on, I'm just going to the toilet," and for about two minutes that ship was in the control of a 17-year-old private from 3 Para. And when he came back, I was like, "Don't f**king ever do that again!" '

Canberra was sailing into weather she was more accustomed to; the sun shone, the temperature rose, her crew changed into the same immaculate whites they wore for cruising, and it all heightened the sense of unreality. This was cruising seen through the looking glass as the passengers began to sprawl around the decks and remaining pools, the Alice Springs and the Lido, to sunbathe. Under the bluest of skies, they stretched out and relaxed while chatting about things never previously spoken about on this ship; no longer the elderly and wealthy fresh from Steiner's hair salon, who talked of dinner, cabaret and shore excursions, but shaven-headed fighting men who swore and laughed and bantered of sex, booze and killing. Such sessions had to be strictly limited; getting too comfortable, too used to the sun, threatened to blunt the fighting edge being sharpened. Officers and NCOs began to grow concerned at the risk of sunburn; medics issued warnings over the loudspeakers, and the men were then told that they could be put on a charge if sunburn impaired their ability to train, particularly if sore shoulders prevented them carrying packs.

But the fine weather and the open sea offered opportunities to step up the training a gear. The sound of gunfire was added to the cacophony of thundering feet and chanting as the troops zeroed in their weapons from the stern. Rubbish bags and empty drinks cans were chucked overboard and left sinking or dancing in *Canberra*'s wake under volleys of accurate fire. There was an accident during live firing; *Elk*, practising manoeuvres around *Canberra*, found herself in the wrong place and a round pinged off her bows into the sea. Mercifully, nobody aboard was hurt.

The training ran through every part of the ship. Up on the bridge, Burne was teaching the P&O crew Naval manoeuvring. The RNR officers were already proficient in this, but it was a steep learning curve for the others. 'The rest of the deck officers had to learn to turn the ship the way the Navy wanted,' said Reed. 'Drive alongside tankers, drive without any radar, lights out, be among a bunch of other ships, strange things.' Just as the civilian crew had learned the language of the troops, now the deck officers learned that of the Navy – corpen, zig zag, zippo one, all the terms and techniques to throw *Canberra* around with the flexibility of a warship instead of a grand lady of the seas who proceeded on her way with unhurried dignity. It was stimulating, exciting and new, and the enthusiasm displayed by the P&O officers made for a happy relationship with their naval counterparts. There was never a quiet moment aboard; fire drills, lifeboat drills, man overboard exercises, a constant bustle of activity. Everybody was learning from each other. 'Within the space of a week, we had come together as a wonderful ship's company,' said Morgan O'Connell.

'They recognised that they weren't experts at going to war; but what they were experts at was running a cruise liner. P&O had this long history of trooping, so they thought this is something our forebears have done, so we can just become a troop ship. Interestingly, we had to teach the *Canberra* one or two things too: when we went to lifeboat stations we were appalled to discover they'd put all the doctors in one lifeboat and we said this was bizarre, we were grouped together because of where our cabins were, but we said "Hang on a minute, what happens if that lifeboat goes down?" You would see people leaning on guard rails which was anathema to the Royal Navy, but on cruise liners guard rails are designed to be leant on, so people would be leaning on them chatting to each other, in the swimming pool, in the bars. I felt I couldn't have been made more welcome if I had been a first-class paying passenger. They just looked after us incredibly well and I would like to think that they thought we looked after them to the best of our ability too; it was a wonderful community.'

Everybody felt all aboard growing closer, more single-minded, and was grateful for it. 'Three or four days in, we were invited for drinks into Martin Reed's cabin as a thank you for making it go as smoothly as it had,' said Brian Faulkner. 'Unfortunately, I sat on his sink, which came off the wall and water was pouring out into the cabin and we had to get a plumber up.' *Canberra* coped cheerfully with such minor mishaps. Thousands of troops put pressure on the fabric of the ship, and carpenters, plumbers and electrical officers were kept busy with running repairs, whether they were toilets blocked by cigarette ends or a lift that plummeted to the bottom of its shaft under the weight of 20 Marines who had packed into it. As she approached Sierra Leone, there was another mishap, which unsettled and saddened those aboard. A whale was sighted half a mile off the starboard bow, and kept coming towards the ship. The officers speculated that *Canberra*'s approach was so quiet that the animal could not hear her; a collision was inevitable, and the bows sliced the whale in half. 'We felt the thud, and saw all the blood in the wake,' said Norman Menzies, the Captain Quartermaster of 3 Para. 'When I leaned over the back, I thought we were sinking, but we were doing the anti-submarine zig zag.'

A flurry of signals preceded *Canberra*'s arrival at Freetown on Saturday 17 April. The government of Sierra Leone had needed to be persuaded by Britain to accept her for refuelling and re-storing because she was carrying troops. Those men were in a state of high excitement; after a week on board, they anticipated a few hours' shore leave, and there was booing when it was announced over the loudspeakers that nobody was to leave the ship. *Canberra* wanted to be in and out of Freetown as quickly as possible. The only people going ashore were the 26 Vospers workmen, flying home after putting the finishing touches to the forward flight deck in the preceding days. The weather was hot and humid, and medics worried about mosquitoes issued anti-malaria tablets.

The men took out their frustration on an unfortunate British family who came to the jetty to cheer the ship and wave Union Jacks. 'This nice family turned up to wave, not realising that two-and-a-half thousand troops would not be too polite in their replies,' said Reed. Indeed they were not; father, portly mother, shapely teenage daughter and lad aged about 10 got the full blast of off-colour soldierly humour. 'Father was offered everything from light tanks to cases of small arms for the loan of his buxom daughter,' wrote Hands. 'Ten-year-old son was ignored, except when he shouted "Rule Britannia" in an attempt to boost morale. The troops replied loudly with such replies as "Piss off, you little queer," or "Here's a fiver, go and fetch your other sisters."' The crestfallen family withdrew. Dug-out bum-boats full of native peddlers offering everything from skins to fruit to monkeys swarmed around *Canberra*; those on board were ordered not to have any contact with them because of the risk of bringing disease aboard, but at least one enterprising P&O crew member managed to buy some cannabis before the ship's fire party was ordered to turn the hoses on the boats to drive them away. That was only partially successful; troops throwing objects at them proved more effective.

Legitimate trade was also taking place; British consular officials and a P&O agent were on board determining what *Canberra* needed. Food and fuel obviously, but amongst the more unusual requests were 50 irons and ironing boards and 10,000 paper bags suitable for packed lunches. It proved to be a long day; the fuelling proceeded slowly, and the delivery of provisions was even slower, as lines of men delivered fresh fruit and vegetables at a languid pace under the scorching sun. The Royal Marines Band helped to pass the time with an impromptu concert on the flight deck, but as the sun set, loading was far from finished. The sticky, sweaty evening dragged on, and it was not until just before midnight that *Canberra* cast off in the darkness and left Africa behind. It had been a week of intense activity, punctuated by ever-gloomier bulletins from the World Service; US Secretary of State Alexander Haig shuttling endlessly between Britain, the UN and Argentina trying to broker a deal, Galtieri insisting that he would not give up the Falklands, Britain imposing a 200-mile maritime exclusion zone around the islands, the task force battle fleet sailing south from Ascension Island. Now *Canberra* was heading for Ascension too, maybe to another phase of a so-far phoney war, or perhaps to something far more testing.

CHAPTER SIX

Pinkers and Clausewitz

ONE CAME with a reputation for eccentricity; the other for aloofness. Either was a big enough personality to dominate the bridge single-handed, yet it contained both. Each made an instant and lasting impression; together they could be disconcerting, as SAS Lieutenant-Colonel Mike Rose, found when he arrived on board *Canberra* by helicopter for dinner at the invitation of Hew Pike. In common with everyone unfamiliar with the ship, he became lost and found his way to the bridge. 'He had an encounter with these two,' said Pike. 'And he came to me and said, "I've just been up to the bridge and I've met these two complete lunatics."'

Captain Dennis John Scott-Masson and Captain Christopher Peter Oldbury Burne were, of course, anything but lunatic, but both took some getting used to. Pike himself had been wrong-footed early on in the voyage when Burne invited him to the bridge. 'He said, "Now you must come up to the bridge and see what we do" and I said thank you very much and when I got up to the bridge and said, "Well, here I am" it's, "Get off my bridge, get off my bridge, we're busy."'

Strictly speaking, it wasn't his bridge. Scott-Masson remained the captain of *Canberra* throughout; Burne was the Senior Naval Officer, with operational control as part of the task force. It was a potentially tricky relationship, but worked out remarkably well, whatever frictions that arose being settled discreetly. 'We came to the conclusion that the best thing to do was treat Chris Burne as the charterer's representative, and that makes Merchant Navy sense,' said Martin Reed. 'The Navy had chartered the ship, so they say where it goes, and Dennis is still fully responsible for her. Dennis would follow whatever Chris wanted, which was fine.' In his turn, Burne formed a view of the command structure of *Canberra*. 'It was really a holiday firm, that's the way it worked, and the first captain was really like the managing director.' They made a striking pair; Scott-Masson tall, broad, imposing, and possessed of a deep, rumbling voice and measured delivery that gave whatever he said an air of gravitas. Burne was taller still, rangy, energetic, with an ebullient, booming manner. They were of the same generation, Scott-Masson, at 52, two years older than Burne, and there was a certain symmetry about their careers, even as their styles of command were diametrically opposed; the one a big-picture man, the other concerned with every detail. But both were products of the age in which they went to sea. 'Dennis was an old-fashioned passenger ship captain,' said Reed. 'They didn't even have to tie their own shoelaces in the old days, there was always a steward looking after you, so you get rather cocooned to that way of life and he'd never really changed from that. He would sit in his cabin and mastermind the whole thing.' John Muxworthy observed of Burne, 'He is a seaman officer of the old kind, in the best possible sense, a gunnery officer and they ran the Navy for a thousand years.'

The commanding officers of the embarked units were acutely aware that the relationship on the bridge had the potential for flashpoints. 'It can't have been easy for either of them,' said Nick Vaux. 'It's to their credit that although they were both individual, private people, that they somehow managed to make it work well.' Scott-Masson, who died in November 2010, got on well with Burne, according to his wife, Anne-Marie. 'He liked Chris very much indeed,' she said. Burne expressed his gratitude to Scott-Masson and his crew in a letter to P&O's marine manager, Captain Peter Love, on 16 April, writing, 'Morale is high throughout the ship – and your deck officers are delighting in the manoeuvres I am schooling them in. As with our experiences ashore, the Captain and crew here could not be more helpful – it is a constant pleasure and relief to me.' Scott-Masson's often hands-off approach was familiar to his senior officers. Burne said, 'One

day, we had to change course and after we'd done it I said to the officer
of the watch, "I wouldn't tell Captain Scott-Masson" and I can see him
now looking at his watch and saying, "Between 9 o'clock at night and 9
o'clock in the morning, we tell him nothing," because he was the managing
director, he wasn't running the ship at the time.'

There were inevitable tensions and pressures arising from the
requirements of the Navy and embarked military force. Vaux said, 'Chris
Burne had huge responsibilities. His responsibility ultimately was to ensure
that *Canberra* operated within the Royal Navy plan, but long before that
he was directly liaising with Dennis Scott-Masson over matters of
protocol, and when did the parochial interest of P&O conflict with the
operational requirements of the task force, and how was that resolved?
And then Chris's other, very complex control had to be exercised over the
requirements of the embarked forces, vis-à-vis the ship and her ship's
company. For example, right from the beginning we were correctly
practising blackouts at night and man overboard and the ship catching fire
and so on, and all of that was quite difficult. You had to decide who laid
down the new rules and how they were implemented. Were P&O officers
in charge? Probably not, because they weren't accustomed to it, so if it
was our blokes who were in charge, then they had to be briefed by him, so
it was not easy.'

Liaison between Scott-Masson, Burne and the military force com-
mander, Tom Seccombe, was key to smoothing out tensions, and that fell
into the remit of Michael Bradford, the deputy captain, who observed drily,
'I would liaise between the two and bounce a few balls hither and thither,
or stop a few if I thought it was necessary.' The RNR experience of
Canberra's most senior officers was also vital in resolving any difficulties.
'The great luck of *Canberra* was having a good command team with Mike
Bradford, Martin Reed and Phil Pickford, for which Dennis of course took
a lot of credit,' said Peter Mayner.

Scott-Masson was justifiably proud of his own RNR service, which
went back almost as far as his time with P&O. The sea was in his blood,
and he was a fine mariner. His father had been at sea, and Scott-Masson

never wanted to do anything other than follow him. He had been with P&O since 1950, after an education at the Nautical College, Pangbourne, and a three-year apprenticeship with the Shaw Savill shipping line. P&O promoted him to captain in 1966, and he had served in many of the company's ships. *Canberra*, though, held a special place in his heart. 'He absolutely loved that ship, and he had spent a great deal of time on it as chief officer, deputy captain and twice in command,' said Anne-Marie Scott-Masson. His service with the RNR began in 1951, and he was promoted captain in 1971, five years after being awarded the Reserve (Officers') Decoration. His crew held him in affection, but were wary.

Reed, who developed a close friendship with Scott-Masson that lasted to the end of his life, said, 'He could be terrifyingly aloof. Talk to some of the young girls who took letters up to him and they'd say he was so scary, and you'd say, "What? Dennis? Scary?" He could be quite imposing, a great character, but certainly distant, and could be quite difficult to work with sometimes.' There was an air about him of belonging to an earlier, grander age, an impression bolstered by the tufts of whiskers he affected on his cheekbones. He liked his routines, one of which was a pink gin at noon – 'pinkers' – which he saw no reason to abandon as *Canberra* headed to war. 'Twelve o'clock was pinkers, in his cabin, regular as clockwork,' added Reed, who noted that the grander aspects of being captain of one of the world's greatest cruise liners also appealed. 'You have to say he was a very big snob; he loved titles and special people, it was the way he was brought up. His visitors' book was always full of titled names; he would always entertain and if a lord or lady turned up, it was, "Put them on my table."' Scott-Masson invariably read the lesson at *Canberra*'s Sunday service from the hefty ship's Bible, which was carried in ceremoniously by a cadet and placed on a lectern. This ritual continued once the troops embarked and the service was held in the ship's cinema to accommodate more people. A music stand served as lectern; soldiers whiffing a hint of pomposity about the whole rigmarole duly sabotaged it, causing it to collapse when the good book was placed upon it.

'He was a bit of a seadog, therefore not necessarily all that approachable,' reflected Vaux. 'But in fact when you got to know him, he was charming and very interesting.' Scott-Masson remained slightly detached from military life on board during the voyage south, and Vaux saw the merit in that. 'I think he struck absolutely the right note with the embarked force, because he never spent a lot of time with them, he never asked to come and see us do anything, but he made regular broadcasts to everybody and explained what was going on, and he did that very well. What he tried to do, and I think successfully, was try to let the embarked force get on with their military thing but every now and then draw together everyone collectively in something like a band concert or a service, or just him talking to people so they felt part of the ship.' As *Canberra*'s captain, there was a degree of distance between him and the military, but he found something of a kindred spirit in the person of Tom Seccombe, added Vaux.

'Tom was a full colonel and older and senior to us all, parachuted in at the last minute and he co-ordinated and controlled the whole thing superbly. He was a wonderful character in his own right. Large, avuncular, highly intelligent, great sense of humour and he kept everyone from falling out with each other and where necessary, he laid the law down. He formed a separate, and very important friendship with Dennis Scott-Masson, because in a sense they were two people isolated from the rest and so, for Dennis, that was quite important because he felt he was neutral from any of the conflicting interests. They were both about the same age and rank and had similar interests, and they got on very well.'

Pike appreciated that Scott-Masson had been unexpectedly presented with huge and unfamiliar challenges.

'Suddenly he'd had his ship hijacked and instead of being full of polite and rather elderly tourists, with the occasional death at sea on his hands if somebody had a heart attack, he had three battalions of testosterone-charged soldiers and the command hierarchy that went with them. It must have been a most astonishing experience for him, like having your precious house invaded by gangsters, but he still very much felt, and quite rightly as well, that it was his ship, his rules ran. Every Sunday, he would give the Captain's talk, and actually we didn't need a Captain's talk, but it was one way to show, "It's my ship, all you Paratroopers and Marines". That was slightly bizarre, but he was a gallant chap.' Pike also had sufficient sympathy for his feelings to quietly reprimand a young officer who bemoaned over dinner with the Captain that the Falklands crisis was interrupting the polo season. 'Scott-Masson's own son was serving in the Guards, and was vegetating somewhere and couldn't get involved in the action, so he was very upset that this arrogant young officer was moaning about missing all the polo. I had a word with him, basically to say it was not very tactful.'

Generally, though, Scott-Masson was blessed with a monumental calmness, according to his wife, which she believed allowed him to take all the upheavals and uncertainties in his stride. 'The greater the drama, the calmer he became,' she said. 'When his ship was being pulled to pieces, his eyebrows were raised at what was happening, but he wasn't alarmed in any way. This is the way he was: the worse things got, the calmer he got. The only thing was, and this was pointed out by the junior officers, that if he was standing on the bridge rubbing the back of his thigh, they knew he was worried about something, but that was the only sign he ever gave.'

The night before *Canberra* sailed, Scott-Masson had been quietly determined. 'Of course at that time, they didn't know if they would be going all the way, but he said to me, "If we go all the way, all I want to do is get them there safely, and come back safely, that's my job" and he also said he would take them in as close as he could.' In the face of uncertainty, Scott-Masson decided to keep everything around him as familiar as he could. 'In a naval ship, they would have cleared everything from their cabins and got ready for battle stations, whereas he went to sea with everything around him in his cabin, which was very spacious and well-furnished and with pictures of his family around and vases of flowers and pink gin poured at lunchtime. Everything stayed as normal as he could keep it, because he thought this was the way he should do it.'

Mrs Scott-Masson did all she could to keep life as normal as possible for him too. As a winter of fighting and sacrifice unfolded in the South Atlantic, her letters described the spring blooming in the garden he loved in Somerset, sometimes enclosing one of the primroses that were coming out. 'It was a habit of sailors' wives not to trouble our husbands at sea: you never told them anything bad, there was nothing they could do but worry themselves silly, so I wouldn't have told him anything controversial.' She made one exception to that rule, informing him that the wife of one of the seamen taken on by *Canberra* to replace an Asian crewman was complaining as the ship headed ever farther south. The man was one of the handful sent back from Ascension. Scott-Masson wrote to his wife every other day, regardless of how often mail could be sent from his ship, the tone of his letters measured. So was the tone of his brief daily message to P&O: 'All fine and well'.

All was fine and well also with the schooling of the P&O crew in naval manoeuvring under the guiding hand of Burne as *Canberra* made steady progress southwards, and her officers became accustomed to, and fond of, this most individual of men. Burne was nicknamed 'Beagle', a moniker that had followed him ever since he had managed the pack of hounds at the Royal Naval College, Dartmouth years before, doubtless with the same boundless energy that he now brought to the bridge. Difficulties that came his way were greeted with a cry of 'Boing, boing', a springy little catchphrase that became very familiar. 'He had this extraordinary approach to problems,' said Reed. 'You always knew that if there was something to think about, you'd hear this "boing, boing". "Oh, bring it over here and we'll sort it out. Boing, boing!" A lot of people thought he was a bit of a fool, but he was an extremely clever man, a very smart brain, and if you wanted to talk to him, he'd talk to anyone at any time about anything. It didn't matter who it was, he would give you the time, he'd talk it through.' A reputation for eccentricity followed him as doggedly as his nickname, thanks to an incident aboard HMS *Coventry*, of which he took command in 1978, and had since assumed something approaching legendary status in the fleet. 'It was man overboard drill,' said Reed. 'So he walked out of the bridge wing, went to the starboard lookout and said, "Jump over the side." "What for sir?". "Man overboard drill, we need someone in the water." "Not a very good swimmer, sir." So Chris says, "Well, hold my hat," gave him his cap and jumped over the side, with this shout of, "Man overboard".' There was a slight delay in rescuing him because the lookout was frozen in astonishment that the Captain had just voluntarily plummeted into the water.

It was, as those around him on *Canberra* began to observe and respect, an example of his impetuousness, demonstrated memorably when a myriad difficulties, concerns and uncertainties began to accumulate. As problems piled up, Burne 'lost the bubble', a submariner's term that loosely translates as losing the plot. 'Things were going a bit crazy,' recalled Reed. 'We weren't too sure what we were going to be doing, worried about this and about that, and suddenly he appeared on the bridge in the most disreputable pair of shorts with an old singlet. "Boing, boing! I've lost the bubble, going for a run, brief me when I get back" and off he went. He ran round the upper deck until he was absolutely knackered, showered, changed, came out, said, "Right, I'm ready, tell me what's going on." He had so much information, it was all confusing, so he'd decided to chuck it all out and start again. I thought it was brilliant. I've done it ever since. If it all gets too much, sod it, forget it, start again.' Burne presided over an evening meeting of the naval officers to discuss the day's signals that became known as the 'Giggle Session' because he so often prompted giggling. Evenings held another ritual. 'It was my job after dinner to put him through to Northwood on the phone,' said Graham Harding. 'He had a booming voice, and everybody on the bridge could hear him, and it sounded like gibberish.' That was for the benefit of the shadowing Russian spy ship, which if it managed to eavesdrop was presumably flummoxed by the peculiar conversations of the British, as when John Muxworthy noted Burne reporting back the successful rendezvous with *Elk* the day after departing Southampton, and some initial problems with her refuelling from *Plumleaf*, the two ships being euphemistically described as cousins. 'Hello Freddie? Freddie! This is Beagle – I'm in my new home and I've got my cousin with me; he's jolly good company, but when he goes on a bicycle ride with my other cousin, he keeps on falling off.' It wasn't all booming. Harding watched as a young naval rating was referred to Burne over an infraction. 'He ushered this lad into his sea cabin and said, "Let's see if we can sort this out" and the door closed. He was like an uncle, quietly shepherding a nephew into his study. He was that sort of person, not somebody who ranted and raved.'

Burne won the admiration of the P&O deck officers with the good humour and clarity he brought to teaching what they needed to know. 'He was a very good communicator, a great guy,' said Philip Pickford. 'A wonderful sense of humour and a wonderful way of keeping us informed, because there were a lot of the guys who were totally unused to military ways.' The tuition quickly had the desired result, said Reed. 'After about two weeks, Chris sent back a signal saying *Canberra* was a fully worked-up ship of the fleet, which is excellent because it takes about three months for a naval ship to get worked up. He was very proud of her.' Merchant marine and naval officers were growing more attuned by the day; Burne even equipped *Canberra*'s navigator, Second Officer Trevor Lane, with RN stripes for his right shoulder to balance the P&O stripes on his left. Burne drilled the need for flexibility into the officers, and his exhortations were echoed to the whole ship over the loudspeakers by his executive officer, Commander Tim Yarker, so often that the cry, 'Stay flexible' took on the status of a catchphrase for everybody aboard.

Burne was omnipresent on the bridge; although he had been allocated the comfortable cruise director's cabin near the purser's office, he preferred the cramped pilot's cabin just aft of the chart room. More often than not, he was to be found in one of the two pilot's chairs on the bridge. 'He claimed one as "my chair" and he would throw himself in the chair and pontificate about this, that and the other, but he could listen as well,' said

Reed. He was fond of quoting the great Prussian military theorist Carl von Clausewitz, especially his dictum, 'Everything is very simple in war, but the simplest thing is very difficult' and was an avid reader throughout the voyage of Norman F. Dixon's *On the Psychology of Military Incompetence*. Burne was an immensely experienced officer; he had joined the Royal Navy as a cadet in September 1945 and his first command had been in 1966. He was promoted to captain ten years later and had served in a variety of staff roles, most recently with the UK Commanders-in-Chief Committees. Vaux already knew him; somewhere along the way, they had met and discovered a mutual interest in field sports. They had also seen each other in Norway, where Burne had taken parties of cadets on expeditions and Vaux was involved with arctic warfare training. 'When we got onto *Canberra* and I discovered he was the Captain, it was a very pleasant surprise and I like to think that because we had a previous relationship, it did help a bit in the early stages. He had a slightly austere and occasionally inflexible approach to arrangements. I was able to go to him and say, "Come on Chris, all we're trying to do is this, and surely . . ." and he'd say, "Oh well, in that case . . ." because part of the strength of his character was that when Chris Burne said something, it was difficult to get him to change his mind.'

The circumstances were as unfamiliar to Burne as to anybody else, and added to the issues he was grappling with was coping with journalists on board, a task he approached with thinly disguised distaste. 'There was a psychological moment when the press came on board and Chris Burne and the naval side wanted to minimise their presence in every way,' said Vaux. 'There was even a suggestion that they would be hived off into a special mess or segregated in some way, and people like Hew Pike and myself said, "That is just nonsense." All correspondents everywhere are treated as if they are visiting officers. They have to be, because that is where they're going to get their information from. That was one real weakness that Chris Burne had: he didn't see any necessity for them, he regarded them as a bloody nuisance and they knew that.' Both Marines and Paras had long experience of dealing with print and broadcast journalists in

Northern Ireland and were much more relaxed about talking to them. 'People like myself had seen that the press were intelligent, resourceful and on the whole even-handed in trying to tell the story, and if you helped them it was easier. Indeed, one or two of the correspondents, like Robert Fox, one had actually come across,' added Vaux.

As luck would have it, the telex machine on which the newspapermen sent their copy was in a small office adjoining Burne's sea cabin just off the bridge and he took to policing it in his own inimitable fashion to ensure that no unauthorised reports left the ship. 'We were constantly trying to get to the machine, or make a joke of getting to it,' said John Shirley. 'Chris Burne was saying, "You can't use the machine" and he's jumping up and down in front of it, partly in jest, and he looks like John Cleese as Basil Fawlty.' The comparison to the manic hotelier of Fawlty Towers stuck. 'We started calling him Captain Fawlty, and somebody sent a piece of copy back and referred to him as Basil Burne, and that got into the papers.' Yet for all their frustrations at the restrictions placed on what they could report, the journalists warmed to Burne because of his directness and honesty. 'He was quite straight,' said Shirley. 'He didn't understand, or didn't want to understand what we wanted to do, which was to send back stories and have access to the phones and the telex, and he wasn't going to let us do that because it was clearly part of his orders to retain security, but because he was quite direct and clear about it, you could relate to that.'

In common with Scott-Masson, Burne got on well with Seccombe, who attracted the affectionate nickname, 'Uncle Tom'. He was a witty, urbane man, who termed anybody he thought might be rocking the boat 'ungodly'. He loved to quote Evelyn Waugh and P.G. Wodehouse, and had the knack of finding the perfectly apt line for any occasion. Robert Fox wrote, 'I once asked him about the difficulties of his job aboard *Canberra*, and he replied with Bertie Wooster's reaction to one of his Aunt Agatha's nastier phone calls: "It's a bit like being hit in the small of the back by the 4.45 from Paddington."' Seccombe enlivened meetings, recalled Pike. 'He was a bit of a lad – in agony, he would cry out in one of our meetings, "I need a woman." A very charming chap.' His humour endeared him to the men, and his charm helped defuse tensions. Vaux reflected, 'Tom Seccombe was very important, because as you might imagine, regimental rivalry apart, there is no one more parochial or protective of their interests than the commander of a battalion, so you had three of those, plus other sub-units like the field hospital, and all of them competing for the best facilities and training programme. It was absolutely crucial to have someone about who was going to control and arbitrate.'

There was an air of quiet satisfaction amongst naval, military and P&O officers at how efficiently *Canberra* had transformed herself from cruise ship to troop carrier as she steamed the 1,000 miles to Ascension. The newly-schooled deck officers performed anti-submarine manoeuvres with increasing confidence as she sailed on in company with *Elk*, and the World Service informed all aboard that the two ships would soon be joined by another P&O vessel, the North Sea ferry MV *Norland*, out of Hull, which would bring the 2nd Battalion, the Parachute Regiment, south, having been requisitioned. The sense of cohesion and co-operation was reinforced on the first evening after *Canberra* departed Freetown by the first formal concert by the Marines band. It was a stirring and memorable performance on the midships flight deck as soldier, sailor and civilian alike found whatever vantage point they could to see and hear the performance. Then, as daylight began to fade, the sunset ceremony took place – no shouts of derision this evening – and 'The Lord's My Shepherd' sung. It was the first of many concerts by the band which would unite all aboard, but the musicians had already made their presence felt, and were winning a lot of friends in the process.

Almost as soon as *Canberra* left Southampton, the bandsmen had retrieved the instruments which had been quietly loaded on board to escape the scrutiny of the press, and set about entertaining. They split up into small groups and toured the bars and public rooms where the soldiers spent their evenings. Whatever the lads wanted, they could deliver. Pop, rock, standards, jazz, sing-alongs, they named it and the bandsmen played it, provided backing for the resident amateur cabaret performer that every drinking-hole seemed to have, or sang themselves. The shouts of 'Oi, bandy, play', followed by a request for a tune were all the bandsmen needed as they drew on the widest and most eclectic of repertoires. These were spontaneous, informal and joyous sessions of music that did much to keep spirits up and bolstered the universal regard in which the band was held. Its director, John Ware, said,

'The musicians became great favourites with the other troops; they got to know them all pretty quickly, and it did become a great morale booster. After a while, I had to tell them to tone it down a bit, because they were doing a lot of hard physical and military training during the day, as well as training for their medical jobs, leading very full days and then going on and carrying on working until late at night. But given that they were doing all these other military tasks that were not really natural to them, it was a sort of therapy for a lot of them to go and play their instruments in the evening and do the thing that they really did well.'

The bandsmen's passion for their music rapidly permeated throughout *Canberra*, and it wafted from some unlikely places. Early in the voyage, Fox was surprised to see a bandsman with a violin under his arm going into one of the women's toilets, and the sound of music coming out as he practised his scales. 'When we got on board, everybody was competing for offices and storage space, and I had to find somewhere for my instrument room and library,' said Ware. 'I sat and thought to myself, "What space isn't going to be used much on this trip?", and it struck me that the ladies' loos wouldn't be. There weren't many women on board, and they were all P&O, so they had their own toilets, so I commandeered one of the public ladies'.'

Canberra crossed the Equator at 5am on Monday 19 April, and passing into the southern hemisphere marked an intensifying of efforts to darken the ship at night. It had proved to be a frustrating business ever since Southampton, despite the optimism expressed in 3 Para's log that it had gone well at the first attempt. It hadn't, not really, and the officers ordered to enforce the blackout for each unit on board loathed the task, which was daunting on a vessel designed to flaunt herself during the hours of darkness. Usually, the only dark area of the ship was forward of the bridge, for navigational reasons; now every part of her must be dimmed. There was little point in her officers executing anti-submarine manoeuvres if she glittered over the sea like a vast illuminated target. Winter was drawing on in the South Atlantic, and if *Canberra* sailed beyond Ascension, the daylight hours would soon shorten, and long nights held increased threats of attack. Don Cole and his fellow electrical officers had already put in days of work, with some success. Lampshades were masked so they glowed rather than shone, and much thought was given to reducing the general level of lighting in public areas while ensuring people could still see where they were going. 'We had to look at the circuitry, as normally *Canberra* was lit up like a Christmas tree, which you really don't want in a war. We spent a lot of time isolating circuits, and we saw how much we could get the lighting down as low as possible while still keeping it safe,' he said. Even though she was no longer the brilliant spectacle she had been on the night the advance planning party had boarded in Gibraltar, light still seemed to pour from window upon window. Basic instructions to close cabin curtains at night were not followed; nor were blackouts made from the rolls of canvas that had been hurriedly loaded at Southampton being used. Officers peering down at the ship from the wings of the bridge despaired as they saw light everywhere. The transgressors included those who should have been setting an example, not least Tom Seccombe, whose luxurious suite amidships on C Deck was amongst the brightest spots to be seen. Scott-Masson later recalled in a lecture aboard *Canberra* how problematic blacking her out proved. 'You've all seen a ship from the shore at night or from another boat, and we are a blaze of light – we want to be a blaze of light, we want to advertise – and we had to achieve at that stage what seemed like the impossible. One evening I do recall, when from the bridge the report came that there was a blaze of light over the ocean and the commander of the embarked military forces, who was in one of the veranda suites, it was obviously his cabin, but the officer concerned in darkening ship was not prepared to knock on his door and tell him so.' Several more weeks of determined effort would pass before *Canberra* was properly darkened and the only brightness to be seen was the white of her paintwork.

As she approached Ascension, the pace of preparations for action was quickening; the day before her scheduled arrival the decision had been taken to transfer first-line ammunition – sufficient for troops to operate for 24 hours – from Elk to *Canberra*, but it would have be stored below, because adding it to the chacons on deck threatened the stability of the already grossly overloaded ship. That Monday evening, as junior officers cursed and grappled yet again with the blackout, their COs were invited for drinks on the bridge. Below decks, a noisy, hotly-contested football quiz was keeping men occupied over their allotted ration of beer. Before he turned in for the night, Hew Pike wrote to his wife, reflecting on the strange juxtaposition of being at sea in the warmth of equatorial waters and what might lie beyond.

The ship's officers threw a drinks party on the bridge – beautiful with the warm evening breeze blowing – hard to imagine sometimes what we are possibly heading for. Certainly the weather will not be as kind as we sail further south, but at present it is lovely. There are lots of flying fish and dolphin, and a few birds.

Dawn the following day brought a glimpse of land on the horizon. Gradually, the jagged profile of Ascension Island grew clearer: a lonely, rocky, arid volcanic outpost in the middle of a vast ocean, valued not for its beauty or history, but purely for its strategic usefulness; a British territory leased to the Americans, its key asset a long airstrip named Wideawake after the colloquial name for the vast colony of sooty terns that bred on the island. *Canberra* let go her anchors at 7.35am, close inshore to Pyramid Point on the western side of Ascension. There were many on board who believed that this was the limit of their adventure; *Canberra* would stay only as long as it took to offload her troops and their stores and then the Navy would take over. 'When we initially sailed, the assumption was that we wouldn't go any farther than Ascension,' said Burne. Despite all the planning, the training, the blackout, the preparation for a fight, the instinct that the combination of continuing diplomatic pressure and threat in the shape of a task force would make Argentina back down was widespread. 'The great thing about amphibious warfare is that you can poise,' said Reed. 'You can just sit there as a threat, and we thought the threat was going to be enough. We were still at that point working under the articles that said, "It is not the present intention of Her Majesty's Government to place the *Canberra* in an area of risk".' Such well-meaning intentions vanished as the days ticked by at Ascension, days that brought tedium, frustration, and tension before decisions were made that changed the lives of everybody aboard.

CHAPTER SEVEN

Our Lads

TO THE crew, they were more than passengers; they were 'our lads', cherished, worried about, fussed over, as near as damn it, family. The relationship that sprang up between the civilians and the embarked military personnel was like nothing either had experienced before, thanks to the odd circumstances in which both groups found themselves. Paying passengers were always treated with the utmost civility and there was even a degree of mutual regard between long-serving crew and guests who returned year after year, yet it had never been like this, nor could be. This was an unspoken closeness, mutual affection and respect that developed spontaneously, a bond that was all the stronger for having been unforced. On the crew's part there was admiration for the challenges the fighting men faced, on the part of military and naval personnel gratitude for the P&O men and women's willing cheerfulness. Each group felt a responsibility for the other and out of that emerged a depth of trust that belied the brief period they had lived side by side. If *Canberra* had felt like a floating city to the men boarding at Southampton, by the time Ascension was reached, it had developed into an entire society of its own making, complete with class divisions, social customs, relationships and gossip. Any private reservations the P&O officers may have harboured about how the soldiers would behave had vanished. Scott-Masson later observed drily, 'It was much easier than having passengers, as they did what they were told.'

As in any society, there were rules to ensure its smooth running. The daily meeting of the adjutants often took on the air of a querulous headmaster laying down the law to a school full of recalcitrant boys as it got to grips with the practicalities of a ship full of soldiers let loose in a novel and, in its way, exciting new environment. Fag-ends and their disposal were a recurring theme of its minutes, their tone akin to reproving miscreants found behind the bike sheds: 'Smoking permitted as exceptional ruling around Alice Springs Bar, but if one cigarette butt found out of ashtray, etc., this will be stopped'; 'Cigarette ends must be extinguished and placed in the proper receptacles – not thrown overboard'; 'Smoking no longer permitted on outside decks – only allowed to smoke in public rooms'. The conduct of troops in search of refreshment after training came up: 'No sweaty bodies in public rooms,' declared the adjutants; 'Coffee areas must be kept tidy or they will cease'. Cleanliness of both men and ship came up again and again: 'There is a shortage of cleaning materials, so please look after the mops etc.'; 'Laundry facilities may be used now between 0600 and 2400 hrs with a gap in the afternoon before and during ship's rounds so that they can be cleaned and emptied. Must take extra care with these driers as there are no replacements or spare parts for them'.

On and on the rules went, but one in particular aimed at ensuring the harmonious operation of *Canberra*; civilian and soldier should not drink together. 'None of the crew were allowed in the military recreation areas, and vice versa,' said Martin Reed. 'It worked very well, but we did have fraternisation periods, if they wanted to invite somebody for a drink or there was a film they wanted to share.' Such restrictions did not apply to officers; drinks in the Crow's Nest played an incalculable part in forming amicable working relationships, as did periodic receptions and parties. For those in the ranks, the no-fraternisation rule was there to be broken, not least because there was no rationing in the crew bar, making it the most attractive of destinations for enterprising spirits determined to get round the daily ration of two cans of beer per man. It was in the nature of soldiers to see what they could get away with, and their officers and NCOs knew what they were up to. 'For the first week or two, you could see there was an element of testing the rules,' said Morgan O'Connell. 'But the rules had been laid down, and they were all founded in common sense.'

The interaction between civilian and soldier was cordial from the moment the men, laden with kit, got on board, especially with those crew at work in public areas of the ship. Thanks to her job in the shop, Sue Wood quickly came to know lots of the men, chatting to them as they queued to buy everyday items like sweets, chocolates, writing paper or washing powder. The shop was also a magnet for those souvenir-hunting, and although it had been stripped of most of its luxury goods left over from cruising at Southampton, stocks of binoculars, watches and waterproof cameras had been left on board – much cheaper to buy than previously, as everything had been reduced to Naafi prices – and they packed in the customers during the twice-daily openings. There was also a brisk trade in T-shirts with '*Canberra* World Tour '82' emblazoned on the chest. The soldiers needed patience, as the queues snaked back a long way from the shop at the aft of the ship. 'It was lovely getting to know the guys,' said Wood. 'It was one big family, and the atmosphere was really positive. You just felt that you'd known them forever, and we seemed to spend all our time feeding them chocolate; I've never seen people eat so much chocolate. There were long, long queues for the shop, but you never heard them moaning, they would queue for as long as it took.' She became one of the most fondly regarded of all the P&O crew by the troops: a down-to-earth, friendly Lancastrian with a smiling, upbeat manner who took extra care to find a few words for the youngest of the soldiers. 'The lady in the shop, she was great,' said Mick Southall. 'She always went out of her way to be very nice to me and my mates because she noticed we were quite young.' The newly-married Wood, on honeymoon in the most unromantic of settings, was to bring a touch of glamour to the lads' lives with her love of singing that was seized on by the bandsmen. Word travelled fast in the closed world of *Canberra*, and it quickly reached the musicians' ears that she was worth hearing. Wood was an enthusiastic participant in crew shows, and after taking their place in the queue at the shop for the chance to have a talk, a group of bandsmen invited her to join their groups touring the bars, performing a few numbers in each before moving on to another. She was greeted rapturously. 'I felt like a modern-day Vera Lynn,' she said. 'I can sing, but I'm not fantastic, but the reception that we got every time we went round these mess rooms was really good. I was due to go into one, and I came down this central staircase, which was just the way in, and they were all cheering. I felt like a movie star. They just appreciated having entertainment and something to do.'

For all the boisterous reception she received, the cheers and the wolf whistles, it was plain that at least part of her appeal lay in reminding them of home and those closest of all; a request she received over and over again was to perform 'Leaving On a Jet Plane', with its lyrics beseeching a lover to await the singer's return.

The crew below officer level largely followed the rules and kept its own company, finding in each other – and in the ship itself – sources of comfort and continuity in the face of uncertainty about what they might have to face. 'We were all very close, and particularly so because we were at sea so much, and although I like being at sea I like getting into ports, and that wasn't happening,' said Wood. 'Everybody supported each other because of the long days. It was our home anyway, but because of the situation you became even closer. You did need the support, because some days you would get a bit down, so there were always people there to build you up again. Unless you read, there wasn't a lot to do when you weren't working.' Her manager in the shop, Leslie Jenkins, also felt that the familiarity of the surroundings and routine was vital in keeping the crew on an even keel emotionally: 'We were doing work that we had done before within an environment that we were accustomed to, and that very much helped.'

Outsiders took some time to grasp just how deeply the connection ran between ship and crew when trying to understand how readily all had volunteered and how matter-of-fact they seemed, at least for now, even as the news worsened, diplomacy faltered and it became clear that a homeward voyage from Ascension was not going to happen any time soon.

'They just said, "This is our ship,"' recalled Kim Sabido. 'That seemed to be a general feeling. I spoke to a man and a woman and they said, "This is our life, this is our home." For them, their lives revolved around what this ship did, and for nine months of the year they were on it. I asked staff about how their families felt about them being here, and a lot of the families were linked to the ship as well. This was their life, and their futures as well. The psychology of that took a lot of getting used to, as I came to realise how close that socio-economic link is between a ship of that size and its staff.'

It soon became apparent to those unused to the Merchant Navy that the ease with which all sides settled into helpful co-operation resulted, at least in part, from the similarities they saw in each other. *Canberra* moved its passengers around the world smoothly, efficiently and safely, and did so because of a tight chain of command and clear hierarchy in which everybody knew the rules and obeyed them.

'I was ready for the military structure, because I'd learned about that from Northern Ireland and I knew how strict they were on rules and regulations,' added Sabido. 'But mentally, I wasn't ready for the way *Canberra* was run. It was, in civilian terms, just like a military operation, and that's why it melded very well with the military on board. Everybody had their place, Scott-Masson's image permeated throughout the ship: you could be disciplined, you could lose your rank, you could even be thrown off the ship, and those staff looked to their line of command to know what was going on.'

No group on board listened more avidly to the captain's Sunday broadcasts than the men and women he commanded, especially those who cleaned or served or cooked or repaired and were out of the loop of the informed gossip and speculation in the Crow's Nest; if there were Marine and Para officers who rolled their eyes when Scott-Masson came over the loudspeakers, the men and women who called *Canberra* home hung on his every word, finding reassurance in what he had to say and the way he said it. For some, though, gnawing worry lay just beneath an outwardly calm appearance, their jumpiness aggravated by a steadily tightening sense of claustrophobia because it was impossible to leave the ship and go ashore, even for an hour or two. Barren as it was, far from home or even the ports familiar from cruises, the sight of Ascension from the anchorage, the pull of dry land frustratingly out of bounds to all but military personnel, proved both tantalising and a reminder that normality lay a long way astern.

Susie West, holding daily surgeries for the crew reporting with run-of-the-mill ailments just like any general practitioner back in Britain, began to detect nervousness and a sense of being boxed in amongst some of the patients she saw, especially those drawn from the pool of unemployed seamen who lacked a close connection to *Canberra*, or friendships forged over the course of numerous voyages.

'Some were thrilled to bits and couldn't wait to get to the latitude where the pay went up, and there were others who thought they'd made entirely the wrong decision, and some who denied that they were told what they were doing, and said, "I just agreed to come and had no idea I was volunteering to go to war". As we went farther and farther south, we had to acclimatise to the fact we were not going to go into port. That was for the foreseeable future; we were not going to touch on dry land and that is a very different concept from going on a cruise ship. You knew if you joined a submarine, you're not going to come up for four months, but to be on a ship you can't get off, even a very big ship, produces a certain amount of claustrophobia, so understanding that was part of the process of submitting to naval command. When you get off the ship on a cruise, you get out of your uniform and you sightsee and you fit in on the ground and you actually feel like that you can self-determine, and if you were terribly unhappy you could get a cab to the nearest airport and go home. But when you are aboard ship, you are just a little ant and you cannot do what you want at all; you will do what the ship does. You will go where the ship goes, and you will do as you are told and I think a lot of the P&O people had a lot of difficulty with it.'

It was fortunate for those struggling to cope with a reality far removed from the idealised notions of gung-ho bravado that swept *Canberra* when her requisitioning was announced that the Navy, increasingly mindful of the emotional toll combat could extract, had included a consultant psychiatrist in the surgical team aboard. There were no crises, no attempts at suicide, but the closeness within both forces and crew, as well as confinement on a ship where secrets were impossible to keep, meant that those showing strain quickly became apparent, whether their personal difficulties manifested themselves in episodes of drunkenness, or in the case of one of the ship's officers an increasing and obsessive concern about emergency procedures. For almost all, their anxieties were managed and they carried on with their jobs.

'I was asked to see formally about 25 people, and they were roughly divided 50/50 Merchant Navy and embarked forces,' said Morgan O'Connell. 'There was one of *Canberra*'s ship's company I was asked to see because people were concerned he was cracking up because he insisted on going to bed with all his clothes on and two lifejackets, and I discovered he'd been sunk three times during the war, and my assessment was he was probably more in touch with reality than the rest of us. There were some who were a bit depressed, and about fifty per cent had some sort of alcohol-related incident afflict them. But there was only the one I had to send home.'

O'Connell had been the subject of some fascination and suspicion on the part of the troops at first, his very presence a source of speculation about what might be going on in this closed, crowded environment.

'People were intrigued, and since you can only run round the deck so many times before you get bored, rumours start,' he recalled. 'All of the doctors took turns at being the duty medical officers for the day, but the men quickly discovered the days when I was on duty and as soon as my name was piped, the rumour would run round the ship that somebody had tried to jump over the side or tried to commit suicide.'

A little subterfuge was called for; the medical officer in charge, Surgeon Captain Roger Wilkes, invented a pseudonym that had a touch of graveyard humour.

'He came up with the idea of calling me Barry Westlake, Barry because I was an Irishman and he presumed that was an Irish name, and Westlake because they were a firm of undertakers just outside Plymouth. So when the pipe went out for Barry Westlake, as opposed to Morgan O'Connell, there was no issue about the psychiatrist being called.'

Anchoring in Ascension made it possible to offload anybody unable to cope, or the simply useless, like the drunken sailor who joined at Southampton and had to be confined to his cabin. A few departures were made reluctantly; a family crisis back in Britain led to the departure of a P&O crewman, and the journalists lost one of their number when the representative of the regional press decided to go no further. All felt that this would be the pause when their fates were decided; homeward and a return to lives they knew or southward to the unknown. Crew with their minds on danger money if *Canberra* headed onwards to the Falklands found themselves the butt of poker-faced wind-ups by soldiers preparing themselves for the worst, who regarded the chatter about a bumper pay-day with amusement tempered by faint irritation. 'They did not believe anything would happen and did not understand what it was about,' said Chris Sheppard, a Marine of 24 itching to get at the Argentines. 'All they talked about was how much money they were going to earn, and I could see that they did not have an inkling that they were going to war, which was understandable; they were civvies, it was just an extra pay cheque, and my response to that was, "I'd do this for no money". I loved saying to them, "The money you're going to earn isn't any use to you, because this ship ain't coming back." That was just my humour, but it was beyond their comprehension anything could happen.'

Rumours – or in services parlance, 'buzzes' – swept the ship endlessly; that *Canberra* was going all the way, or heading home; the Argies were about to give up, or were digging in; a plan to retake the islands had been settled, or could not be decided; the Paras were going to stage an airborne assault, or go in by sea; America was coming in on Britain's side, or staying on the fence. Everyone claimed an impeccable source for their information, and much time and energy was expended on tracking down the latest version of the truth. 'Angela and I would have a walk round to see what we could find out, because there was always this competitive aspect of finding out what the next thing was,' said Rosie Elsdon. 'You'd hear all these buzzes and so we'd try to find out from our sources and be the first to know.' Certain areas of the ship buzzed more vigorously than others; the bureau, where there always seemed to be fresh coffee on the go, was a popular stopping-off point. So too was the hospital, where often enough the medical staff found that a discussion of the latest rumours proved to be a sidelong approach to needing a sympathetic ear. 'Part of it was quite social,' added Elsdon. 'People would pop down, say hello and want a coffee or a drink, we'd always have the door open and they felt they could just have a chat, and it was quite helpful that we were there. Everyone was uncertain, or they were concerned for their families, and it was good to be able to share that. A lot of them had wives and children at home, so it was really hard for them.'

Elsdon and Angela Devine, close friends, had adjoining cabins and did much to keep each other's spirits up. Devine was blessed with a sparky sense of humour and her ability to make those around her laugh was much prized. 'It was almost as if I wasn't taking it seriously,' she said. 'I think it was also because I was older and there's a lot to be said for that, because if I'd died I'd had a very good life up to that point.'

The buzzes were not confined to word of mouth; they made it into print, thanks to a scurrilously funny daily newsletter that sprang from the fertile minds of a couple of young officers. *The Canberra Buzz* was started by Lieutenant-Commander Nick Brown and Lieutenant Tony Miklinski early in the voyage and became one of the most affectionately-held aspects of life on board, copies of its few sheets of typed A4 being run off in *Canberra*'s print shop. It set out to entertain, and succeeded spectacularly, thanks to its earthy tone and irreverent spirit. Jokes, poems, buzzes, cartoons, titbits of scandal, the hurling of insults between Marines and Paras and the football results from back home were its stock-in-trade, and it was the source of much uproarious laughter. Nobody was safe from its scrutiny; Jeremy Hands recalled how, with the terse query, 'Who's a randy boy, then, Harry, RN?', it compounded the embarrassment of an officer glimpsed pleasuring himself in his cabin with the aid of one of the top-shelf magazines helpfully provided by W H Smith. *The Canberra Buzz* was one of the great morale-boosters on board; a cartoon showing a two-headed soldier wearing the insignia of both the Marines and Paras inserting a tin of corned beef into the backside of an Argentine general raised ribald laughter, as did the back-and-forth of rivalry between the units, like the bon mot, 'Far better to keep your mouth shut and let people think you're half-witted, than it is to open your mouth and wear the green beret and prove it'. It had a cod advice section to make the politically-correct brigade back home wince:

Dear Dr Golly,
    I was told that if my wife jumped up and down after intercourse, this would prevent pregnancy. After constant breast feeding, if my wife jumped up and down, she would finish up with two black eyes and eventually knock herself unconscious.
    Yours
    Gormless

Dear Gormless,
    Lead weights may solve the problem.

The same issue, from April 28, poked fun at the northerners aboard, with 'Ode to a Marine on Board SS *Canberra* (To be read with a North Country accent)', which began:

> I were sitting in the Naafi
> A-chewing on me lunch
> A nice fat hunk of corned beef
> By God, it packed a punch.

> Then someone turned around and said
> "What do you think you're doing?
> The Argies are stepping out of line
> There's a spot of trouble brewing"

> I hurled me corned beef to the floor
> Me little knees were knocking
> And as I legged it to the door
> I thought, Oo Eck, it's shocking!

Several stanzas later, the ee-ba-gum ode concluded with a kick in the direction of Nicanor Costa Mendez, Argentina's foreign minister, who was a familiar figure on television news bulletins as efforts at mediation dragged on at the UN:

> We're sailing for the Falklands now
> So watch out the Argentines
> You'll never get us out tha knows
> For we're the Royal Marines

We'll sort you out and chuck you off
I pity your defenders
You haven't got a hope in hell
So up yours Mr Mendez!!

Eventually, though, inter-unit sniping and snide remarks that were a little too personal spelled the end of *The Canberra Buzz*, as the senior military officers on board decided enough was enough. Nevertheless, this energetic and fearless little publication that reflected the spirit and salty humour of the embarked forces so accurately left a potent legacy, in the form of a nickname that worked its way into the national psyche. In one of the early issues, Jeremy Hands wrote a short piece that nodded towards Moby-Dick in referring to *Canberra* as the 'White Whale', because of its trademark gleaming paintwork. The name struck a chord with everybody aboard, and it stuck; Hands would later elaborate on it in his dispatches for ITN and the ship became 'The Great White Whale', a soubriquet that quickly became universal, embraced enthusiastically both by the public which was to take the liner and all aboard to its heart, and the press. It was the fondest of nicknames, and followed *Canberra* for the rest of her days, not just in the minds of those who sailed with the task force but amongst cruise passengers as well, the mention of it enough to prompt smiles of warm recollection.

The rivalry between Marines and Paras that made for such lively exchanges in *The Canberra Buzz* was only too plain to see when men pounded the Promenade Deck, the surface of which was by now badly cracked and scarred by the endless punishment. It was not just the deck suffering; the 3 Para log noted that the soles of the men's trainers were wearing thin from the constant laps, and a request went to the American authorities on Ascension for replacements. 'If you heard that some Marines had been round the deck four times in 12 minutes, we said, "Right, we're going to do better than that"', said Mick Southall, the young Para and enthusiastic runner. 'The Paras were all rough-looking lads off the council estates and the Marines were all good-looking. They'd have a guy with a massive six-pack, and you'd have a Para come out, put his fag out, and then run him round the deck for four hours. We fostered that elitism and rivalry, but it was good humoured.'

There was, however, some concern amongst the commanding officers that the rivalry that sprang from fierce pride on both sides – sharpened by intensive training for war that pumped up minds as well as bodies – could boil over into fights, especially under the influence of drink, hence the separation between bars. 'We had a potentially dangerous mix,' recalled Nick Vaux. 'Royal Marines and Paras don't normally get on, and people like Hew Pike and myself very quickly realised that we had to prevent anything starting, and the way that we did that was by mixing the training. The Paras are very good at some techniques, and vice versa, and that went really well, so quite soon you had a group of Royal Marines being given a presentation by a Parachute Regiment senior NCO, and once they got used to that, it made a big difference. Not a hand in anger was raised all the way down.' Pike said, 'At officer level, we got on very well with the Marines, but at the soldier level the relationship is quite different. They are very tribal and very suspicious of each other. I was delighted that we were going to be taking part in an amphibious operation, but from the point of view of the Toms, it was, "This is insulting, why aren't we parachuting, why are we doing this silly business with Marines?", and of course some of the boys were very young, only 18, 19, 20.' The NCOs were ever-watchful. 'The sergeants and sergeant majors knew what to look for and nipped anything in the bud,' said Norman Menzies. 'Some of these soldiers would go off at a tangent and that's where the sergeants and corporals came into their own in keeping a tight grip on them. There was a buddy system as well, so if you went on deck, you couldn't go on your own: you had to go as a pair, so you knew where everybody was.' Unbidden, a self-imposed segregation had sprung up between Marines and Paras at the beginning of the voyage, which gradually broke down under the influence of training. 'At first, we didn't want anything to do with them and they didn't want anything to do with us,' said Southall. 'We do our thing and they do theirs. As we started training together, the respect was there. I think it was there beforehand, but nobody wanted to acknowledge it.' If the Paras referred to their rivals as 'Royal Latrines', the Marines demonstrated that *The Canberra Buzz* was not the only forum for doggerel with a scathing ditty which subverted the cadences of 'Twinkle, Twinkle Little Star' to insulting effect:

> Para, Para in the sky
> Living proof that shit can fly
> If you've got a low IQ
> You could be a Para too.
>
> Para, Para flying high
> Drops like bird shit from the sky
> Thick as f**k and tough as heck
> Hope you break your f**king neck.

One of the sergeants keeping an eye on any potential flashpoints was Steve Brabham, of the Paras. 'For as much as there's always rivalry, I wouldn't want to go to war with anybody less,' he reflected. 'The Marines are, like we are, a right bunch of arrogant bastards, but the best at their trade, so we had some fiery comments, but no fisticuffs.' As segregation broke down, inter-unit entertainment evenings sprang up, in which Marines and Paras took turns at staging sketches, often enough propelled by some robust banter between the two sides. 'A lad called Chris Phelan was up telling jokes,' said Brabham. 'And he was being heckled by this big Marine, so Chris has enough and says, "What's your size, mate?" and he says six-foot-four, and Chris replied, "I didn't think they stacked shit that high, now sit down." Well, of course the place just erupted. It was a free for all, good humorous banter, people having a laugh on both sides.'

Marines and Paras alike fell for straight-faced practical jokes. As *Canberra* rolled gently through a swell, Laurie Bland, a 3 Para Corporal, and his oppos posted a notice advertising a pool tournament, which generated excited interest amongst men for whom the sight of a table in a

114

pub back home was a magnet. 'A pool competition; on a boat,' recalled Bland. 'You should have seen the names, "Oh yeah, I used to play pool" and you think, "Dickheads". One of them asked how you're going to play pool on a boat, so we said, "The table's in a gyroscope, like the ship's compass" and they said, "We didn't know that." No, you wouldn't do. Loads of them were putting their names down, and when they got the mickey taken out of them, they're saying, "I knew, I knew." 'Course you did.'

Keeping the troops entertained and occupied once training was over for the day was a key factor in preventing any trouble. 'The night-times were always worrying for me,' said Lawrie Ashbridge, 3 Para's RSM. 'I always felt there could be a problem, so we got some quiz nights organised, made use of the *Canberra*'s library, and I acted as judge to make sure there was no fighting.' Inventive spirits came up with more ambitious ideas. Bland devised an ingenious cabaret intended to make use of the state-of-the-art Clansman radios that Pike had argued so hard to get, involving a couple of men doing what appeared to be a mind-reading act. 'He was going to be dressed like a genie, with a big turban and a blindfold, and Ned would be the compere, go round the audience saying "Give us your watch", hold it up and I'd be in the balcony with binoculars, looking at it. He'd have the radio headset on under the turban, and I'd have another one and say, "Steve, it's a comb, it's a clasp knife" or whatever. In rehearsals, it was quite good.' Rehearsal was as far as it got before the idea was stamped on as too frivolous, as was a gang show inspired by the death of theatre producer Ralph Reader that spring, the memory of his massed ranks of boy scouts belting out 'Riding Along on the Crest of a Wave' on television decade after decade prompting Bland and his mates to consider *Canberra* the perfect setting to reprise that anthem.

Inevitably, card games loomed large, soaking up both time and a great deal of money. 'I watched a couple of card schools where a lot of money was going in, the biggest was about £600,' said Brabham. 'It's not supposed to happen, but it does and what are you supposed to do if you walk in to the middle of a card game, there's five or six people playing, and there's all that money? How do you divvy it out? I watched one, and then said, "Right, that's enough."' There was also much time to be whiled away – and fun to be found – in the sackfuls of mail arriving on board from Britain. Besides the letters from home and loved ones, post was pouring in from young women responding enthusiastically to exhortations in the newspapers to write to the brave boys of the task force. Some of the letters were sweetly innocent, others explicitly raunchy and full of promises of what awaited the lucky troops on their return. Many enclosed photographs of themselves in various stages of undress, even rivalling the magazine spreads taped to cabin bulkheads. This was manna for the young soldiers, real girls ready to make dates once whatever happened was all over, and the clamour for the latest letters was intense. A filtering system quickly established itself; letters without pictures received no replies, while those with the sexiest poses received fulsome responses. Some who had set out to bring succour to the lads became unwitting victims of the same poker-faced humour meted out to crew already dreaming of how they would spend their danger money. The units' resident comedians spent consider - able time and effort searching for letters which, to judge from the photographs, came from the most unattractive girls. They too received full and suggestive replies inviting further correspondence – in somebody else's name.

To their delight, the men found that *Canberra*'s cinema remained operational and had a well-stocked library. Dinner, followed by a film, and then a couple of beers before bed became the routine for the lucky ones whose training schedules allowed an evening to follow a settled pattern. There were two, and sometimes three, screenings of the film, beginning at 4.30pm to allow as many men as possible to see it, especially if it was of the favoured variety. 'They loved watching war films, the bloodier the better,' said Martin Reed. 'They did an awful lot of work during the day, so not many of them stayed up late.' Action films were the biggest draw, with Sam Peckinpah's grim and explicit *Cross of Iron* about German soldiers fighting on the Russian front during World War Two proving especially popular. For the Paras, Richard Attenborough's

A Bridge Too Far, the epic story of the airborne assault on Arnhem in 1944, was a source of pride. Another Peckinpah movie, *Straw Dogs*, in which a timid academic takes bloody revenge on a group of men who rape his wife, received approving cheers.

It was not all blood and guts; *Canberra*'s stock of videotapes suitable for cruise passengers included hit television comedies of the day like *Last of the Summer Wine*, with its trio of ageing adolescents getting up to mischief in the Yorkshire countryside, and *To the Manor Born*, mining its laughs from the on-off romance between an impoverished aristocrat and her nouveau-riche neighbour, and both provided escapist fun. Mail drops from home also brought new tapes including recordings of football matches, which attracted avid attention. Predictably enough, other videos mysteriously appeared, leading to another headmasterly ruling from the adjutants: 'No blue movies will be shown in any of the public rooms'. There was music as well, in the form of taped British Forces Broadcasting Service programmes piped into the cabins. So was a cheerfully amateurish request programme started by two young Marines using the records on board; it would, like *The Canberra Buzz*, be silenced when the undertone of needling rivalry became plain in too many of the messages being read out. The pace of training during daylight hours meant that evenings were often much more sedate than a P&O crew braced for the shenanigans of boisterous young troops expected. 'Most nights, the guys were so shattered, the busiest part of the ship was the cinema,' said Southall. 'A lot of guys spent a lot of time in their cabins listening to the music being played through the stereo. I read an awful lot of books. We were told to make sure we got our rest.' The younger soldiers, of which there were many, new to life in their battalion or commando and desperate to prove themselves in these extraordinary circumstances, gravitated to each other. 'The guys who'd just passed out of training would meet up,' added Southall. 'We'd talk about how it was going, if you'd dropped any bollocks, how we felt. We were in our own little group, providing support for each other because we were the newest guys. Most of us were under-18 or only just turned 18, and we were concerned about not letting ourselves down and not letting our corporals and sergeants down.'

Such youngsters were useful to older comrades determined to make the most of their evenings, especially if, like Southall, they did not drink. Considerable ingenuity was expended on circumventing the two cans rule, and the allocation to non-drinkers was quickly snapped up. The British soldier's unswerving devotion to having a drink, and his determination in getting as much as he fancied, was to result in a constant headache for both the naval party and the civilian pursers, as supplies dwindled with alarming rapidity in the face of unending efforts on the part of troops to outwit the ration and slake thirsts worked up by energetic training. Even if the men had stuck to their allocation, that meant 300 cases of beer being drunk every day, and the troops had no intention of limiting their intake. Supplies were running low by the time *Canberra* anchored at Ascension, and buzzes about a large consignment sent out to the island by a brewery back home for the men aboard ships having been purloined by the RAF gained such currency that Tom Seccombe even went ashore to try to pull rank and establish where it was, without success. One solution lay in the pockets of *Canberra*'s catering officer, Nigel Horn. 'He came back with a large consignment of beer that he had to pay for,' said Maurice Rudderham. 'The Naafi would only accept his personal cheque, which he was a bit worried about as he wasn't sure he had enough money in his account to pay for several cases of beer – we had to send a hurried message off to London saying "Please authorise for the deputy purser's cheque to be honoured, and pay this money into his account" – that taught us early on that we were going to have to look around for supplies.'

The men were also looking around for supplies with no less diligence, and had been since dumping their kit at Southampton. Three days out, the adjutants' meeting noted, 'Last night there was an incident involving a Marine and a member of the ship's crew. He was in their bar without being invited by an official invitation. He offered violence after he had drunk too much and then insulted one of the women, who is a ships' cleaner.' It kept on happening; the approach to Ascension found the 3 Para log noting,

'RSM reports that the 40 CDO RM were all absolutely drunk last night in the William Fawcett Room'. It added, for those unable to put two and two cans together, 'They are obviously not adhering to the 2-can rule.' The officers did their best to enforce it; NCOs were posted behind bars to check off the names of those collecting their two cans. That didn't work. A note of resignation crept into the adjutants' minutes: 'New system for the bars – a scheme starting today whereby enough cans of 2 per man based on average attendance figures would be started. Have to wait and see how it works.'

The battle of wits between the soldiers and the rules in pursuit of what Marines and Paras were united in terming a 'wet' was inevitable; at the end of gruelling, demanding, exhausting days during which every hour drilled in the danger and risk of what might lie ahead, the men needed to relax and let off steam, and drinking was part of it, not least because *Canberra*, even in its stripped-down state, invited leisure, especially on these warm equatorial evenings. The senior NCOs, like Lawrie Ashbridge, recognised their lads' needs and indulged them provided matters did not get out of hand. 'Yes, some of them got rat-arsed, but so what, that's what life's all about,' he said. 'They weren't supposed to, but come on, we weren't going to stop that. As long as they weren't harming anyone, it was not a problem, and a ship like the *Canberra* lent itself to people enjoying themselves.' The RSM was a figure to watch; if he could be persuaded to have an extra drink or two, the men took it as the signal to do likewise. Bland recalled enquiring in a tone of innocence, '"Are you having a can, sir?", and he says, "I've already had two, Corporal". "Are you having another, sir?" "Aye, go on then." You hear this phssst of all the cans being opened. If it's good enough for the RSM . . .'

Policing the two-can rule fell to the Marines, who were stationed outside the bars at closing time to prevent beer being taken to cabins. Fines for infractions, or drunkenness, were imposed, but smuggling drink out was easy. 'We had it all sewn up,' added Bland. 'We'd get the carry out at opening time and go and stash it.' Getting beer in volume was equally easy; sending a fresh-faced young soldier to the bar to explain that he was collecting multiple cans for a group of his mates worked every time. The P&O crew serving knew exactly what was going on and played along; their fondness for the soldiers saw to that, and also meant regular invitations to their own bar, where nobody was on hand to count the number of cans and beer was not the only drink on offer.

Full though she was, *Canberra* still held plenty of nooks and crannies where scrutiny was even less likely. Ashbridge's instincts when he first boarded had been correct; men could lose themselves on board, if only for a while. For Bland and his mates, that meant an empty cabin way down on G Deck, forward of the engine room and, ironically enough, near the locked beer and minerals store, where cans smuggled out of the bar could be drunk in peace, if not comfort as men packed in until it was so tight there was hardly room to bend an elbow far enough to get a drink to the lips. 'That became the speakeasy,' said Bland. 'There were four bunks and a chest of drawers, and they'd pull the bottom two out and sit on them, and then the top two, and sit on them as well. A guy sat behind them, three or four on each bunk and you could end up with maybe 30 blokes in there, smoking away, no windows, and just partying.' For now, there was still time to party, as the days at Ascension dragged on.

CHAPTER EIGHT

Waiting and Wondering

HELICOPTERS HOVERED over her constantly, and so too did the air of uncertainty as day followed day. *Canberra* lay at anchor off Ascension, still gleaming white in the bright sunshine, vast, sleek, utterly incongruous in the company of the dull grey tankers and ungainly supply ships that surrounded her, but at one with them in the grip of a powerful South Atlantic swell ceaselessly dashing itself on the jagged, forbidding shoreline. Tenders laden with fresh and frozen food supplies rose and fell at her sea doors as the loading ramp screeched and scraped against the movement, the men trying to move cases and cartons up it sweating and swearing as they strained. Now and again, the swell subsided sufficiently for the loading to be merely fraught and not dangerous; often enough, it left crew staring down the sheer precipice of *Canberra*'s hull as she seemed to soar and the tenders fell away. Airlifts were the most reliable deliveries, the pilots cautious, judging their moments as the landing pads rose and fell. The clatter of rotor blades was endless and the buffeting of downdraughts constant; even a civilised pinkers could not be taken in peace as aircrews made their approach, lowered their loads and gunned their engines, wheeling away so the next in the queue could take their place. 'We were having helicopter movements every five seconds at some times,' said Scott-Masson, 'And the forward landing pad was just outside my cabin, and I can tell you the noise is indescribable.' Ton upon ton of stores and ammunition arrived hour after hour until the sun started to set and quiet descended as the last helicopter of the day headed back to the island. The polished teak of the Sun Deck, barely visible beneath the containers occupying almost every square foot, showed signs of sagging and had to be shored up with timber.

Canberra was giving as well as receiving; besides the ships struggling to offload stores, others approached in need of the most basic commodity of all, water. The task force moored at Ascension was running worryingly low, and had cause to be grateful for the presence in its midst of a liner that for twenty years had revelled in the quality of the water she produced, so pure that soap and shampoo lathered far more luxuriously than it ever did on land. *Canberra* kept a reserve of 1,000 tonnes, and made hundreds more every day from her purification plant. Even so, the demands of troops showering away the sweat of punishing training, laundering their kit and gulping down pint upon pint to stay hydrated in the hot weather was putting the supply under pressure. Consumption on board had to be closely monitored. More than once, the adjutants issued sharp warnings that not a drop should be wasted as the volume used on a daily basis was exceeding what was being made. Nevertheless, whatever *Canberra* had, she shared; every request for water was willingly met, busy little tugs riding the swell ferrying consignments around the anchorage to ships unable to come alongside. The ceaseless activity in the air and the waters around her drew soldier and civilian alike to the guard rails in their spare moments. If lucky, they caught a glimpse of the occasional shark nosing around or watched fascinated as the sea seethed with shoals of black fish whenever food was dumped, or the plumbing flushed out the soldiers' waste after breakfast, leading to them being christened 'shit fish'. In the distance, the sound of firing could be heard as troops got their feet on dry land after more than ten days at sea and began weapons training.

While they did so, their commanding officers attended a round of meetings with brigade to discuss options for landing and re-taking the islands, all underscored by the grim commentary of the World Service bulletins as April wore on; South American states siding with Argentina, Alexander Haig doggedly to-ing and fro-ing in search of a peaceful settlement, Margaret Thatcher telling a sombre House of Commons that force could not be ruled out, Britain declaring that the exclusion zone around the Falklands now extended to Argentina's aircraft.

Yet despite all the activity, the detailed planning of an amphibious operation, and the news reports that seemed increasingly to point towards hostilities, an air of unreality persisted on board for the first few days at Ascension. There remained a touch of the champagne campaign about it all; lunch for the officers could still be preceded by the cracking open of a half-bottle of bubbly to sharpen the appetite, and evenings in the Crow's Nest amid the scaffolding jacks were as convivial as ever. Privations were limited to stocks of certain drinks running low; the tequila had all gone, but there was plenty of cognac, which meant the brandy-and-ginger favoured by many was in no danger of disappearing. The wine list, however, was beginning to show gaps; all the Mercier champagne had gone, along with the Chateau La Tour St Vincent and the Bourgogne Aligote-Bouchard Pere et Fils. Still, there remained healthy stocks of both reds and whites that helped the conversation along. 'It's quite a social milieu, the military and Navy, so that's what you'd expect to do in the evening, have a drink or two or three,' observed Roger Patton, the second-in-command of 3 Para. 'The atmosphere was a bit surreal, it was just a very strange way to go to war, but I'd rather do that than jump out of a plane into the teeth of the enemy. That was what we were trained for; this was altogether different.'

That slightly surreal air was underscored by the quiet but resolute determination of the waiters, resplendent in full uniform, complete with bow ties, to behave exactly as they would on any other cruise. Khaki had supplanted tuxedos, and rolled-up sleeves carefully shot cuffs; the waiters studiously chose not to notice. The Pacific Restaurant was set with the same care and attention to detail; no flowers on the table on this cruise, but otherwise indistinguishable, cutlery and crockery sparkling, tablecloths freshly laundered, smiles welcoming but never over-familiar. 'Nice table for you sir', they murmured as they seated the officers or senior NCOs, serving the meals and pouring the wine with punctiliousness, even if they were bringing grilled liver with boiled cabbage rather than the roast fillet of beef Saxon with choron sauce of only a few weeks before. 'It was completely strange to us all,' said Brian Faulkner. 'The waiters would look after two or three tables as they normally did, and there was absolutely no difference whatsoever in their behaviour towards us to the way they would behave to passengers who had paid thousands of pounds for a world cruise.'

Life was rather less genteel for the men queuing up at the canteen servery and then finding a seat in the Atlantic Restaurant, even though they were eating the same meals as their officers. 'We ate off trays with four holes in them, one for your soup, one for your main course, and so on, and if it was rough weather, your soup got mixed up with your custard, which was interesting', noted Marine Bungy Williams. No matter; trays and plates alike were cleaned of the plain, unfussy meals by officers and men ravenous after bouts of intense training. 'The food was good and there was plenty of it,' recalled Laurie Bland. 'Squaddies don't care; if you get fed three times a day, that's what matters, you just stodge out.' The ship's officers, accustomed to dining with passengers on the finest that *Canberra*'s galley could produce, admired what it was producing in difficult circumstances. 'It was good honest food,' said Graham Harding, 'Good quality, and just enough, so that nothing was wasted. I thought it was excellent.' Some begged to differ. Inevitably, as time passed, the vegetables loaded at Southampton and Freetown began to deteriorate, and the arrival of a black potato on his plate prompted Max Hastings of the *Evening Standard* to be scathing in print about what was being fed to the country's fighting men, much to the annoyance of P&O: 'The sort of thing we used to find on the table in my old house at Charterhouse on one of the cook's less contented days.'

There were brighter interludes; Maurice Rudderham's jealously guarded stock of fillet steak, left in store during the hurried departure, appeared on occasional special evenings that were eagerly anticipated and offered at least a brief glimpse of what life aboard was usually like, the adjutants' meeting noting with relish of one such scheduled event, 'Good meal – steak and chips for soldiers next Wednesday.' Keeping the food coming meant long and gruelling days for the galley, which was feeding far more people than usual with far fewer hands. *Canberra* had always baked its bread, and going to war made no difference to that. 'We were working from 6am until 8pm, with breaks in the middle,' said Roy Paddison, a 39-year-old baker who turned out thousands of rolls served with breakfast, lunch and dinner, which proved a favourite with the troops who wolfed them down. 'We had a job keeping up with the production of the rolls, but you'd just step up and be doing a few extra hours. It was good stuff that we were feeding them, and the troops would help us, humping bags of flour around.'

Mixing over dinner was an essential part of forging a sense of common purpose. There was no set seating; companions at table varied from day to day, and the interaction helped keep the bush telegraph busy. Not all the buzz concerned the overriding question of whether there would be fighting, as Susie West found to her chagrin when she tried to break out of the familiar nightly routine of dining in a group and making conversation with them all. 'It became very difficult to have any sort of private life. I arranged to have dinner with one of the journalists, and instead of going on one of the general tables, we'd go and have dinner at a table for two in the corner and pretend we were in an Italian restaurant. I wasn't naive, but of course it was totally misconstrued and the next morning it's going round the ship that the assistant surgeon and so-and-so are having a sexual relationship. I realised it wasn't the thing to do, and if I was going to have dinner with somebody and just have a one-to-one conversation, the only place it could be was my cabin. Trying to carve out any sense of privacy was a challenge for everyone.' The handful of female officers who ate in the Pacific Restaurant were the most sought-after companions over a meal; they brought a different flavour to the conver - sation, their presence providing a brief respite from the intensely focussed all-male atmosphere of units preparing for war. Those mentally bracing themselves for a fight far from home were drawn to the women of the hospital or the bureau when they needed to talk to somebody and found that chatting over a meal helped soothe their tensions, especially if there was a little gentle, harmless flirting. The instincts of the men were to be at their most charming and chivalrous when women were around, and this spread throughout the ship. The routine effing and blinding of troops joshing each other or working up a sweat in training largely vanished whenever a female came into view, being replaced with smiles and good manners.

The decision to accept female volunteers when *Canberra* was requisitioned was turning out to be unexpectedly prescient. Small in number though they were, female medics, bureau staff or cabin stewards evoked memories of home, lightened the mood. 'Having those girls on board was the best thing that could have happened,' said Martin Reed. 'It made everything seem so much more normal. All the troops moderated their language when the girls were around. The mere sight of a woman was enough to bring a sense of civilisation to the whole thing.' The commanding officers of the embarked units had been acutely aware of the potential for their men to be a nuisance to the women, and they were warned in no uncertain terms that any such behaviour would be dealt with harshly. 'It was one of the very, very rare times in my life where I was able to say, "If I get any problems, I will send you home"', said Nick Vaux. 'That had such an effect, because they were all hell-bent on going. The message was passed down that all these girls had volunteered to stay on, even though we're likely to be going to a war zone, and they deserved respect. The other half of the equation was that the girls had to play their part as well, and they did, they were fantastic.'

Nevertheless, it was impossible to confine thousands of fit young men who had magazine centrefolds taped up in their cabins and letters containing pictures of girls back home in their pockets in the pressure-cooker atmosphere of a closed troopship without their eyes and thoughts turning to the few women on board. Sue Wood, attracting cheers and wolf whistles as she sang, became accustomed to finding notes from love-struck soldiers when she arrived to open the shop. 'I kept getting these letters from squaddies pushed underneath the door, because they didn't know I was married. Whenever you went into a room, all eyes were on you because you're a female among a lot of men. I could handle it, but somebody who was a bit shy might have struggled; but anyone who'd gone into that situation wouldn't have been a shy person anyway.'

At least one of the women learned the hard way that for all the courtesy, boys will be boys, when her daily keep-fit exercises on the fo'c'sle were brought to an abrupt end by the ribald shouts of a group of soldiers. Others did their best not to put temptation in the men's way, but even so were aware of the attention they attracted. During lulls in the long days at Ascension, the nurses sunbathed, and to escape prying eyes used an area on top of the bridge known as Monkey Island. 'It was the only place not overlooked by 3,000 men,' said Rosie Elsdon. 'When we'd been sunbathing for a couple of days, we realised that the helicopters taking off and landing had changed their flight path so they could come in really close and down so they had a better view of us.' The drinking on board loosened inhibitions as well as tongues, and some of the women had to endure their backsides being slapped by leering squaddies emboldened by more than their two cans.

Despite the effective prohibition on anything other than social intercourse between military and civilian, liaisons did take place. There were some men and women aboard *Canberra* no different to those who had faced impending wars down the ages in finding that danger and uncertainty drew them together and intensified their passion. Most of the relationships were fleeting; a few grew into much more. Those that came to light were the subject of gossip in the Crow's Nest or the Marines and Paras bars, the trysts being euphemistically referred to as 'cabin activity'. Roger Patten became aware that one of his officers had become involved, but chose not to intervene. He said, 'It didn't seem to do much harm, I don't think. I don't know how you stop something like that anyway; you just put people under more pressure than they're under already.' Couples kept their involvement as discreet as they could, no easy task in an environment where secrets tended not to stay hidden for long. There was only one embarrassing scene, when an officer became convinced that he was in love with a woman who had given him neither cause nor encouragement to believe that his feelings would be reciprocated. The man made a fool of himself, barging into her cabin, refusing to leave and eventually having to be ejected. Other than that, all aboard left the couples in peace, shrugged their shoulders and got on with their jobs.

If the commanding officers had been alive to how unusual it was for a troopship to sail with female crew and the need to make sure the environment did not become too brutally masculine for their comfort, one aspect of life aboard a cruise liner took them by surprise. It showed itself early; four days out from Southampton, item 25 of the daily adjutants' meeting ordered that henceforth, Marines and Paras queuing for the showers must no longer do so naked. 'No "bare buff" whilst waiting for showers – minimum of towel. The problem isn't the women, but the male mess deck hands!' The adjutants could not resist the exclamation mark; if being waited on was slightly surreal, this was positively bizarre. The lines of young men without a stitch on were attracting a swooning audience from among one of the more colourful social groupings within the *Canberra* family, the gay men. 'It was a fact of life on those ships,' reflected Graham Harding. 'There were always quite a few homosexuals, and they tended to stick together and have their own little group.' Among them were some who were outrageously camp, even wearing make-up on occasion, and they lost no time in making their interest in the troops plain, gravitating to the showers barely had *Canberra* lost sight of the English coastline. 'We had a few who liked to touch the lads,' said Brian Faulkner. 'There was one incident when one of the stewards came into a cabin, this Para's quite well built, and he started rubbing his shoulders and saying "You're a strong boy" and he ended up having to throw him out.' Some took to appearing out of nowhere at bottlenecks in the corridors when groups of men were on the move, accidentally and unavoidably brushing against them as they rushed along in response to orders. The just-turned-18 Bungy Williams had his eyes opened when detailed to the 'grease pit', the washing-up area of the galley.

'You had all the waiters coming in who were serving the officers, and I jokingly turned round to the bloke I was working with and said, "He looks a bit gay, doesn't he?" and this civilian bloke says, "We all are." I said, "You're joking," and he says, "No, if you're not gay, you won't get promotion." I said, "What about this lad here then?", and he says, "I don't know about him, I've not had him." I said, "I thought you said you were married with a couple of kids," and he says, "Well, yes I am, but if I don't do it, I won't get promoted".'

The importunate behaviour of some of the male crew was a worry to officers who knew how their aggressively heterosexual young soldiers might react. 'There's always a danger that when the lads are together and they sense there's a little community like that, they will tend to go after them,' said Vaux. It was another thing for the NCOs to monitor after dark when drink had been taken, and a sergeant felt the need to warn Reed that certain individuals were risking injury as a result of their blatant attempts at seduction. Soldiers were on sentry duty around the ship. They were lonely postings, and under cover of the increasingly effective blackout once the ship had quietened down for the night, there were those on the prowl eager to provide some company. One of the crew had crept up on a sentry and touched him, a hazardous strategy. The young soldier, keyed up to any threat, was badly startled. Even so, he showed commendable restraint. 'He was told to politely remove himself,' said Reed. 'Then one of our boys appeared on the sick list. He'd done the same thing, crept up behind the sentry and put his hand round this bloke's leg. His face had been altered.' It was a vicious attack; the culprit, a Marine from 42 Commando, was sent home. There was another episode of violence; a Para invited a steward back to his cabin and they started to become intimate. Then the soldier changed his mind about the assignation and attacked the unfortunate civilian, who got away without being too badly hurt and chose not make a fuss about what had happened. Older hands knew there were gay soldiers in their ranks, even though homosexuality was frowned upon; their encounters with crew were conducted with even more discretion than those between men and women. Their comrades accepted it as the way of the world and kept quiet about what they knew.

Overwhelmingly though, the troops after being initially disconcerted by the full-on sexual attention they were receiving, formed a bantering rapport with the gays. They knew they were objects of desire and the sheer absurdity of having to slap away the wandering hands of a well-fed steward wearing a come-on smile and mascara in between lectures on survival or pounding round the Promenade Deck rendered it impossible to take offence, as did the bawdy, camp humour on display as rules about fraternising were blithely ignored and soldiers' bars adopted. 'Each bar had a couple of mascots who were gay,' said Chris Sheppard. 'They were happy just to be amongst men, we didn't mind and it was all good fun because they knew how to make people laugh.' The sheer cheek they displayed made many friends. 'They took the mickey out of us more than we did out of them,' noted Williams. 'They were great, they knew nobody was going to hurt them, they'd say. "You've got a nice bum", and the guy would look round and say, "Oh, cheers mate".' The discourse was a little less like a Carry On film up in the Crow's Nest, but it too had its moments; Jeremy Hands writing that when the lighting failed during a lecture to Marines and the room fell quiet, a voice broke the silence: 'Ooo, fancy me in the dark with all these soldiers!'

All those soldiers had much to occupy them. Hardly had *Canberra* dropped anchor than the mammoth task of rearranging the stores loaded in such haste at Southampton began, and that meant donkey work. The helicopters were transferring loads between ships in the anchorage as well as resupplying, the landing craft ferried back and forth. 'The loading had been ad hoc,' said Scott-Masson, 'And of course you had what you wanted first at the bottom of one ship, and probably not the right ship, and what you wanted last you had at the top of the ship you did not want it in, so there was an enormous amount of trans-decking, and this went on all day and every day.' Human chains passed stores hand-to-hand across the decks as order was imposed, but even with hundreds of men pressed into service, keeping up with the loads arriving minute after minute was a problem. Steve Brabham was busy organising the stacking of hundreds of cases of mortar bombs. 'The Sea Kings were queuing up at the back of *Canberra*, and as fast as we were unloading them, there would be another one plonked down, and we had this snake moving around the ship, all shifting ammunition boxes.' Officers watching the loading worried about the number of flying hours the helicopters were clocking up. 'I thought, "God, these helicopters are going to be knackered by the time we get to the Falklands"', said Hew Pike. 'An awful lot of things were in the wrong places. The Rapier missiles were too far down in the ship for a final outload to a beach head.' The jumble was not confined to *Canberra*. Brabham and a corporal were ordered over to Elk to retrieve munitions needed for training ashore. 'We were shown where the ammunition was and we looked down into this hole and the rough sea had dislodged some of the load, so instead of neat pallets, everything was stuck in the middle. It was like looking for a needle in a haystack. The hatch was open, the sun was coming down, and it was like a sweat box in there. We must have lost three pounds in fluid just looking for what we were after.'

The sweat was pouring off the men going ashore as well, as they got their first taste of what an amphibious landing on the Falklands would entail. Landing craft cut through the swell towards *Canberra* as soldiers lined up by the galley doors to leap aboard. For now, boarding was relatively easy; the soldiers were not carrying full kit, and jumping down onto the deck as the craft rose towards the ship on the waves went smoothly. The landing craft ran into the beach, beyond which the men and their officers found a blasted, bleak landscape of ash and clinker, the only vegetation an area of forest and greenery high above at the very summit of the island. Overhead, planes and helicopters made their ascents from or final approaches to the airstrip, now the busiest in the world, with more than 300 flights a day, even surpassing Chicago's O'Hare Airport, which held the record. It was good to get off the ship, to be on solid ground, able to run and march not on the monotonous merry-go-round of the Promenade Deck, but on roads heading upwards and across the island. Better still was the chance to fire not at bags of rubbish thrown from the stern, but at the derelict vehicles that littered the Wideawake range. Tens of thousands of rounds were fired off as the men once again zeroed their weapons, scores of mortar rounds, and equipment unearthed from the bowels of *Canberra* was demonstrated, notably the Milan anti-tank missile, which many of the men had never seen because at £4,000 each, they were considered too expensive to be used other than sparingly in training. The first was reassuringly devastating, streaking towards its target more than a mile distant and demolishing it with a roar that provoked cheering and sent thousands of screeching Wideawake terns whirling into the air. A second had a similarly satisfying effect, and the confidence of the men in the weaponry they would take ashore soared. The training could be hairy and deafening. Brabham was ordered to demonstrate a Bangalore torpedo, a charge assembled in sections and pushed along the ground towards obstacles to be cleared. Finding cover at a safe distance on the rocky, featureless terrain was touch and go. 'We were hiding in this little fold in the ground, and when it went bang, it was bloody horrendous, we were shouting for the next two hours and lip-reading. When you get to that stage, you start thinking this is bloody serious stuff, this isn't a birthday cruise any more.'

The commanding officers felt the tempo quickening too, not least because of the planning meetings that were getting to grips with the logistics of landing on the Falklands. 'We were much more preoccupied than we had been,' said Vaux. 'We were getting ready for something that we now knew was likely to happen, and we were desperate to achieve as much live firing as possible and get all our equipment sorted.' The commanding officers paced their men; an hour or two was found for the troops to relax on Ascension's beach, to catch some sun, even to swim. Vaux and Tom Seccombe also gave themselves a couple of hours off, borrowed Pike's Land Rover and took a ride up to the lush greenery of Ascension's summit, there just to wander in the forest for a while and, in a moment when gallantry intruded on preparations for war, to gather wildflowers for some of *Canberra*'s women, to the amusement of a couple of senior NCOs who went with them, including Warrant Officer Bob Brown, of the Royal Marines Police, known as 'The Sheriff'. Vaux wrote, 'Mr Brown's grin became somewhat lopsided when Tom decided that he, personally, ought not to appear with a bunch of flowers in a crowded landing craft alongside the ship . . . Later, we swung on board with an aggressive-looking "Sheriff" gingerly clutching his posy; mine was furtively shoved down the front of my shirt.'

Hostilities seemed distant at such moments, but the enemy was closer than anybody realised. Late in the afternoon of Friday 23 April, Graham Harding stepped outside onto the bridge wing for a smoke, and began chatting to Mike Austen, the senior Royal Fleet Auxiliary radio officer, the two men gazing out over the sea and enjoying the sunshine. Away on the northern horizon, something caught Harding's eye. 'We had a huge World War Two gunnery binocular set on a plinth, and we saw this thing approaching; it came into full view and then turned 90 degrees to the west,' he said. Austen made a quick sketch on the back of his hand as it faded from view; cargo ship, bipod masts, dark funnel with a slanting white stripe. After initial puzzlement as to why it had abruptly changed course, the two men thought nothing more about it. Thirty-six hours later, on the Sunday morning, Harding was out on the bridge wing again, this time with his own binoculars. As he slowly scanned around the horizon, he froze; dark funnel, white stripe. 'This bloody thing suddenly appeared and I went berserk because I recognised it and said, "What the hell has that been doing for the last day and a half?"' He shot back into the bridge and raised the alarm, sending the anchorage onto full alert; within minutes, a helicopter was scrambled to identify the ship and the frigate HMS *Antelope*, her gas turbines whining ever louder as she gathered speed, came past in pursuit as the ship disappeared over the horizon. Harding had spotted MV *Rio de Plata*, out of Buenos Aires, which had slipped unnoticed past the Royal Navy to gauge the strength of the task force gathering at Ascension. A tense twelve hours followed, as signals flashed back and forth to Northwood; how could a spy ship have got so close? How much had she seen? Was the anchorage secure? Above all, had Argentine divers been landed to carry out underwater attacks? Intelligence suggested that Argentina had some form of midget submarine that could be used against shipping. The risk was too great to leave to chance. Limpet mines could send men and ships to the bottom as they lay at anchor at night, crippling the task force, and the biggest target of them all, ghostly white in the moonlight, was there for the taking. At 1am on the Monday, *Canberra* was ordered to the relative safety of the open sea, beyond the reach of underwater sabotage. 'That was the pattern of our life during the next few days while we were still there,' said Scott-Masson, 'going to sea at night and coming back in the daytime to continue troop transfers.' She zig-zagged through the darkness, slowly steaming a hundred and more miles every night, no slackers on the blackout now, the sentries at her rails more alert than ever, straining their eyes and ears for any unusual movement in the sea surging quietly past far below, armed not only with their weapons but also powerful lamps to shine downwards if they thought they heard or glimpsed anything.

Abruptly, the phoney war was over. The shadow of an enemy beyond the horizon cast by the spy ship revealed itself as the shooting started. As *Canberra* spent the nights hidden in the darkness of the ocean, the World Service announced that South Georgia had been retaken in an audacious operation involving the SAS and 42 Commando's M Company; the buzz around the ship was that the SAS and the Special Boat Squadron were now ashore on the Falklands gathering intelligence. Everything pointed towards a fight, each day making a peaceful settlement less likely. Haig's shuttle diplomacy was at its end, as Argentina rejected yet another compromise and the United States announced its support for Britain. On the last day of April, those at the guard rails watched silently as the landing ships (logistics) sailed for the total exclusion zone before *Canberra* put to sea for refuelling, an eight-hour operation that in the swell of the South Atlantic required enormous skill because of her bulk. 'Normally, in a replenishment at sea, the frigate or naval ship approaches the tanker which maintains a steady course and speed, and the replenishing ship does the manoeuvring,' said Scott-Masson. 'But we had to change that technique because from the bridge of *Canberra* the tanker was so relatively small that we couldn't even see it, so the only way to do it was for the tanker to approach us and we stayed on a steady course and speed and he did the manoeuvring.' That same day, *Canberra* acquired a third landing pad to take small helicopters; the flat roof of the air conditioning unit just forward of the funnels was shored up and tested.

A series of arrivals on board reinforced the sense that action was now inevitable, not least that of Naval Party 8901, only recently repatriated from being taken prisoner by the Argentines after putting up brave resistance on the first day of the invasion. They were the subject of intense curiosity from Marines and Paras alike from the moment they boarded after flying to Ascension, scrutinised and questioned by soldiers who wanted to know every detail of what had happened and how it had felt. Twenty-three-year-old Corporal David Armour – nicknamed 'Lou', which was short for 'Loopy' – had been right in the thick of it, leading his section under fire as he broke through to Government House. 'When we first got on, and we weren't attached to anyone, we were very popular,' he said. 'The other troops wanted to know what it was like. But a bit later on, there was a lot of nudging about who was going to see action, it was, "You guys have been there, you've had your bit, now it's our turn".' News reports made much of NP8901 vowing to go back and settle the score, but such tub-thumping was ignorant of the uncertain position of its men, who did not know which unit they belonged to or what their role would be, and whose accommodation made them feel like an afterthought. 'They didn't know what to do with us,' said Armour. 'It was plain that it was a political move having us going back at them, because once we were on board ship, it was, "Who's looking after them, what are they going to do?" We were in the bowels of the ship, and we were saying, "F**k me, if anything hits us, we've had it", because we were right down by the watertight systems in the bilges, and we just knew once everything was locked down, there was no way we were going to get out because those doors wouldn't be opened. There were massive cogs and rail systems and the doors were different to anything else on the ship.'

The answer lay with 42 Commando, which with M Company on South Georgia, was under strength. NP8901, under the command of Major Mike Norman, formed the nucleus of the new J Company, which also absorbed other Marines who had been sent to *Canberra* in the hours before she sailed to be allocated as required.

Other new faces were appearing. The colourful figure of Major Ewen Southby-Tailyour RM arrived from HMS *Fearless*. He was an accomplished yachtsman who had spent a posting to the Falklands compiling a book on the inshore navigation of the islands; with the exception of the local fishermen, nobody knew their coastline as thoroughly and his expertise was essential to the planning of any landing. He was an old friend of Vaux, whose stateroom sofa he made use of as a vast improvement over the bath he was obliged to sleep in aboard the crowded *Fearless*. Vaux wrote of him, 'A suave, gregarious bon viveur, he instantly adapted to *Canberra*'s social scene and contrived to spend as much time with us as possible.' He made an immediate and lasting impression on all who met him, Robert Fox noting, 'He was a fund of stories and anecdotes, most told against himself. The clearest image I have is of his mane of white hair appearing round some corridor or bulkhead in the *Canberra* with the invitation, "I say, come and share a glass of port in my cabin".'

Conversation in the Crow's Nest was further enriched by the presence of the commanding officer of 2 Para, who flew ahead of his men, sailing for Ascension aboard the *Norland*, to join the briefings at brigade as he awaited their arrival. Forty-one-year-old Lieutenant Colonel 'H' Jones – he preferred the initial to his loathed first name, Herbert – lost no time in plunging into animated discussions of military history with Fox and Max Hastings. Hew Pike noted that Jones had brought only one book with him, Sir Edward Creasey's 1851 *The Fifteen Decisive Battles of the World*. Pike's relationship with his fellow Para officer was a touch prickly. 'He was very argumentative, but then so am I for my sins. You occasionally meet people who really have a sense of destiny, and he had this sense that this was his moment and he was going to make the most of it.' Hastings noted Jones's intensity, writing, 'He was a Roman, for all his twinkling laughter, who yearned for the opportunity to show his own steel on the battlefield . . . But none of us doubted his passionate yearning for distinction, nor his inevitable rivalry with Hew Pike . . . a sharp, crisp, clever, equally ambitious soldier in a more conventional pattern, who was plainly destined for higher things in the army.'

There was a contrast, too, with Vaux, who knew only too well the hazards of the operation that loomed, because of his experiences during the Suez crisis as a young officer. 'Nick was one of those impish, understated professionals whom men find easy to follow in war,' wrote Hastings. 'They command confidence, because they know their business with no need to show off about it, and their chief ambition is to bring back alive the men whom they lead.' Now that diplomacy appeared exhausted, the COs were impatient to get on with the job. 'Why should they not?' observed Hastings. 'They were professional warriors, men who had spent years training in Norway, Germany, Wiltshire, Northern Ireland, Canada, Kenya for one eventuality: battle. This did not make them cruel or bloodthirsty, still less insensitive. They simply saw in those April and May days of 1982 the glow on the southern horizon of a chance to fulfil the promise and preparation of a lifetime.' Nobody could have known it, but for the few days Jones was on board, *Canberra* was the temporary home of the two men who would be awarded posthumous VCs for their bravery in the Falklands. As Jones talked military history in the Crow's Nest, Sgt Ian McKay, of 3 Para, talked football in the Meridian Room.

The desire for the waiting to be done with ran through all ranks; the men were ready for action, fit, positive, confident, aggressive, eager to fight, willing to do whatever it took to win. Wires used for cutting the cheese served after dinner began disappearing from the galley, proffed for conversion into garrottes; Rudderham ultimately had to stand guard, issuing them as the cheese was sliced and then locking them away. Those with workbenches around the ship, in the engineering and radio departments, or the carpenters' shop, found themselves chatted up by smiling soldiers laying on the charm to get a keener edge on a blade or a sharper point. A bloodthirsty song, credited to Marine Maurice 'Moz' Tombs of 42 Commando began doing the rounds, taken up with equal relish by the Paras and belted out in the drinking holes, with or without the accompaniment of the touring bandies. It subverted the relentlessly bouncy tune of Cliff Richard's 'Summer Holiday' to gruesome effect, its chorus going:

> We're all going to the Malvinas,
> We're all going to kill a spic or two,
> We're all going on a pusser's holiday,
> For a month or two-oo-oo,
> Or three or four.

The verses detailed inventively brutal variations on what the invaders could expect, one offering:

> We're going to kill the wops with phosphorous,
> We'll get them with our GPMGs,
> They'd better not try to take cover,
> 'Cos there ain't no f**king trees.

The chorus – only that, the verses being too savage – eventually found its way onto television back home, and if it made more politically correct viewers wince, so be it; the lustiness with which it was sung and the uproarious laughter and cheering that followed its every rendition was an expression of the spirit of young men primed and conditioned to do whatever was asked of them. Their commanding officers were at one in agreeing that if, for whatever reason, Argentina relinquished the Falklands without a fight, a large-scale exercise would have to be mounted to vent the pent-up energy before the Marines and Paras could be safely landed back in Britain. They also worried that the longer *Canberra* paused at Ascension, the greater the danger that the men would pass the peak of readiness. Pike wrote to his wife on 28 April: 'It is now just midnight, and I have switched on the news and it all sounds pretty belligerent, with the Argentines now threatening to shoot down aircraft over the Falklands. But don't worry – we are brimming with confidence and just wish we could be allowed to get on with it. The longer the politicians wait, the more difficult the task ultimately becomes, so I do hope there isn't a long delay. The sooner we get the job done, the sooner we will be home.'

The troops on board felt instinctively that the voyage they had joked would circle the Isle of Wight a few times before going back to Southampton was taking them towards the greatest challenge of their lives, whether they were in their teens or had decades of service behind them. 'I knew, I just knew,' Lawrie Ashbridge reflected. 'I'd been in the army 22 years, been in a few fracas, but I just knew that in my 22nd year, I'm going on the biggie. I remember H. Jones and Hew Pike and myself sitting on this ledge at Ascension watching our anti-tanks firing and thinking, "What the frigging hell are we doing here?"' *Canberra*'s officers caught the mood and braced themselves; yet for many of the crew – and their families at home – there remained a failure to appreciate the course on which they were set, lulled into believing that no danger faced them by the P&O newsletter, even though the company knew before April was over that she was bound for hostile waters. Almost a week into May, it told its audience, 'As you know and as reiterated in our last newsletter, the Royal Navy have stated that they do not intend placing the *Canberra* in a hazardous situation, which means that she is not likely to be so vulnerable to military dangers as the front line task force units.' The blandest, most clumsily unrealistic assessment of the crew's emotional state followed: 'Their greatest problem seems to be overcoming the natural feeling of boredom which prevails on board and we are actively endeavouring to assist the situation by providing staff to organise more entertainment, which we feel would relieve the situation.' They never got their entertainment, but the much discussed danger money was about to start being paid.

CHAPTER NINE

Going All the Way

IT WAS an uncomfortable trip across the anchorage as the boat bumped through the swell towards HMS *Fearless*, where the perilous-looking rope ladder hanging over the carrier's side and the long haul up it to the deck promised to do nothing for the dignity of a cruise ship captain of a certain age. 'I couldn't see any other way of getting on board so I presumed this must be for me,' said Scott-Masson. 'With me was the deputy captain and the senior naval officer and none of us were in the first flush of youth. A helicopter decided to come in and land on the deck above us and its rotor blades kicked up all the water and of course we got saturated. In true naval style they were going to welcome us by piping us onboard, so there was a sailor standing there with his pipe but he forgot the fact that we had to go on our hands and knees to crawl over the edge of the gunwale onto the deck, and he was far more busy piping to help us. All we wanted was someone to help us up.'

Their awkward entrance was quickly forgotten as the three men were swept up in the tense atmosphere on board, the result of weeks of meetings to weigh options for winning back the Falklands that had culminated in decisions those responsible knew could cost British lives. Landing sites for the forces aboard *Canberra* had been considered and discarded, a list of 19 possibilities whittled down to three, one of which was submitted to the chiefs of staff and the Cabinet for approval. A window in mid-May had been identified as the optimum time to mount the operation, and now the details were being settled, which was why Commodore Michael Clapp summoned Scott-Masson: he needed to ask a question. 'At the end of the

140

briefing he asked me, would I be prepared to take the troops into wherever they were landed,' said Scott-Masson. 'And did I think that P&O would be prepared to let the ship go down into the landing area. I was a little nonplussed and I thought for a few minutes. I was certain the ship's company would back me and be prepared to go in and I thought, "Well, I'm sure the P&O management would agree we should do what was required of us".' If Scott-Masson was temporarily knocked off balance by being asked to take *Canberra* all the way in, he quickly recovered his equilibrium. This had not been part of the plan; he had sailed on the clear understanding that the troops he carried would be transferred to naval ships well clear of any war zone. To his everlasting credit, he did not flinch; he had told his wife that he would do whatever was asked of him, and said the same thing publicly. He was as good as his word, and the RNR officer in him appreciated the problems the task force faced as Clapp outlined them. The naval assault ships were already full to bursting, and transferring *Canberra*'s Marines and Paras to them for what remained a long voyage south would make conditions aboard impossible, as well as degrading the men's fitness. Nor was there the capacity to transport the huge tonnage of stores that the overloaded liner bore by any other means. Similar considerations meant that *Norland*, with 2 Para aboard, would also have to go in.

Clapp kept certain things to himself; he did not reveal the landing site, or that his staff had, like P&O in London, thought the unthinkable and considered the possibility of *Canberra* being sunk. Her officers subsequently learned that the Navy calculated – and hoped – that *Canberra*'s majestic height would help those aboard if disaster struck; the anchorage identified was shallow enough for her keel to rest on the bottom whilst the upper decks remained above water, increasing the chances of getting people off alive, as well as holding out the possibility that her flight decks could still be used.

Scott-Masson's instincts were correct; his crew received the news that they were continuing southward calmly. Their ties to the ship and to each other buoyed up their spirits, and the prospect of staying with the troops they held in such affectionate regard made whatever lay ahead less daunting. 'I think everyone believed wholeheartedly in what they were doing, and what amazed everyone was the spirit of the youngsters,' said Michael Bradford. 'There were no anti feelings at all; I think it was a question of if we have got to go, then let's get on with it and get it over as quickly as possible.' Martin Reed had noticed a subtle change in the crew after almost a month in close proximity to the soldiers, going through the same survival drills, and absorbing their mindset. 'We weren't really civilians any more,' said Reed. 'We were a ship's company and we were as trained as we possibly could be. I think they'd have been upset if you called them civilians. You couldn't call them armed forces, but they were no longer civilians.' *Canberra* was at six hours' notice to sail as May began, which brought with it the news that a lone Vulcan bomber from Ascension had carried out a daring raid on Port Stanley airfield, followed up by 20 Harriers from HMS *Hermes* and HMS *Invincible* attacking Argentine positions that had also been bombarded from the sea. It felt like a good omen, that Britain was carrying the fight to the enemy, and the sight of Ascension's anchorage filling up with yet more task force ships instilled confidence in everybody aboard. The next few days were to demonstrate just how brittle emotions on board could be underneath that optimistic surface.

On the evening of Sunday 2 May, as the last troops clambered back aboard *Canberra* after yet another's day's training and she prepared to put to sea for the night, the nuclear-powered submarine HMS *Conqueror* spotted the Argentine cruiser *General Belgrano* skirting the southern edge of the total exclusion zone around the Falklands. She was an old ship, in a previous incarnation USS *Phoenix*, a survivor of the 1941 Japanese attack on Pearl Harbor that brought America into the Second World War. She stood no chance; 200 men died in the initial explosions caused by the two torpedoes fired by *Conqueror*, and 850 scrambled for the liferafts as the cruiser began to sink. It would take more than a day for all the survivors to be rescued, and by then the tally of the dead stood at 321.

There was a moment's silence when the news reached *Canberra*, as men and women took in the loss of life and its implications; and then the whoops of exultation went up, at least among the troops. 'I thought, "Yeah, great",' said Mick Southall. 'It never occurred to me that they were somebody's sons.' There was no such elation amongst the crew, or the naval party, who knew what it was to be a seafarer and could all too easily imagine the horror of the sinking, just a grim acceptance of its necessity. 'We were quite quiet,' said Reed. 'Anyone involved with the sea knows that something like that is horrendous, and we were feeling more for the people involved rather than the overall effect. Then we thought, "Well, there's a big piece shifted off the chessboard."' All realised there would be an attempt at reprisal, and the jitters started. 'I thought, "Bloody hell, that's torn it",' said Graham Harding. 'I wasn't exactly full of beans mentally, I was getting somewhat nervy about what was coming once we left Ascension.'

Men steeled for retaliation from Argentina found their nerves on edge. 'I thought, "What's the biggest thing they can hit?"' said Steve Brabham. 'The *Canberra*, or one of the big military ships? We were in the Pacific Lounge watching a film, and every so often you get this rogue wave that slaps the side of the boat, and this thing hits *Canberra* and we looked at each other as if to say, "Have we been f**king hit?" It made such a crack. There was like a pregnant pause, nothing happened, no alarm bells ringing, and then one of the civilian crew said, "It's just a wave slapping on the side", and we thought thank Christ for that.' The sinking of the *Belgrano* prompted an infamous headline in the *Sun*, which screamed, 'Gotcha!' When word of it reached *Canberra*, it provoked fury, and those raging at its crass inappropriateness turned on the journalists aboard. 'We came in for a huge amount of stick,' said Kim Sabido. 'Losses on any side are not to be celebrated or rejoiced in. When the papers were shipped to us a few days later, some of the naval and military set fire to the *Sun* and they were throwing it over the side. They absolutely hated that headline because it demeaned life, and it was a cardinal sin to celebrate death and destruction.' Derek Hudson, of the *Yorkshire Post*, who had flown out to Ascension to join *Canberra* as the new representative of the regional press, observed that the reporters were equally appalled. 'The entire press party signed a joint message to the editor of the *Sun* protesting about his headline and asked for extra supplies of his tabloid because supplies of toilet rolls were running low.'

As if to underline the gravity of what was unfolding, the government announced that an additional brigade was being sent to join the task force. To get it there, the 67,000-ton *Queen Elizabeth II* was requisitioned from Cunard. A degree of not entirely friendly rivalry existed between that company and P&O, and there were officers aboard *Canberra* who referred dismissively to the *QE2* as 'The Black Pig', or derided its familiar role of cruising to the US as being the work of 'a North Atlantic ferry'. Within weeks, the rivalry would degenerate into outright animosity.

Revenge for the *Belgrano* was swift. HMS *Sheffield* was one of three Type 42 destroyers, along with *Glasgow* and *Coventry*, providing a defence screen for carriers 50 miles south-east of the Falklands on the morning of Tuesday 4 May when two Argentine Super Etendard warplanes searching for HMS *Hermes* found her instead. From a range of six miles, they fired two French-built sea-skimming Exocet missiles. One missed; the other hit *Sheffield* at approaching 700mph eight feet above the waterline near the forward engine room on the starboard side, tearing a jagged hole in the hull and starting fires that raged through the ship. The crew fought them with reckless bravery, but with the water main destroyed could not hope to win. Four hours later, *Sheffield* was abandoned, 20 of her 281 men dead and a further 26 injured. She remained afloat, burned out and blackened, being taken under tow on 9 May, with the aim of getting her to South Georgia and then homeward. At dawn the following day, she began to list in worsening weather. Dense fog veiled the end; nobody saw her slip away into the chill of the South Atlantic with the remains of 19 men still aboard. She became their war grave, the first Royal Navy ship sunk by enemy action since World War Two.

Canberra was going about her usual routine when the news that *Sheffield* had been hit reached her at about 5pm; men were checking their kit, showering after yet more training, reading or chatting to their oppos over a smoke at the guard rails. In the Alice Springs Bar, 3 Para were getting the evening's entertainment underway with a game of bingo, and in the Pacific Restaurant, the waiters showed officers to their tables for an early dinner. Then it all stopped; everybody froze, shocked into silence as the news spread from deck to deck and cabin to cabin faster than any buzz. 'Despondency. Sheer bloody despondency,' reflected Reed. 'We all thought, "Bloody hell, this is going to be nasty now", we're going to take casualties, not only in personnel, but in ships.'

In an instant, everybody realised that there was no going back, no easy course, that loose talk in the papers back home jeering at 'Argies' and 'spics' who would run away in the face of plucky Brits had been exposed as just so much jingoistic nonsense by determined opponents who had destroyed one of the Navy's most modern and well-armed warships. 'We were in the middle of dinner and it just swept through the restaurant,' said Rosie Elsdon. 'That was the moment when we all thought, "Golly, this is actually going to happen", it all suddenly hit us that what we had been training for and all the troops had spent their lives training for was going to happen.' The Naval personnel were the most profoundly shaken of all. Lawrie Ashbridge went into 3 Para's bar to see how his men were taking the news, and was immediately buttonholed. 'One of them said, "Have you seen, sir, some of them Navy lads, they're crying", and I hadn't, so I went for a wander round and came across a few of them crying, and I could understand it. I said to my lads, "Put it into perspective, they've never been to Northern Ireland like you; you've seen more action in the few years you've been in than a chief petty officer who's been in for 20 years."'

For Don Cole, there was the pang of personal loss; he had helped build *Sheffield* at Barrow-in-Furness in 1974, and she had shaped the course his life had taken. 'I had even been on sea trials with her; she was my first time at sea and I think what inspired me to seek a career at sea. I remember standing on her aft mooring deck during speed trials in the Clyde and not being able to see anything but a wall of foaming white water all around the aft end as she hit full speed with her twin Olympus gas turbines screaming away at full power.' What Cole knew of *Sheffield* made him pessimistic about *Canberra*'s chances if she came under similar attack. 'It was hard to believe that a ship like that, a ship I knew so well, could be destroyed in a single action. A ship like that has armoured plates; an Exocet would go straight through *Canberra* and there'd be a lot of fatalities, so I was very concerned.'

Sabido found himself the target of a violent demonstration of how raw emotions were at the loss of lives. He had taken his typewriter with him to the Crow's Nest, and made the mistake of sitting down to write a dispatch about the mood on *Canberra*. Doing so in public was a bad misjudgement, coming so soon after the anger at the 'Gotcha!' headline. Over his shoulder, the bar quietened as men read what he was typing, and tempers boiled over. He was hauled out of his chair by a group of young officers and pinioned, unable to free himself. 'I actually feared for my life because the atmosphere was so venomous. My arms were pinned behind my back. One got hold of me and the other had his face up to mine. It frightened the shit out of me. He wasn't negotiable with, debatable with, calmable. They saw us as almost like being the Devil incarnate, as joining in with the blood and lust of war without respecting – and that was a big word for them, respect – their positions as fighting men and comrades in arms because you're writing about military losses and deaths.' Senior officers intervened to free him before any real damage could be done, but the incident illustrated the hair-trigger state of soldiers primed for action by weeks in a closed environment now coming to terms with the shooting starting in earnest and killing men they could identify with. 'It was that intensity, both mental and physical, of being cooped up in that ship,' added Sabido. 'It was a spark that showed how intense everybody was feeling, and how on edge as well, being shut in this claustrophobic atmosphere, not being fully aware of what was happening around you and not knowing what was going to happen.'

The sense of being in the grip of a dangerous and unpredictable situation led men to exercise whatever control they could over their surroundings; that evening, Southall began what was to become an obsessive checking of his kit. 'You'd have checked it only two hours ago, but you'd drag your web gear out and put it on your bunk and check it again, and you'd go for dinner or watch a film, and before you went to bed you'd get it out and check it again. I found myself doing that a lot, checking that my gear was ready to go.'

The waiting was over; after 17 days at Ascension, *Canberra* was ordered to sail south to join the task force on Thursday 6 May. There were no banners to bid her farewell this time, but there was music and cheering; marches played over her loudspeakers as she weighed anchor in the late-afternoon sun a few minutes before 5pm and got under way, gliding through an unusually calm sea past HMS *Fearless* and HMS *Intrepid* whose crews had gathered to shout noisy encouragement, the men at *Canberra*'s rails waving back and giving thumbs-up signs. Her course took her for the first time past Wideawake Airfield, revealing the scale of the air operation underway and explaining the ever-present flights over the island. Every inch of it was jammed; reconnaissance Nimrods, Hercules transports, Harriers, the Vulcan that had bombed Stanley's airstrip and the Victor tankers that had refuelled it in mid-air. Even as she passed, helicopters were lifting off and heading out to her; a last consignment of beer, another load of food lowered by aircrews who waved their own good wishes as they returned to the island.

Canberra was not alone; *Elk* and the frigates *Ardent* and *Argonaut* were in company, as was the tanker *Tidepool*, which would spend the evening refuelling her. The jagged profile of Ascension rapidly fell astern, the last dry land *Canberra*'s soldiers would see until they set foot on shores held by an enemy dug in and waiting for them, 4,000 miles away.

There had been enough worry and tension over the past few days. Tonight, there would be a party; music, dancing, drinks, the chance for officers with too much on their minds to let off some steam and relax, courtesy of P&O. The incongruity of the event in the hours after leaving Ascension was not lost on anybody there. Outside, a blacked-out *Canberra* ploughing south towards danger under the protection of two warships more watchful than ever since *Sheffield*'s loss, her sentries with lamps jumpy knowing that a British ship could be sunk; inside, colourful paper streamers decorating the low-ceilinged officers' wardroom, a quartet of bandsmen shoehorned into a corner, the din of laughter, chatter and clinking glasses, so packed that people had to leave to allow others in; Naval and military men taking it in turns to ask the women to dance and savouring the few minutes of each number, which for nearly all was the first physical contact, however innocent, with a member of the opposite sex in weeks. It was an interlude of normality amid disorientating uncertainty, and all the sweeter for it. In the morning, the preparations for war, and understanding of the human toll it might extract, would intensify.

The 7th began with a call for blood donors, and it sent the buzzes into overdrive. The shrewdest of the troops knew that they needed about 10 days to recuperate, which meant any landings were unlikely until around the 17th; they also knew that the medics could not store the blood for more than a few weeks, so there was every chance of going into action soon after that date. The surgical team aimed to take 1,000 pints of blood, to be kept in bar fridges that once held champagne; in the event, they could have had much more than that as so many volunteers came forward, dozens having to be turned away. 'The soldiers were great,' said Peter Mayner. 'In they came, and they were full of jokes about us being careful to keep hold of their blood as they might want it back later.' In common with the rest of his P&O medical team, the voyage had been an intensive period of learning for him; although their principal role was to look after the crew, they were quickly integrated into the Naval surgical squadron and taught how to deal with battlefield injuries, assimilating the hard-won experience of military surgeons in Northern Ireland. Mayner had something of a head start; as a young doctor he worked in a casualty unit close to the SAS headquarters in Hereford where he had seen the effects of gunshots, becoming familiar with how high-velocity rounds sucked dirt and fragments of clothing into wounds.

For his colleagues, though, this was entirely alien, a world away not just from their normal routine of dealing with sunburn or seasickness, or stabilising elderly coronary patients until they could be got ashore, but from anything they had experienced in training. Learning all this here, in the setting of a converted nightclub where they had laughed and taken in shows, was both unnerving and sombre. 'I'd never come across a shrapnel wound in all my years,' said Rosie Elsdon. 'They had this system of what they called delayed primary suture for these really nasty wounds that are horrible, filthy. You clean them all out, pack them and leave them for five days and then you take the pack out and stitch it all together, and then it heals really well. If you stitch it all together straight away, it goes septic and doesn't heal. There were some gruesome pictures, and it did make you think, "Gosh, that might happen", and we all just hoped that we'd be able to cope with it if it came.' There were lectures from specialists accompanied by detailed notes to absorb; primary care for eye injuries, how to treat cases of exposure.

The bandsmen were learning too, putting in long, draining days for their role as medical orderlies. (This was something of a British military tradition; bandsmen had been employed as stretcher bearers in the First World War.) P&O crew enthusiastically answered a call for volunteers with first aid experience, attending training sessions in the afternoons that required a strong stomach, as bakers, cleaners and waiters saw things that nothing in their lives aboard a cruise ship could possibly have prepared them for. A consignment of instruction films on treating shooting and blast injuries in Korea and Vietnam had come aboard at Ascension, and they were shown in the Crow's Nest. 'We dragged all the girls up there to watch one on sucking chest wounds, which was very graphic,' said Reed. 'So it kicks off very quickly with this bloke sitting on the side of his bed with blood pumping out of his chest, and I'm thinking, "Whoah, this is a bit rough", and it carried on with how you treat it straight away, and there's this huge crash behind me. This enormous Marine had passed out completely. One or two of the girls had to leave, but it prepared them for looking after people in hospital.' There was more; a bullet being removed from an eye, a grenade lodged in a jaw, deeply disturbing images of suffering and disfigurement flickering in a darkened bar before an audience flinching but forcing themselves to watch.

Similarly graphic instruction was being given to the troops. An illustrated lecture by Rick Jolly became known as 'Doc Jolly's Horror Show' as the men learned how to treat injuries in the field. The journalists were undergoing the same training. Derek Hudson said, 'Leading Medical Assistant Terry Bradford drew the short straw and was instructed to give the hacks a first aid briefing about the battlefield uses of phials of morphine, treating sucking chest wounds and burns, applying tourniquets without strangling anybody and other useful snippets. Afterwards, we had a written test and mine came back marked nine out of 20, so it was just as well more experienced hands were available when I was near any casualties later on.'

The transformation of The Stadium into the hospital was all but complete. The carpet was being taken up to expose a polished dance floor that could be scrubbed clean of bodily fluids, and the bandsmen were about to start scraping absorbent tiles from around the bar to create another hard surface. Reminders of the hazards *Canberra* faced were constant; the carpet was hauled up against the windows around the Games Deck, already criss-crossed with tape against shattering, to offer at least some protection against a blast unleashing a blizzard of broken glass. 'We were using electric wire to hoist this heavy carpet over the windows and securing it to pipes going overhead when a ship's engineer came past,' said Morgan O'Connell. 'He said those pipes carried pressure and behind the panelling where they were is 20 years of dust, which is a fire hazard, and one of our greatest fears was fire. You couldn't effect any fire control on this ship, I was petrified of fire, and we didn't have the means to protect ourselves.' For now, the hospital was not kept set up all the time, even though its first operation had already been carried out at Ascension, on a crewman from *Elk* who collapsed with a perforated ulcer. The medical team whittled the time taken to get everything in place down to 17 minutes from scratch; whenever the date for going ashore was announced, they would do so one last time and leave it in place to receive casualties. Like everybody else, the surgical squadron was ready, and as part of keeping themselves occupied, word was put round the ship that anybody with minor medical

The ship of the future takes shape in the Harland and Wolff yard in Belfast. The Promenade Deck around which troops would pound on the way to the Falklands is being built.
© P&O Heritage Collection

above: The towering aluminium superstructure rises towards the skyline; *Canberra* would have one of the highest bridges in the world, 108ft above the waterline.
© TopFoto

Wednesday 16 March, 1960: thousands gathered at the Harland and Wolff yard cheered as *Canberra* was named and she rumbled down the slipway, entering the channel with a crash. *© P&O Heritage Collection*

'Every ship is ar
individual with
distinct persona
Sir Hugh Casso
design brief of
cool elegance is
here in this artis
impression of ho
the Meridian R
would look.

© *Illustrated London
News Ltd/Mary Eva*

The Crow's Nest, for first-class
passengers, at the top of *Canberra*,
with its 41 floor-to-ceiling windows,
stylised furniture and decorative
buoys that would later take the fancy
of airmen returning from war.

© *P&O Heritage Collection*

Even tourist class was luxurious.
The William Fawcett Room on t
Promenade Deck, with its mould
plywood chairs.

© *P&O Heritage Collection*

The design for the
Bonito Pool on
the Arena Deck.

© *Illustrated London
News Ltd/Mary Evans*

Berthed at Sydney for he first time, 9 June 1961. Crowds lined the shoreline and a fleet of boats escorted her into the harbour.
© P&O Heritage Collection

A resolutely British ship: Alec Bedser and other members of the England team get some light-hearted practice on the Sun Deck en route to Australia for the 1962/3 Ashes series. © TopFoto

boats escort Canberra into New York for he first time, August 1962. BC broadcast a television cial devoted to her.
Popperfoto/Getty Images

top left: 'I shall take the ship wherever the Commander-in-Chief of the Royal Navy decides to send me.' Captain Dennis Scott-Masson on the quayside at Southampton af *Canberra* was requisitioned. Press Association Im

above: Canberra converted for war: a mushroom of girders fills the Bonito Pool to support the main flight deck. Troops would suspend climbing ropes from them as part o training. Imperial War Museum

above: 'They seemed like giant snails carrying mountains of equipment on their backs.' Troops preparing to board. Crew were waiting to guide them through the labyrinth of passageways to cabins.
Imperial War Museum

A Vosper Thornycroft welder works on the steel plates of the flight deck forward of the bridge.
Imperial War Museum

ere had been no scene like it since the end of Empire, a troopship bound for war. The evening Good Friday, 9 April 1982 as *Canberra* leaves Southampton for the South Atlantic, seen off crowds and lines of parked cars flashing headlights to wish her luck. *Imperial War Museum*

w right: Naval Party 1710 took over Steiner's Hairdressing Salon, decorated in a tasteful de of purple, as its office. The Senior Naval Officer, Captain Christopher Burne, is seated he right, and supply officer Lieutenant-Commander John Muxworthy is at the desk. The rdryers were removed before *Canberra* sailed.

w: Canberra's cooks, o produced 600,000 als, in the galley. With m are deputy captain chael Bradford cond left, front row) d next to him, assistant geon Susie West. *&O Heritage Collection*

Putting up a show of lights: Martin Reed (second right) helps position a general purpo machine gun on the bridge wing. It would b loaded with tracer ammunition in the hope that glowing bursts of fire deterred attacking pilots. *Courtesy of Martin Reed*

below: Waiting and wondering at Ascension *Canberra* paused at Ascension Island for 17 days as her troops went ashore for weapons training. The armoured vehicles of the Blues and Royals were used as well as anti-tank weapons that many of the men had never see fired. *Press Association Images; © Adrian Brown/Alamy*

w it's hurting, yes it is.' Soldiers chanted as they hefted heavy beams above their heads to
d upper body strength as part of the incessant training on board, here around the midships
ht deck. *Imperial War Museum*

right: Every available corner was used for training: here, men have taken over part of a deck
ractice stripping down a heavy machine gun. *Imperial War Museum*

w: Men of 3 Para disembark through the sea doors into a landing craft. *Imperial War Museum*

Four times round equals a mile: Soldiers
pounded the Promenade Deck from dawn
until dusk to maintain fitness. The deck
broke up under the impact of their boots,
which set the ship's superstructure shaking.

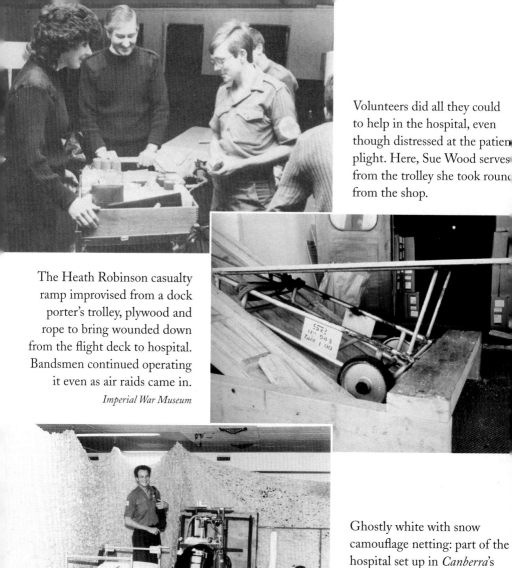

Volunteers did all they could to help in the hospital, even though distressed at the patient plight. Here, Sue Wood serves from the trolley she took round from the shop.

The Heath Robinson casualty ramp improvised from a dock porter's trolley, plywood and rope to bring wounded down from the flight deck to hospital. Bandsmen continued operating it even as air raids came in.
Imperial War Museum

Ghostly white with snow camouflage netting: part of the hospital set up in *Canberra*'s theatre, The Stadium and the adjoining Bonito Club.
Imperial War Museum

Thirty-nine different roles, and the greatest boost to morale on board. The Royal Marines Band of Commando Forces, directed by Captain John Ware, plays amid the scaffolding supports of the Crow's Nest.

right and below: Rendezvous in South Georgia: *Canberra* with the *QE2* at anchor at Grytviken. Below, an airlift takes off for her from *QE2*. Relations between the two ships would be as frosty as the weather.

Imperial War Museum; Getty Images

'I lived on a diet of adrenaline and cheese-and-onion sandwiches.' *Canberra*'s chief officer, Martin Reed.

scruffy but unbowed: Canberra, streaked by rust after weeks at sea, at anchor off Port Stanley in the days before bringing troops back to Britain.

Courtesy of Roy Paddison

above: Men of 5 Brigade at Port
San Carlos after being landed from
Canberra. The ship's company would
enraged by a BBC broadcast that gav
credit to the *QE2* for getting the troo
ashore. *Imperial War Museum*

left: L Company of 42 Commando r
outside Stanley in a building damage
by cluster bombs.

below: Piles of Argentine weapons in
Port Stanley. *Canberra's* officers arme
themselves with surrendered pistols
before loading prisoners of war.

'You couldn't help feeling sorry for them.' Filthy, bedraggled, frightened and hungry Argentine prisoners shortly after being brought aboard *Canberra*.

The details of every prisoner were recorded by the military in the Meridian Room under the supervision of the Red Cross.
Imperial War Museum

'We even found children's colouring books in some of their packs.' The prisoners were fed twice a day. The P&O luggage label used to tag each man is visible on this young soldier's shoulder.

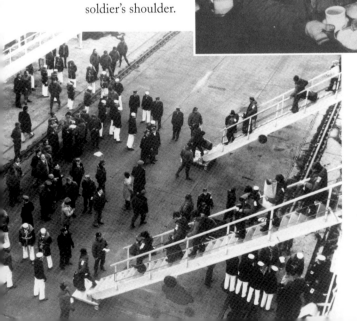

Puerto Madryn, the isolated port in Argentina where *Canberra* disembarked the prisoners. The first few down the gangways were congratulated by a senior officer, who quickly tired of it; the rest trooped quietly away to be loaded onto trucks and buses.
Imperial War Museum

Lieutenant Colonel Nick Vaux (centre, front row) and the men of 42 Commando toast the birth of Prince William on the voyage home.

'Everybody wanted to look fit for the birds.' The Sun Deck packed with sunbathing troops on the voyage home. The journey allowed them time to talk through their experiences.
Imperial War Museum

Prince Charles flew aboard to meet crew, leaving before *Canberra* docked so as not to distract any attention from them.
Imperial War Museum

The sheer spectacle of *Canberra* steaming majestically home surrounded by vessels was captured from helicopters and broadcast live to millions watching on television. © *TopFoto*

A sea of people: The view of the dockside at Southampton from *Canberra*. An estimated 20,000 well wishers gathered to welcome her home.

'She was like a mother bringing her children home.' There had been no homecoming in living memory to match it; 120,000 people had lined the shoreline to cheer the Great White Whale's return. *PA Photos*

The view from the bridge: as the Marines band played and men of Naval Party 1710 lined the forward flight deck, the scale of the welcome began to become clear. *Imperial War Museum*

Britain's favourite ship: A poster advertising *Canberra*'s return to cruising. The Government paid the £689,000 cost of P&O's marketing campaign to announce that she was back in service. © *P&O Heritage Collection*

A band played *Canberra* off on her first voyage after being refitted, as streamers rained down from the decks. © *TopFoto*

Britain's favourite ship: Pristine once more, *Canberra* ready for her first cruise after returning to service. Her role in the Falklands kept her fully booked for years afterwards.
© *P&O Heritage Collection*

Canberra arriving into Berth 106 at Southampton for the last time on 30 September 1997.
© *P&O Heritage Collection*

left: Toasted in champagne as she went to her end: *Canberra* beached in Pakistan awaiting scrapping. She ran aground so quietly and smoothly that her crew was unsure it had happened

© *P&O Heritage Collection*

below: Fading away: Bit by bit, she was dismantled, the superstructure, then the funnels, then the hull until nothing remained. Dennis Scott-Masson's widow kept pictures of *Canberra*'s scrapping from him.

© *P&O Heritage Collection*

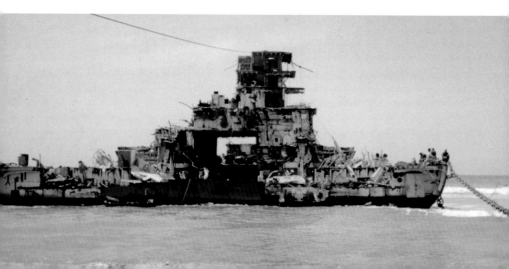

problems such as warts, ingrowing toenails or toothache should report to them as they would be only too happy to deal with them.

The first aid training was concentrating the minds of the troops. O'Connell noticed that they were confronting their darkest fears: 'I was particularly interested to observe these Marines and Paras doing in effect what we would call in medicine anticipatory grief work; they were preparing not only for the death of themselves and their colleagues but also the thought of being grievously injured, which was their greatest fear. They didn't mind being killed, except for the effect it would have on their families, but being horribly injured and not being able to wear their red beret or their green beret any more did bother them, and there was a lot of very healthy preparation work going on.' Running parallel with the medical lectures were the military briefings, on weapons, mines, tactics, and survival. Every public room was in use as men were gathered at session after session; in between, corridors and vestibules became impromptu lecture theatres, the brown paper bags used for rubbish were slit open, folded out and taped up to form makeshift blackboards on which NCOs chalked instructions. Diagrams of Argentine regiments, insignia and rank structure were stuck above urinals, identification charts with the silhouettes of the Royal Navy's ships began to appear on bulkheads.

One of the star turns was Sergeant Roy Pennington, a fearsome-looking old hand whose numerous missing teeth spoke of a long history of conflicts. He fixed the young Marines and Paras with a ferocious glare as he set out to educate them in how to survive in a harsh environment, going into gut-wrenching detail and tapping the palm of one hand with a bayonet to emphasise his points as his audience listened wide-eyed and open-mouthed to the colourfully-expressed instructions, liberally peppered with profanities. Jeremy Hands recorded one passage on taking shelter.

'Right. So find yourself a bit of ground that's dry and looks like it's firm beneath. Then dig away with your little shovels and home, sweet home is made. Failing that, of course, you can always live in a hollowed-out elephant seal, which you will of course have killed first.

But you've got to watch these, 'cos they're bad bastards, and might not entirely go along with your ideas. Always approach these big buggers from the front. They are not known for their nimbleness. But should you be c**t enough to try to surprise it from behind you should remember it is well able to roll backwards quickly and be on you. If that happens, you are well f**ked.'

Hudson said, 'The sergeant told them to get their spoon edges sharpened so they would also serve as knives, to cut four inches from rubber sleeping mats and tuck the pieces around the elbows under a combat jacket for protection against lying down on the rocky Falklands, take sugar, salt, sweets and a rabbit snare, which would also "make quite a nice weapon for strangling some poor bastard". Other pointers came thick and fast; always purify water, because Falkland streams and pools were rife with liver fluke, which caused growths the size of walnuts.'

As if that was not enough to make his audience wince, Pennington never failed to cause a stir by unfurling a large diagram of a sheep and explaining in forensic detail how to kill, skin and butcher it. Hudson noted what followed, as he took his mesmerised audience on a whistle-stop tour of living off the land.

'When you kill a sheep, never eat the offal, cut off the head and throw it away. My granny likes it in broth, but it takes too long to cook. Keep your fish head, nice soup. A gutted cow can become a refuge from extreme cold. Just crawl inside and keep warm like old Buffalo Bill did. Keep rendered-down sheep fat for smearing on the face and lips to prevent chapping, and for making candles which can keep a snow hole slightly above freezing point. Stones should be placed under your fires so that the blaze does not sink four feet into damp peat, just as it would in snow. Use these stones when they have been cooled from white hot to warm to dry out sodden boots. Go to the ship's chemists and buy a Durex: it holds a pint and a half of water and is a real morale booster, it feels just like a nice tit. Five types of penguin breed in the Falkland Islands and their flesh is fishy but edible. The eggs are nutritious and can be preserved by being buried in the sand. Penguins such as rock hoppers and gentoos are easily caught, especially when returning from a day at sea fishing for krill. Their bellies can be slit open and the krill inside eaten. Seals' eyes have enough vitamins to sustain a human being for a week, cormorants are delicious, but do not eat seagulls unless there is no alternative. Take a few mousetraps along for catching birds. Try to get hold of some women's tights from the *Canberra* shop. They will help to keep you warm and I often wear them.'

Pennington concluded disarmingly, 'I don't like killing anything; I only kill for survival.' Never, in 20 years, even given all the oddities and eccentricities amongst the hundreds of thousands of passengers she had carried, had anything remotely like this been heard in *Canberra*'s tastefully-appointed public rooms, the savagery of the imagery all the more unsettling for its setting. The verbal blood-spattering of his lectures had tremendous impact, but did not meet with universal approval. Some officers felt the sergeant was being lurid to the point of cartoonish for the sake of it, rather than imparting useful information, and the more experienced soldiers scoffed at his most outlandish advice, such as eating seals' eyes and hollowing out animals for shelter; going into battle against Argentine troops would be difficult enough without picking a fight with elephant seals as well. It was also pointed out with some force that for all its many resources, *Canberra* was unlikely to be able to provide either rabbit snares or mousetraps. Nevertheless, certain points hit home; Sue Wood suddenly and bafflingly found the queue at her shop full of gruff, embarrassed young men clutching pairs of sheer women's tights in every shade available, stocks of which were quickly exhausted. The adjutants' meeting of 10 May noted wearily that another tip had been taken to heart. 'There are presently 1,100 spoons missing from the Atlantic Restaurant – P&O can usually make up three sets of cutlery – but at the moment they are finding it difficult to make one full set for a setting. These deficits amongst other things mean the soldiers have to queue longer whilst the one set of cutlery is washed.' Pennington's advice to take salt ashore had also been heeded; 45 salt cellars had vanished.

There was less startling survival advice offered to men facing the ravages of a South Atlantic winter than embarking on the wholesale slaughter of marine life and the islanders' precious farm animals. Forget about the tough-looking skinhead cuts, let hair grow to help keep the scalp warm; shave at night so the skin is hardened against the winds by morning; check your oppo's face for any signs of frostbite, and get him to do the same for you; keep at least one pair of socks dry by taking them into your sleeping bag at night. There were hazards to watch for underfoot, mounds of tussock grass concealing holes in which ankles could be sprained or broken, and, above all, mines. Men whom O'Connell had noticed worrying most of all about being maimed listened attentively to lectures on identifying and dealing with mines from Steve Brabham, who sat up for nights on end preparing his text. 'I ended up telling every unit on the boat what to look for; packaging, dead animals, craters, knowing how to identify it, what to do, how to clear yourself, actions on a casualty. In all honesty, the action on a casualty is to leave him and get yourself out first and then come back. It sounds gruesome, but it's no good staying in a minefield that's covered by indirect or direct fire stopping a bloke bleeding to death if you're going to take it yourself.' Brabham raised a nervous chuckle by explaining that if the lads stepped on the thumbnail-sized area of a mine visible with their toes, they'd be lucky; it would only take their foot off. Step on it with your heel, and your leg would be gone. What he said stuck; months later, a Para newly fitted with an artificial leg greeted him in a pub with the words, 'Brab, you're right. Mines do blow your f**king legs off.'

Mike Norman's hour-long lectures in the Meridian Room on facing the Argentine forces drew rapt attention from his audiences, conscious that this was a man who had been in the thick of what awaited them. Leavened with dark humour, they were insightful and informative. Hudson recalled, 'Tough young Paras in their late teens and early 20s and their slightly older

NCOs looked quite out of place sitting on the pretty pink upholstery as Mike would announce with a grin, "I was in charge when we won a silver medal at the Stanley Games. It is nice of you to come back with us and get the island back. We were beginning to think of you all as the British policeman. You can never find one when you want one".' Norman had to laugh a day before *Canberra* left Ascension when a memo from the Ministry of Defence dated April 23 marked 'urgent' arrived on board. It politely asked for the receipt for five new tyres for the Land Rover he had been allocated in the Falklands, as it was required for audit purposes. 'They should have sent this to the bloody Argies, they're driving the sodding Land Rover now,' he told Hudson.

The Navy was also busy lecturing, paying special attention to the Paras, less familiar with the sea than the Marines. The instructions about abandoning ship and survival in the freezing ocean were blunt. Laurie Bland said, 'The Navy guy says, "Hands up if you're overweight", and the blokes were going, "Him, him, him", and he says, "Well if you are, you'll last a lot longer than the racing snakes. The racing snakes, with no meat on them, you'll last a minute before you die of hypothermia. The fatties, you've got a minute-and-a-half". They were so matter-of-fact, they said, "If you're told to abandon ship, go over the rail, or if there's gates, open the gates and go in an orderly fashion; it's just like parachuting. But don't make the mistake of putting your life preserver on until you're in the water, because what'll happen is that if you've got this rubber yoke round your neck, you hit the water, it wants to stay up, your head'll come off. If your head doesn't come off, it'll still kill you, because you're jumping sixty feet. Don't do what you see on the telly, throw it in and try and dive into it, you're not a performing dolphin"'. The never-ending litany of death and danger was treated with characteristic black humour by the men, who took to chanting, 'We're doomed, we're doomed,' in the manner of the lugubrious Private Frazer from *Dad's Army*. Others though, were at pains to maintain their sang-froid, Robert Fox writing, 'There were moments of peculiar Englishness. In the bar, two aristocratic cavalry officers were overheard, one lamenting the opening of the polo season, and the other was more worried about whether his bronze sculpture would be accepted for the Royal Academy Summer Exhibition than anything that might or might not await them in the Falkland Islands.'

The weather was cooling and the seas roughening as *Canberra* zig-zagged south at a steady 15 knots. The wind began to gust with such force that deck officers who climbed up to the exposed emergency conning position between the funnels to test steering from there via the engine room, in the event of the bridge being put out of action, needed safety harnesses. A last respite from training and lectures took everybody's minds off what drew closer with every mile steamed, carrying with it a faint echo of the games played on deck by cruise passengers in normal times. An inter-unit sports day would give the Marines and Paras the chance to exercise their rivalry in tug-of-war, deck quoits and the 10,000 metres – 24 times round the Promenade Deck – on Sunday 9 May, timed to coincide with the London Marathon. The escorting *Ardent* saluted *Canberra* with a flourish as the event got underway by speeding along the starboard quarter for a firepower demonstration, five deafening rounds from her 4.5-inch gun that made everybody start and raised plumes of water, followed by the firing of flares which were shot at with her cannon, a dashing display to remind and reassure all aboard that they were sailing under her protection.

It was a fiercely contested day, troops conditioned to give their all in battle showing the same full-blooded determination to win the events. Unsurprisingly, the P&O team long used to coaching the blue-rinses in quoits beat all comers with no difficulty, and a team of heavyweights from the engine room put up a valiant show in the tug-of-war before 42 Commando won it. There was a touch of the school sports day about it all; the 10,000 metres, gruelling even for those who knew every inch of the battered deck, run against a clamour of encouragement from everybody watching, officers bickering over the merits of runners, and exhorting their men to try harder in the manner of competitive dads. The crew's cheers were for *Canberra*'s 'ringer', laundryman Frank Taylor, a formidable and experienced marathon runner, who caught the soldiers off guard as he streaked to the front of the pack and stayed there to loud encouragement from his wife, Anna, who worked in the Bureau. Military pride could not countenance being outrun by a civilian, even as they recognised he was a fine athlete; 3 Para were the army cross-country champions and its best gained ground steadily, beating him into third place. There was substantial compensation, though, noted Hands. 'But Frank was the only runner to end the race in the arms of a beautiful woman, being smothered in kisses. "There's no f**king justice", said the winner as he trooped off to collect his certificate.' 42 Commando won the team prize, and a cheque for their welfare fund donated by the reporters. That evening, the band played a concert to cheers. It had been the final day on which it was possible to relax. Within 24 hours, *Canberra*'s destination would be finalised.

CHAPTER TEN

A Sea Full of Ships

SHE was no longer brilliant white; weeks at sea had begrimed her signature pristine paintwork, the spray now lashing against her hull leaving it salt-encrusted and starting to streak with rust that crept down towards the waterline, overlaying her elegant lines with an air of grubby ruggedness. She began to creak and groan, pitching even with her stabilisers in use, as the sea grew heavier and soldiers still pounding the Promenade Deck ran uphill and then down with the motion of the waves, no longer soaked in sweat from exerting themselves in sub-tropical temperatures, but chilled and clammy from the spray that swept in at them lap after lap. *Canberra*'s men and women felt the difference in their ship as she ploughed deeper into the late autumn of the southern hemisphere, watching as general purpose machine guns (GPMGs) were mounted and tested, and for the first time going to red alert in response to a submarine threat after a lookout on HMS *Intrepid* thought he saw a periscope break the surface of the sea, spending the next hour-and-a-half until they were stood down wondering if there would be a juddering impact, an explosion, a dash for the lifeboats that was real and not an exercise.

The changes in the weather and ship seemed to prompt changes in themselves; everybody was quieter, more introverted, their smiles a little tighter. Swapping the light summer clothing they habitually wore on cruises for woollens and waterproofs against the cold and damp had been another reminder of their destination. They needed each other's company more than ever now; it was not good to be alone. Evenings brought gatherings all over the P&O quarters, amongst officers and crew alike.

Not parties; just groups of friends who felt a little safer, a little less scared for spending an hour or two with others who were feeling the same. Tension made sleep fitful, and manifested itself in niggling problems. Kevin Mountney, a 25-year-old steward, developed a nervous stomach as worry and loneliness crowded in on him: 'You're not getting enough decent food down, you're tired, your sleep patterns are all over the place, the weather's closing in, exercise is a problem. I'd lost my cabin mate in Ascension, he was flown home because of a problem in his family, and I felt very lonely. Where my cabin was, they'd closed the watertight doors for the integrity of the ship, which was a constant reminder of what might happen, and to get to the mess room I had to go up the stairs, over the top and all the way back down.' Don Cole also found the routine and increasing number of alerts exhausting. 'You'd be working 12 hours and then get eight hours off, but in that eight hours you'd have to feed yourself and try to get some sleep before you're back to work, and the alerts cut into your sleep time, and that became draining.' Everybody developed their own way of coping; for Susie West it was writing letters, and a diary intended for her twin sister. 'I wrote copiously. I'd had no idea of the importance of post in keeping up morale until then, and I always assumed that the next post that went out would be the last. If I heard at 2 o'clock that the post was going out by helicopter at three, I'd rush to my cabin and write something else. I wrote to every member of the family, to old school friends I hadn't heard from in 15 years, I wrote masses.'

It was striking how the level of chatter and the noise of the crew fell away. 'There was a general hush among the civilians,' said Kim Sabido. 'The staff you saw on the corridors had become very subdued. There was a cleaner, an Irish chap, who told me that everybody had looked on it as a paid holiday when they left Southampton, but now everything was so real. He said, "I'm cleaning these corridors. There might not be a floor to clean tomorrow, the *Sheffield* was hit by a bomb." He was sweating, I could see the fear in him, so I started to back off questioning him because I could see every question I was asking him made him question himself and what he was doing here.' Everybody was haunted by what had befallen the

Sheffield and every day brought reminders of it, ratcheting up the pressure. A few had worn old gas masks for the finale of the crew show only weeks before in what seemed like another life; now all the crew were issued with them and given instruction in their use. Chemical attack was unlikely, it was explained, but the respirators would give a few extra precious minutes to save themselves if *Canberra* was hit and engulfed by smoke as *Sheffield* had been. Those with beards were ordered to shave them off, as more than a day or two's growth of stubble compromised the airtight seal of the masks. With them came dog-tags to be worn without fail; identifying bodies blown apart, burned or recovered from the sea could not be left to chance. Then, on the 15th, the ship was declared to be on 'active service', which put her on a war footing and brought all civilians under the control of the Naval Discipline Act, even though in practical terms they remained subject to normal P&O regulations.

A scramble for kit frayed nerves and tempers even further; there simply was not enough to go round. Graham Harding was issued with an anti-flash hood to protect his head from fire; it was stolen when he went to lunch. 'We were told to pack an emergency bag in case we had to evacuate,' said West. 'It had to contain the following things, and we didn't have the following things. We didn't have foul weather gear, we were told that all personnel should carry a torch at all times, and there weren't enough torches on the ship to give us all one. The P&O staff did feel a bit like second-class citizens because we didn't have all the gear the military people were told they needed.' A promised consignment of winter wear for the women from SS *Uganda* never materialised, and they had to make do with ill-fitting men's clothing. 'Rosie and I always wore our P&O scarves to maintain a bit of femininity,' said Angela Devine. 'They said if you had to abandon ship, you could take a small bag, which started off as quite a big small bag and then it got smaller and smaller until they said you can't take any bags at all. In the end it got down to a lipstick and Rosie and I took a couple of Tampax because we thought that might be a good idea, and that was it. We used to imagine the scenario if we were floating and got picked up by another ship and of course it would be full of men, so it would be quite nice to have a bit of femininity and put on our lipstick. Stupid, really.'

Shortages of kit were not confined to the crew. 3 Para was still waiting for its winter clothing, which was eventually airlifted on board during a force six gale after being flown out to Ascension. When Norman Menzies got it down to his quartermaster's store, he was aghast. The story of Britain's unpreparedness to fight a war far from home was told in heaps of scruffy, none-too-clean gear. It had come straight off the backs of another regiment and much of it was in tatters. 'It was total rubbish. Mildew on the boots, and they'd taken on the shape of the person's foot who had been wearing them. Useless, we threw them over the side.' Trousers and jackets were little better; legs falling off, tears, fastenings coming away. As so often in the past weeks, the only answer lay in improvisation, ingenuity, and, in this instance, a stroke of luck. The sheer incongruity of sailing to war on a liner devoted to its passengers' every pleasure turned out to be a blessing; needlework was one of the pastimes available to the more sedentary, and the Paras made use of the reels of cotton and cloth still on board. So a tough, lean, fighting man who happened to belong to a long lineage of tailors sat at a sewing machine for hours on end surrounded by a pile of tatty uniforms, mending them and finishing off by hand with some neat, robust needlework that would have been the envy of the blue-rinses. 'We had enough green cotton in the hobbies centre,' said Menzies. 'I was fortunate to have in my section an ex-parachute rigger who was a dab hand at sewing, so we started repairing it and did what we could with what we had. But there wasn't enough to go round, only about 75 per cent of what we needed, which was a disgrace.'

For 42 Commando, one of the issues that had occupied its officers and men was too much gear rather than too little. Nick Vaux had been concerned at the huge weight of ammunition that each of his men would have to carry, and that deepened when in early trials Marines had fallen over as they shouldered their packs. Trial and error to rebalance the load continued after Ascension. Vaux wrote, 'Eventually an assembly was devised, which was tabulated and photographed, and then circulated to the rest of the Commando. By the time of the landings, fighting-order and rucksacks had been adjusted to individual requirements. When those adjustments were complete, the stooped owner "promenaded" with his burden until he was satisfied with the fit.' Weight was also an issue for helicopter movements once troops got ashore; men stood fully laden on a set of scales as air operations officers calculated maximum loads.

Like the crew, the troops grew quieter. Theirs was the quiet not of fear, but of concentration. Two cans was plenty; beating the system in search of a skinful had been left behind with getting a tan, the will-they-won't-they phony war, the half-expected turn for home, slumping down in the sun after a final knackering circuit of the Promenade Deck. A last blowout had taken place shortly before leaving Ascension; each unit held a 'smoker' at which officers and senior NCOs joined the men to eat in the Atlantic Restaurant, after which there were songs – not least the bloodthirsty adaptation of 'Summer Holiday', belted out with gusto – stand-up routines by the resident comedians that poked fun at the officers and rousing choruses of patriotic songs accompanied by the Marines band. The evenings were raucous expressions of camaraderie, the more fervent for everyone acknowledging there would be no more larking about after training finished for the day from here on. 'I had absolutely no doubt that the aggression was there, and the question was of controlling it in the right way,' reflected Vaux. 'These smokers were all part of working everybody up into the right frame of mind to go out and get on with it, and one did enjoy it. They wanted to see that you approved of the idea.' All distractions were discarded as the focus on action intensified. 'The porn pictures started coming down,' recalled John Shirley. 'When it all started, you could go into Marines' cabins, even lieutenants, and there were lots of pictures, not hard-core porn, but top-shelf stuff that you'd expect lads to have around, but as we got closer to the islands, the pictures started coming down. I think people started to cut off from women as sexual; the sense was this is something you're just not going to get, so put it out of your mind, it's too painful.'

It was not a few extra cans making Marines and Paras sway now, but the movement of the ship in ever-heavier seas as they headed to their tables once enough cutlery had been washed to go round; the hot stodgy meal slopping about on the trays, mixing gravy and custard into a yellowy-brown goo, was nevertheless more welcome than ever on evenings growing colder, darker and rougher. Sodden and shivering lookouts returning from duty on the bridge wings were a nightly reminder of the forbidding conditions and the threats that might be lurking. Food, a film, bed; get your rest while you can lads, you'll need it, their sergeants and corporals told them, and they heeded the advice, even if they did not sleep. Just lying there under the orange bedspreads that contrasted so sharply with the drab olive of their kit hung about the cluttered little four-berth cabins, staring at the ceiling or the base of the bunk above for an hour, helped them prepare. Digesting everything learned during the day felt useful, improved their odds, gave them the edge over the enemy; the lecture on the topography of the Falklands from Ewen Southby-Tailyour that made them feel as if they knew the ground before even having sight of it; the session on running fluids into a wounded oppo, rectally if necessary, that would once have made them snigger now possibly the saving of their own life. There were chaplains to talk to if they wished, nothing formal about it, just a chat in passing. Best of all, there was the company of the three others sharing the cabin.

The need for companionship of friends was not confined to the youngest troops; older, more experienced NCOs to whom they looked for guidance felt it too. Brian Faulkner had taken advantage of going on board with the advance party at Gibraltar to bag himself a plum single cabin; as time passed, its quiet had begun to grow lonely, and he moved in with two fellow sergeants, Ray Butters and Ian McKay. All were from Yorkshire, and Faulkner and McKay had the shared heritage of growing up in the neighbouring industrial powerhouses of Sheffield and Rotherham. 'He was easy to get on with, and he adored his wife and his young daughter, Melanie,' said Faulkner. 'He'd talk about Melanie every hour of every day, what he was going to do with her when he got back, a very knowledgeable, kind, considerate man, a real nice, bubbly Yorkshireman.' Young officers looked to their elders for advice, just as the men they led did. Menzies, in the Paras since 1958, gave it freely. 'I told the young lieutenants to get their admin right – dry socks, have a foot inspection even in the trenches. They did it back in the barracks, but in the field it was surely more important to look after yourself. I always used to stress on them that sleep is a phase of war; on exercise, you'd get COs who hadn't had their sleeping bags open for days, they couldn't miss what was going on. I told them they were a bloody disgrace. We don't want tired commanders, we want people whose brains are switched on.'

All wanted to be off this ship now; physically and psychologically ready to put into practice everything they had trained for, their impatience to get on with the landings was sharpened by the sense of danger that had been constant ever since *Sheffield* was hit. During daylight, if it was clear enough, out of the corners of their eyes they sometimes caught a momentary flash of sunlight reflected from the silver wings of a Soviet surveillance aircraft from Angola that periodically flew high overhead, plotting the course of the task force heading ever southwards, the chalk mark of *Canberra* on the sea unmistakeable from the air. Being watched from above, as well as potentially from below by a stalking submarine, reinforced the urge to be ashore. 'We were more and more aware of the threat,' said Vaux. 'A lot of us were increasingly conscious that this was not a warship, so that if somebody torpedoed her, or if there were air attacks, she would be damaged very, very rapidly. So we felt more vulnerable as we were going down, and we knew by then we were going to land, so motivation at every level was much higher, and the two pressures were anxiety and the motivation that one wanted to get ashore and get on with it.'

Men muttered increasingly about the white paintwork making the ship a prime target. On the bridge, though, the Senior Naval Officer was rather more sanguine about that. 'Down in southern waters, white funnily enough is a very good camouflage,' said Christopher Burne. 'There were times at sea when we could see the grey warships quite distinctly, and the white of *Canberra* in misty, murky conditions is a very effective cover; something dark stands out, something light melds into it.' The tension manifested itself in small ways; men fidgeted more than they had, yawned nervously and became irritable. Testy little spats, sprang out of nowhere, even at the most senior level. A discussion between Tom Seccombe and Burne in his sea cabin about defending *Canberra* with her meagre complement of three GPMGs on each bridge wing and a couple more at the stern quickly degenerated into a squabble about who was in charge of them; the thin partition walls muffled nothing, and all on the bridge fell quiet as they listened. John Muxworthy said, 'Beagle Burne said, "It's my ship, and I'll give the order to open fire," so Tom Seccombe said, "Well, they're my men and my guns, so I'll give the order." They were going at it like a pair of children, and Beagle picked up an orange and threw it at Seccombe, who threw it back, Burne ducks and hits his head on a cabinet. He came out covered in blood, *Canberra*'s first casualty.'

Much thought and discussion went into the most effective way to deploy those few weapons, woefully inadequate in the face of fast attacking aircraft. Shooting down modern warplanes with machine gun fire as they streaked past in the blink of an eye was the stuff of fond imagination; it only happened in films peddling the fantasy that the good guy always comes out on top. There were no such clichéd certainties here, aboard a cruise ship neither built nor equipped to repulse or withstand attack; the best *Canberra* could do was to deter and unnerve, and in doing so settled on a plan of action that was a surreal reflection of her normal routine. In peace, she announced herself with lights; in war, she would rely on them for defence. 'We decided that lights in the sky was the way to go,' said Vaux. 'I remembered a pilot had said to me once that the thing that frightened him when attacking was when he saw lights of any sort, because you didn't know what they were.' One in every four rounds of the ammunition belts for the GPMGs was tracer, the glowing bullets visible to the shooter, allowing corrections in aiming. The belts were reloaded with tracer every other round; the bursts of fire hosing up towards attacking aircraft would be blazing, distracting and hopefully intimidating enough to drive them off. 'When it's coming up towards pilots, it does discourage them,' said Burne. 'They can see it, and in some ways that sort of flak in low-level attacks is more effective than things like Blowpipe missiles that they don't actually see.' Flares from Very pistols would also be fired, adding to the unpredictable light shield. Shoulder-borne anti-aircraft Blowpipes were coming aboard as well, with an air defence troop transferred from *Europic Ferry*.

The conclusion that a pyrotechnic display offered the best defence only deepened the sense of vulnerability aboard *Canberra*; everybody knew they were under naval escort, but when the weather closed in, or at night, when no other ships were visible, the feeling that she was alone in the middle of a vast and hostile ocean, across which a missile could come skimming with deadly consequences at any second, bore down. The word 'Exocet' had passed into *Canberra*'s everyday vocabulary, just as it had back in Britain. In the evenings, one or more of the naval party who had attended Burne's 'Giggle Session' usually popped into Martin Reed's cabin on the Captain's Deck, one level below the bridge, to let him know what had transpired; Reed was then in the habit of going down to see his friend Peter Mayner, nine decks below and right in the firing line. 'We'd sit and have a drink and I'd try to keep him up to scratch about what was going on, and he was down on D Deck, which was known as Exocet Alley, because it was ten feet above the waterline, which is where an Exocet would hit. We were always told that we weren't alone, that there was always someone looking out for us, but when you look around and it's a huge area of sea, and there's nothing there, you think, "What do you mean there's someone looking after us?" We'd sit there, and the steelwork around us would pick up any sonar around us, and we'd suddenly hear this noise, this "ping", and think, "There is someone there, it's a submarine" and that was comfortable.'

Up in the luxurious cabins of C Deck, the troops' commanding officers were doing their own share of staring at the ceiling and thinking. At last, after all these weeks, the COs knew exactly what they were expected to do and it was time to issue orders to their officers, who packed into the staterooms, bagging seats on the red or cream sofas, leaning forward expectantly to listen. Twenty-four hours after the sports day, Malcolm Hunt, Hew Pike and Vaux had boarded a helicopter for HMS *Fearless*. That day, the 10th, London had approved the recommended option for the landing site; the three officers already knew what it was from the briefings they had attended at Ascension. *Canberra* was bound for San Carlos Bay, on the westward side of East Falkland, 50 miles from Port Stanley. It had two inlets surrounded by hills, and reconnaissance by the SBS had found no Argentine forces there apart from an outpost on high ground at Fanning Head, overlooking the approach, which would have to be destroyed before the ships went in. The Cabinet was yet to give the final go-ahead for the landings, so no date beyond some time after 19 May was fixed. On the 12th, written Brigade Operations orders were delivered to Hunt, Pike and Vaux, and they returned to *Fearless* the following day for Brigadier Julian Thompson's formal orders group for Operation SUTTON, the repossession of the Falkland Islands. In the first phase, Hunt's 40 Commando and 45 Commando were to land and secure San Carlos Settlement and Ajax Bay. They would be followed ashore by Pike's 3 Para and 2 Para to secure Sussex Mountain and Port San Carlos. Vaux's 42 Commando would remain aboard *Canberra* as the brigade reserve, on instant notice to deploy ashore as needed.

Pike gathered his officers at 2pm on the 14th to issue orders for the landings. Later that day, he wrote to his wife.

We are not allowed to brief the soldiers on what is planned at present, which is a bore, as life is getting fairly monotonous now, as you can imagine, and I don't want them to go off the boil. Eventually, it is unavoidable, but I hope we will be let off the leash long before then. The mail is becoming more intermittent, however, and there's been none for a few days now, probably not as long as I think, but one loses track of day and date, quite honestly. In many ways a good thing, I suppose – I certainly haven't found time dragging, though I suspect the next few days might a bit. The news does not sound too encouraging at the moment and I just don't know what sort of a fight the Argies will put up – there are enough of them there, and we'll just have to see. I'm well able to look after myself and you mustn't worry. I know how much more difficult it all is, when you are sitting at home wondering what on earth is going on – but try not to let all this waiting get you down. I'm sure the children and all their requirements, dates, plans etc., are a great comfort to you and provide such a vital role for you – they are utterly dependent on you, of course, and my trust in you is total. Well I'd better stop now, I think of you all constantly and please don't carry too heavy a burden of worry – we are all fine, and I just hope we all come home soon, having seen them off the FIs.

Scott-Masson and his senior officers had also been briefed. *Canberra* was alive with buzzes; everybody sensed that landings were near. A confession and reconciliation church service was full; many more sat down in the quiet of their cabins to write what might be a last letter to loved ones, even though they had no idea when it might leave the ship. 'Everybody was put in touch with the padre and asked if they wanted to have absolution before we reached the exclusion zone,' said Sabido. 'I wrote a final letter to my parents. I wasn't religious, but not a total atheist, and we all did the same thing, letters home. All introverted, all serious, even the military. Everybody was closing down within themselves. This was now a military operation and people were going to die.'

Sabido and the other journalists were by now keenly attuned to the mood amongst the fighting men; in spite of the altercation in the Crow's Nest after the *Sheffield* was hit, a closeness and understanding had developed between military and press that would result in the reporting of the Falklands War being amongst the most insightful of any conflict. Drinks as they relaxed in the bucket chairs of the bar, talking, gazing across the sea through the giant picture windows almost at the very top of the ship, or playing Scrabble to while away evenings on the long voyage south, had created mutual trust and the beginnings of enduring friendships. There had been the occasional hiccup; photographer Tom Smith, a guest in the sergeants' mess, made the mistake of thinking it funny to refer to Paras as 'fairies' and mocking their parachute smocks as 'Para frocks' after too much hospitality. The black eye that resulted led to him being nicknamed 'The Panda'. Overall, though, the two sides got on well; despite the frustrations of getting reports past the often ham-fisted and arbitrary censorship of Ministry of Defence minders, the reporters had told the story of life on board effectively and with understanding. Derek Hudson found a signal for the attention of the minders that had been dropped in a corridor. It said, 'The impression being given from embarked media of a professional and serious preparation by the fleet, as well as the human stories, is proving most important to the whole operation.' Officers and men were thankful that a public they felt supported them wholeheartedly was being kept informed of how determined they were to right the wrong of the invasion, grateful too for the favours the press did for those who waited and worried back home. Jeremy Hands and his crew made films of life aboard not for broadcast, but for private viewing amongst groups of families, and Hudson name-checked individual soldiers letting their loved ones know they were safe and well.

The reporters were to be allocated to individual units in the event of landings, and a particularly strong bond grew between the troops and those who realised that if they were to keep up with supremely fit men force-marching across the rugged terrain of the Falklands, they had better get in shape; amongst them Patrick Bishop, Robert Fox, Max Hastings, Sabido and John Shirley. Vaux had one of his heartiest laughs of the entire voyage when approached by reporters who asked if they could start training. He allocated them to an instructor. 'This officer said, "Look, you're going to do this on your own, you're not going to do it with the men, because you'll just die"', said Shirley. 'So we used to go out there about seven in the morning and do an hour's PE. It was nothing like the Marines were doing, but it was certainly improving us. I actually thought after a week of it, I was going to die. I remember lying in bed for a whole day, I couldn't get up, it was absolutely appalling, but of course it got a lot better. The really important thing was that on the first day, there was a lot of ribbing from the people running round the deck, but they didn't carry on taking the piss, they liked us for it. It really changed the atmosphere; they began to realise that we were prepared to make an effort, that we were in this thing too. It changed the way they thought of us, and that was crucial.'

For now, though, there could be no more training on deck for either troops or reporters. *Canberra* had run into the foul and frightening weather of one of the world's most fearsome tracts of ocean, the Roaring Forties, between the latitudes of 40 degrees and 50 degrees south. Storms laid siege; mountainous seas sent huge waves crashing over her bows as she pitched fifteen feet or more in force nine gales driving vicious squalls of rain and spray. Nobody could go on deck without being roped and harnessed against being swept away. Even with her stabilisers, she heaved and groaned and shook, her furniture sliding and crashing until secured, the piled-up tin canteen trays clattering to the deck of the galley, those moving about the ship staggering and putting a hand out to the bulkheads for support. Sailing in convoy was becoming ever more treacherous as mist isolated her. It was impossible to see other ships, and even radar was blinded by the conditions, the sea so heavy that the wave-crests cluttered the screen with echoes. Nightfall increased the risk of collisions as blacked-out ships zig-zagged against the submarine threat through the raging storm; the troops aboard thought they had grown used to the sea, but there had been nothing like this. Increasingly frequent air raid or underwater threats already had them on edge; now this furious weather filled them with foreboding. Men lying in their bunks rolled with the ship, struggling to sleep as the unceasing rat-a-tat of rain and spray drummed against the windows; those trying to distract themselves with a film listened as much to the creaking of the wood-panelled walls of the cinema as they did to the dialogue. Outside on this filthy night, a lonely sentinel, terrifyingly exposed, was to be glimpsed at the emergency conning position. 'You could see the pilot up there between the two funnels, strapped on, just see him occasionally in the dark,' said Shirley, who went briefly – roped and harnessed – on deck, where he struggled to keep his footing. 'It was one of those really turbulent nights, and I thought, this is like God clearing his throat, and if God hiccups then we will die, just like that. Even on this enormous ship, you had this sense of the sea being this mighty force that could just swallow you up as it has done hundreds of thousands of people and nobody would know where you were, you'd just go.'

Church that Sunday, the 16th, was interrupted by an air raid warning that sent the GPMG teams onto yellow alert, ready to light up the grey sky with luminous tracer and flares fired from the pitching bridge wings as *Canberra* continued to take a battering from the storm. The congregation's eyes flicked up to the loudspeakers as the metallic, disembodied voice sounded the alert, then down again to their orders of service and the words to the next hymn as the band struck up; 'For Those in Peril on the Sea'. The weather was so bad that a scheduled rendezvous with more ships joining the convoy had to be delayed until the afternoon, when they appeared out of the murk and mist, among them the flat-bottomed landing ships (logistic) *Sir Lancelot*, *Sir Geraint*, *Sir Galahad*, *Sir Percivale* and *Sir Tristram*, suffering badly in the merciless conditions. It grew a little clearer, though no less rough, as the day wore on, and gradually out of the gloom, an extraordinary spectacle emerged. It seemed like a snapshot of a bygone age as those aboard *Canberra* watched.

The sea was full of ships – to port, to starboard, ahead, astern, stretching away to the horizon, destroyers, frigates, landing ships, tankers – all colour drained from them by the flat light of the stormy sky until they were dark shapes against a darker ocean, akin to the silhouettes on the identification charts, ploughing implacably onwards towards a waiting enemy, their battle for now against pounding seas breaking over the bows. It could have been a newsreel of naval might from the Second World War. 'I thought, "This is just like the movies I've seen",' said Chris Sheppard. 'And it was in black and white because of the grey sky, the grey sea. I thought, "This is what you've seen on television, and now you're part of it."' For the men aboard the warships, there was the most unmistakeable reminder that this was not a scene somehow summoned from history; a vast, rust-stained, off-white liner in the midst of the convoy. Nevertheless, there were reminders of an earlier generation braving attack in a hostile Atlantic; the threat of surveillance by spy planes prohibited radio communication and the ships turned to more rudimentary methods to send messages flickering back and forth. 'You went back very much to the Second World War,' said Scott-Masson. 'We had to go back to the primitive ways and we found that the ten-inch Morse lamp was the only really effective way of communicating with each other. We even at one stage tried semaphore flags, and that failed because the chap on the other ship couldn't read semaphore.'

That evening, he broadcast to *Canberra*, treading a careful line between preparing his crew for landings that were now likely only a few days ahead, and not giving too much away. Incongruous though it was, his matter-of-fact tone was exactly as it would have been when announcing that Naples or Madeira was the next port of call; he saw absolutely no reason to deviate from his normal manner, even though he lifted them at the end by relaying preposterous propaganda about Prince Andrew, serving with the task force as a helicopter pilot and Rear Admiral John 'Sandy' Woodward, the battle group commander. They listened more avidly than ever, in the Pig and Whistle, or with friends in their cabins, surrounded now not just by pictures of loved ones and mementos of home, but by gas masks and lifejackets always within reach.

'I believe that this coming week will probably prove interesting and stimulating but I cannot give you more precise details than that and we will wait for the events to unfold, both on the diplomatic and military fronts . . . One amusing report I heard on the BBC: it was claimed by the Argentine that Prince Andrew was a prisoner of war and Rear Admiral Woodward had committed suicide. On that lighter note, I will say good evening and wish you a successful week ahead.'

They did not need their Captain to tell them that action was imminent;

the signs were there all around them. Working parties of Marines and Paras who had humped bags of flour for the cooks or tackled the washing up in the galley were being withdrawn; there was talk about maps having to be taped together because sod's law dictated that the landing site lay at the junction of four separate sheets. Clues were gathered, buzzes pondered, conclusions reached among both the crew and the young soldiers yet to be briefed. A few stumbled across some unmistakeable pointers that landings were coming in the next day or two, including Bungy Williams. His knowledge was hard-won; toothache and an extraction as ship, dentist and chair gripped with whitened knuckles rolled and pitched. 'Nobody knew when we were going ashore, it was all hush-hush. I had pain, went to see the dentist, and he said my wisdom tooth would have to come out. I could see him thinking. I thought, "He obviously knows when we're going," and he says, "We'll have to do it tomorrow." The next morning, it was blowing a force seven, and everything was on the floor, completely trashed. He picked the chair up, picked the drill up, and said, "Right, sit down".'

Canberra was on the edge of the total exclusion zone as 18 May dawned, only 200 miles north-east of Port Stanley, where she rendezvoused with the carrier task force and drew comfort from the sight of air cover as Sea Harriers instead of spy planes appeared overhead. As darkness fell, the perils of the ever-expanding convoy sailing in darkness and radio silence once again became apparent; a collision with *Stromness* and *Appleleaf* as they refuelled was narrowly avoided. 'We were all dark ship in poor visibility, dodging around like dodgem cars not even seeing where the other dodgem was,' said Scott-Masson. 'I'm very pleased to say that no-one hit anyone else, but it was probably all by good luck than by good judgement.'

That was only the first jolt of the night; the second came with a signal from Northwood in the early hours of the following day as those aboard grabbed what sleep they could. Two of her three embarked units, 40 Commando and 3 Para, were to be transferred to HMS *Fearless* and HMS *Intrepid*, it having belatedly dawned on London that if *Canberra* were sunk with the bulk of the landing force still on board, any hope of regaining the Falklands would go down with her. The unit commanding officers immediately saw the sense in the decision, but were appalled at how it was to be carried out. The weather had eased a little, but it was still far too rough for landing craft to cross-deck their men; moving them by helicopter was out of the question, as it would use up precious flying hours needed for the landings. There was only one other way: jackstay transfer, in which steel hawsers were rigged between ships and men winched across in a harness one at a time, a massive and time-consuming operation for about 1,500 men. At one a minute, it would take hours. 'It produced howls of derision,' said Reed. 'The weather was crap, and these whizz-kids at the MoD come up with this ridiculous idea.' Worse than that; in these conditions, the naval personnel were convinced men would die. Pike went up to the bridge and found Burne making calculations on the back of a brown envelope about the maximum weight of man plus equipment the lines could bear. 'He was very excited, he said, "You know, this is going to be a Royal Navy first, this will be the first time we have ever cross-decked a unit by one man at a time by jackstay transfer." I said, "I don't think that sounds like a very good idea to me."'

The hours approaching dawn were frantic and full of worry as the men of 40 Commando and 3 Para gathered their kit in the still-rolling ship. *Canberra* and all aboard had suffered over the past few days because of the weather; now, unexpectedly, it granted a reprieve exactly when they needed it. As the horizon lightened, the sea began to calm, and the wind to drop; there remained a stiff swell and a bitterly cold breeze. The opportunity had to be taken, and swiftly, before the weather closed in again. It would be difficult, even hazardous, but just possible; teetering on the limits of safety, landing craft could undertake the transfers. Each took 140 men, and as they chugged across a thousand yards of choppy water towards *Canberra*, circling her and waiting their turn to come alongside, soldiers of 40 Commando braced themselves to be first to board from the galley doors on Exocet Alley.

A couple of days before, they had packed into the Meridian Room, finding space to sit where they could: young men, so many of them still in their teens, cross-legged on the hardboard that covered the carpets, a few leaning back against the piano still on board that had been tinkled politely as the backdrop to conversation over morning coffee or afternoon tea only a few weeks previously, crowded around the foot of the spiral staircase that led to the Crow's Nest three decks up. All hushed, expectant, concentrating on every word about tactics, the enemy, courage and camaraderie, they had listened to their CO, Malcolm Hunt, with rapt attention as he spoke about what awaited them, closing his briefing with the words, 'Good luck, and may your God go with you.' Now they were going, the single-file queue snaking from where he had spoken down the staircases and along the passageways of three decks, shuffling forward a few steps at a time, burdened by bergens and equipment heavy enough to make them buckle, waiting their turn as crew, cheerful as ever, making the best of it whatever their worries, said good luck, see you soon, give them what for, moving forward, starting to feel the chill of the breeze as they neared the galley.

At the front of the queue, standing by the open doors, looking down at the grey swell, they needed every good wish. The lines securing the landing craft to *Canberra* soared fifty feet overhead; the jump across each man must make was to a vessel constantly in motion, daring them to pick their moment as it pitched and rolled, rising and falling by five feet or more, receding and then thudding against her side with an impact that sent reverberations along the whole deck, the freezing water splashing at them. The briefings about racing snakes lasting a minute and the fat bastards a minute and a half ran through their heads. Bergens and weapons went down first, dropped to waiting hands, before the leap across. Tricky this, not like the drills in the seas around Ascension. One by one, each gauged the gap, registering the upturned faces and shouts of encouragement, took the breath, now's the time, just a step, here we go, and did it; a thumping, jarring landing, caught and helped to stay upright by oppos, straighten up, face upwards and do for the next what's just been done for you. Shout him into it, I've done it, come on, don't piss about, we'll catch you. Easy, once you've done it. It never became routine; nothing could be taken for granted, each leap had to be finely judged against the unpredictable swell, which abruptly dragged the landing craft downwards and away from the doors at the moment a young Marine jumped, missed and crashed into the water with a cry of panic, going under and flailing back up. 'Swim, you bugger!' bellowed a sergeant as men stretched over the side of the landing craft, using the butts of their rifles to try to fend it off *Canberra*'s hull, fighting the sea to give him the room to get clear as he splashed and spluttered for his life before it smacked back and snuffed him out. 'The wave sucked him or pushed him out just before the stern came back in,' said Reed, craning over in horror, high above on the bridge wing. 'How he didn't sink, I don't know. The guys at the back end were quick enough to see they had to stop the stern coming back in, and they managed to haul him in round the other side. Being soaked in cold water and stood in that wind was no joke. The coxswain was very good, got this bloke, ripped his pack off and shoved him in the engine room, which is the only warm place, because he couldn't stop the flow of people coming in.' The soldier, shocked, pale and shaking uncontrollably as hypothermia began to overtake him, was bundled back aboard *Canberra* and put into a hot bath, lucky to be alive.

There were no more mishaps, but the break in the weather was over; the landing craft rose and fell ever more precipitously as the day wore on, making the cross-decking increasingly dangerous. Darkness was starting to close in as the last of 3 Para were transferred, their officers going across by helicopter. As he said his farewells to the crew who were around, Menzies was surprised and touched to be approached by one of the campest stewards, with whom he often chatted. 'He gave me a plastic bag with provisions, coffee, melons and a bottle of wine. I said, "That's very kind," and he said, "Enjoy, and don't get shot".'

That evening, Scott-Masson broadcast to his ship again: 'If there is a landing, I can assure you we will be in the safest possible place and this will be close and more or less surrounded by land. During our approach, which will obviously be under the cover of darkness, we will be impressively escorted by the Navy and other service elements . . . I am sure the embarked military force will now look after us and ensure our safe return to Southampton and I am certain I speak for all of us in hoping we have the honour of returning with the same forces as we have brought out . . . Good luck to all of you in the embarked forces in your future deployment from all of us in *Canberra*. Keep your feet dry.'

Before he spoke, aboard *Hermes*, the decision was received and acknowledged. As troops made the leap across, so had government; land at your discretion. The weather that had broken briefly, fortuitously, was closing in again. This time, it was welcome. Fog, rain, and glowering black clouds were the best protection a great white ship could have. She would sail the next night and go in for the landings on 21 May.

CHAPTER ELEVEN

Take Cover, Take Cover

STEAK WAS served at breakfast, lunch and dinner on May 20, and if that had about it the air of a condemned man being offered a special meal before going to the gallows, then it chimed with the tension and clock-watching. Temporarily returning to cruise-ship fare for men about to go into action seemed entirely appropriate to *Canberra*'s officers; heaven alone knew what lay ashore, so the best they could do was give them the finest food on board, and as much of it as the soldiers wanted. Rudderham's stock of fillet steak took a battering as the men of 42 Commando, for whom it had been an occasional treat, devoured it in the morning, afternoon and evening, all the more gleefully for knowing that the best 40 Commando and 3 Para could expect in the horribly cramped conditions of *Fearless* and *Intrepid* was stew.

Early on, the announcement over the loudspeakers that the landings would commence that night was all but redundant; everybody already knew and it had kept them awake. Nobody slept well, even though *Canberra* had left the storm behind. They tossed and turned, some too hot because they had gone to bed fully dressed just in case, most too keyed up to drop off. Rosie Elsdon woke very early. 'I heard that the most likely time for an air raid was just as it was getting light, and I thought, "If I'm going to be bombed, I don't want to be fast asleep in my nightie in bed," so I got up before dawn and had a wash and got dressed and then just lay on my bed.'

Dawn brought the blessing that the convoy needed; a murky, bleak day of low cloud, fog and rain that hid the ships from Argentine aircraft and at times from each other as well. Those closest were reduced to dim outlines that could just be made out on the sea; the rest of the fleet was invisible as it headed westwards at a steady twelve knots, helicopters sometimes audible but unseen, out ahead probing for submarines. The best thing was to stay busy. The crew set to cleaning the cabins vacated by 3 Para and 40 Commando, and the passageways and stairs were full of 42 Commando shifting grenades and ammunition to the top of the ship in readiness for landing. Their cabins seemed more cramped than ever as men bustled about, packing kit they were not taking ashore and stowing it away until – if – they returned from the islands now less than 100 miles away. In the middle of the afternoon, as the light faded, a small Wasp helicopter emerged from the gloom, and settled on the flight deck, its arrival darkening the mood of all on board as word spread of its mission. It bore the corpse of a Royal Marines corporal who was among 21 men killed the previous day when a Sea King helicopter crashed into the sea as it transferred men from *Hermes* to *Intrepid* at dusk. Even though rescuers were dispatched immediately from *Intrepid*, which was close by, the icy South Atlantic was too swift for them; only nine of the 30 men aboard survived. Eighteen of the dead were SAS.

Word went round the fleet that an albatross had hit the helicopter, its remains jamming the engine and causing the crash; it later emerged the more likely cause was a combination of overloading and an exhausted crew that momentarily lost concentration. The bandsmen winched the body bag down *Canberra*'s casualty ramp, lifted it with the utmost care on to a trolley and took it into the hospital. Peter Mayner, the cruise ship surgeon, was a cheerful and reassuring figure for patients with sunburn and seasickness, or the old losing the gamble that frailty would not overtake them, occasionally having to deal with a sexually-transmitted disease amongst the friskier; he was now part of a front-line surgical squadron versed in the worst that military technology could inflict and assigned to issue death certificates. He had seen bodies at sea before, usually the elderly whose holiday of a lifetime had brought its end, but not like this; not a young man in uniform on active service hauled from the water. The paperwork completed, the Marine was taken down into the bowels of the ship, where in the stark accounting of the price of regaining the Falklands, cold storage that once held treats for overstuffed passengers with expanding waistlines had been set aside as a makeshift mortuary. The Ministry of Defence had decreed that there would be no repatriation of the fallen, so burial in the sea that had claimed him awaited. Within 24 hours, Mayner would sign three more death certificates.

Darkness descended early under the overcast sky, and by late afternoon, *Canberra* was blacked out. The weather still favoured the fleet as it closed on the Falklands undetected, the hours counting down until the time came for it to form up into three waves in preparation for the final approach. Orders issued endlessly from the loudspeakers, emphasising and re-emphasising that at 10pm, the ship would go to alert state red – its highest level of preparedness – and all personnel would report to general emergency stations, mustered and ready to board the lifeboats. They must have their emergency kit with them at all times. Before then, it was time for the last steaks of the day. There was no wine with dinner tonight in the Pacific Restaurant, and precious little conversation either. The waiters were as smartly turned out and attentive as ever but quieter, smoothing any wrinkles out of the linen, straightening the cutlery. War or not, standards had to be maintained, even if waterproofs and lifejackets were discreetly to hand, ready to be put on over dress uniforms and bow ties. The restaurant felt oddly empty since the departure of 40 Commando and 3 Para; just the ship's officers and those of 42 Commando, preoccupied and beyond small talk. Shortly before eight o'clock, all looked up from their plates and watched in silence as a group of men carrying bags and their own lifejackets trooped in and headed for the doors at the aft end. It was changeover time in the engine room, and for the next four hours they would be shut in, 20 or more feet below the waterline; if *Canberra* was torpedoed, their chances were negligible. All her watertight doors had been closed, and the only way in and out of the engine spaces on G and H Decks was through the restaurant. A few minutes later, the watch they had relieved emerged, more animated than the men on their way down, glad to be coming back up from what might be a tomb, like everyone else watching the clock, counting down to 10pm.

It was time for Vaux to address his men, in a setting surreally at odds with what he had to say; as they sat before him in a genteel, pink-upholstered passenger lounge with its piano and ornate lights, its picture windows blacked out with canvas, he spoke of hitting the Argentines hard, steeling themselves to leave wounded comrades to wait for help because the advance could not be slowed, the necessity of killing the enemy to prevent him killing you. Only a week or two earlier, they had all packed into the Atlantic Restaurant for jokes, laughter and songs. Even by the standards of the Marines, 42 was an especially close-knit commando. Deployment to the Falklands came immediately after it returned from four months' training in Norway; officers and men had been together for almost a year, getting to know each other especially well. Now, as he looked out at the hundreds of familiar, determined faces watching him with total concentration, it was impossible for Vaux not to wonder how many of these young men would die or be wounded. The gruelling weeks that followed were to blot out Vaux's precise memory of much of what he said, but one of his themes was the aggression that had been fostered over the course of the voyage, whether it manifested itself in the vigour of training or the laughter of the Malvinas Song. 'I said that very few of us had been to war, so we don't understand until it happens that ultimately you have to kill people, because if you don't, they will kill you. You've got to blank out a lot of scruples and hesitations and limitations that you've all been brought up with in peacetime.' There was a bit of banter in his address, a few laughs here and there to momentarily break the tension of the grim message that this was the hardest, most hazardous operation they had ever undertaken, a world away from fighting in Northern Ireland, which they all knew. John Shirley noted that he closed with a grin and the driest of understated wit, wishing his men, 'A very short and very decisive holiday – good luck to you.'

Vaux returned to his cabin on C Deck to pack his own gear and then try to get a few hours' sleep. The men took a last glance around their cabins to make sure they had left nothing behind, and then hefted bergens and weapons to make their way to bars and public rooms allocated to each company. Where the blue-rinses and silver-haired gentlemen in full evening wear had sipped cocktails before dinner and pondered the evening's entertainment amid polished panelling and pastel shades, relaxing on faux-leather furniture, now hard, supremely fit Marines in full fighting order dumped heavy packs with a thud, propped their rifles against the wall or the chairs and settled down to make themselves as comfortable as they could. The bounty from *Canberra*'s galley was tucked away in their battledress; sharpened spoons and cheese wires. The women's tights bought from the shop were already on under camouflage trousers. Their packs gave them something to lean against as they stretched out on the grubby and scuffed hardboard flooring; no beer for them tonight, just tea and coffee. Stewards were still on duty, stepping daintily over and between the legs of sprawling soldiers as they tidied away cups; as in the restaurant, there was no reason to let standards slip just because there were fearsome-looking fighting men ready for battle everywhere and boxes of grenades stacked on a table. Videos of war films or comedies played for those who wanted to watch; others shoved their berets down over their eyes and dozed. It would be a long night, but they had eaten well and were relatively comfortable, unlike the men aboard *Fearless* and *Intrepid*, packed in so tight that it was almost impossible to move around the ship. Even officers struggled to find space; Norman Menzies had wedged himself into a corner, and grabbed a heavy white sheet from a convenient pile to wrap around himself for warmth as he tried to sleep. A passing padre pointed out that it was a shroud; Menzies shrugged and shut his eyes.

The night was starting to clear as *Canberra* manoeuvred into her position within the new formation as the fleet passed the point on the chart designated Oscar; she was in the second wave with HMS *Brilliant* and HMS *Plymouth*; *Fearless* and *Intrepid* made up the first, and the landing ships (logistic) were astern in the third. It was a drawn-out and at times frustrating process. 'A long old day,' said Martin Reed. 'We'd had a briefing about where we were going to be, but it just went on and on.

Things did work, but then *Fearless* lost her way.' It took three-quarters of an hour for her to regain position, as the rest of the fleet slowed. For the first time in days, *Canberra* was sailing through calm waters as she came under the lee of the Falklands. At 10pm, the loudspeakers ordered all personnel to general emergency stations.

The figures bustling along the passageways and decks appeared instantly to have piled on weight since dinner, suddenly bulkier and less agile because of the swaddling multiple layers they donned in response to a day of exhortations from the bridge to wear their warmest clothes. For Susie West, that meant two pairs of trousers, sweatshirt, two sweaters, uniform, then fleece-lined tracksuit top, all of which disappeared under the oversized combat jacket she had been given, her family photos tucked into one of its multiple pockets, hat and torch clutched in one hand, lifejacket in the other. The P&O medical team, close anyway, stuck together; Angela Devine, lipstick and tampon in her own pocket, was on form and broke the tension by getting the rest laughing. Others were doing likewise; more than ever, the company of friends who jollied along or reassured was to be treasured. Jokes about earning the danger money, or so-and-so looking as if they were setting off for the North Pole helped a little. They brought pillows and cushions from their cabins to try to make the night as comfortable as possible, and shared whatever they had; even the odd camp bed appeared. Gradually, the ship quietened and the crew settled as best they could, trying to sleep like the Marines were in their bars. It was eerily quiet, and once the wisecracks ran out, subdued and tense, more claustrophobic than ever; dingy lighting, blacked-out windows, shadowy and unnerving, no way of knowing what was happening outside this room full of people sweating under layer upon layer of woollens when they should have been in whites soaking up the warmth of a Mediterranean spring. They strained their ears for any clue about what was happening, but none came. The noise and chatter of troops moving around that they had grown used to was absent, and so were the creaks and groans of the passage through the storm; *Canberra* sailed as smoothly and silently as if she was cruising the Pacific.

Silence and darkness was everything as the fleet crept towards the islands and reached the point designated X Ray, just north of land. Twelve minutes after the crew were called to alert, *Canberra* began breaking out of the formation ready to enter Falkland Sound, the fleet line ahead, a mile separating each ship. The frigate HMS *Plymouth* led, *Norland* followed, then *Canberra*, *Stromness*, *Fort Austin* and a second frigate, HMS *Brilliant*. *Fearless* and *Intrepid* were already heading into the sound carrying men those aboard *Canberra* had come to count as friends when she began her own passage at 11pm; less than half an hour would take her to Point Alpha, there to alter course into the mouth of San Carlos Water, and anchor a mile-and-a-half off Fanning Head, where an Argentine force would have to be dealt with.

The bridge was even darker than the rooms where the crew huddled, the faint glow of instruments providing the only illumination. Radio and radar silence was being observed by all the ships; *Canberra*'s only eyes were those of the lookouts, straining to penetrate the blackness for any sight or sound that could spell danger. Everybody was watchful; Scott-Masson, contained and impassive, Burne, all concentration and pent-up energy. It was the blackest of nights, moonless and clear now, the last wisps of mists gone and the southern hemisphere's unfamiliar pattern of stars out, so soundless that the men on the bridge wings could hear the waves lapping gently at the hull a hundred feet below as *Canberra* glided ghostly white through the darkness. Everyone moving about the bridge did so cautiously to make as little sound as possible, and orders were issued in low, muted tones, as if the enemy somewhere out there might somehow overhear anything louder, or a footstep could betray the presence of a vast liner.

Bit by bit, as the sweep hands of the clocks took *Canberra* towards 21 May second by second, all began to register a deeper blackness ahead, a different quality of darkness; 8,000 miles and six weeks distant from home, the Falklands were sighted, the outline of Fanning Head just visible against the sky, a forbidding fortress that the bridge knew held an Argentine garrison waiting and watching for an assault from the sea. No glimpse of light or movement was to be seen as the headland was scanned and re-scanned through binoculars and night-sights, only utter stillness; if the invaders had detected the ships, they showed no sign of it. Cautiously, deliberately, she nosed towards her anchorage. Involuntarily, the officers drew breath sharply and held it as the rattle of the anchor chains went down at 12.17am, seemingly deafeningly loud after the hours of silence. The lookouts scanned the land again for any sign that *Canberra* had given herself away as the minutes passed; still nothing, no gunfire, no explosions. They began daring to hope *Canberra* had got away with it; that somehow, a 45,000-ton liner dwarfing so many of the ships of the task force had managed to slip past an enemy guarding a stolen land as quietly as a dinghy. The hours ahead promised to be as testing and tense as those just past; she must now wait at her anchorage until 5am and the approach of dawn, whilst the landings went ahead. The plan had been amended; 40 and 45 Commandos and 2 and 3 Paras would not now go ashore in successive phases, but simultaneously at 2.30am.

Those too on edge to sleep at their muster points had felt the ship slowing and then anchoring; there had been no emergency, no dash to the boats. Nerves eased a little, helped by the word being passed at about 1am that everybody should settle down and try to rest, as the ship would not be weighing anchor for several hours yet. Waiting, waiting; everybody wished away the time, willing the dawn to arrive and banish the threat of this night passing excruciatingly slowly. Susie West turned the lights off in her cabin and drew the blackout aside from the window; the starlight and the gentle ripples of the sea played tricks and she thought she glimpsed figures in the water. John Muxworthy was with two of the female assistant pursers and the master-at-arms, a nerveless old hand who kept up a non-stop stream of banter and jokes that eventually became wearing. 'He was bloody good at it, he was like he was going out to a party,' said Muxworthy, 'But I got to the stage where I thought, "I wish he'd shut up".' Graham Harding crept out onto the flight deck for a few minutes, staying in the shadows, just to feel the cold night air and catch sight of the land that had occupied his imagination since Southampton. In his cabin, Vaux awoke from a fitful few hours' sleep feeling the urge to be at the heart of whatever was happening, and headed up to the bridge. At his muster point, Roy Paddison was awake and ready to go down to the bakery on F Deck, right at the waterline, there to put on his whites and make an early start on working the dough in the big stainless-steel mixing vats. Come what may, *Canberra* would serve breakfast with fresh, warm bread rolls as usual.

It was about 2am. Hours of nervous anticipation had left many drained to the point of exhaustion; heads began to nod and eyelids drooped, until a crackling, tearing, roaring whoosh in the air over *Canberra* snapped them open, followed an instant later by a crashing explosion. 'This f**king great bang, and we all jumped,' said Reed. 'I felt the hairs on the back of my neck just go voom, flat as a pancake, the most extraordinary feeling, and then we twigged what it was: it was shelling and it was going in the right direction.' The first blast was followed by another, then another, yet more, the rushing overhead felt as much as heard every few seconds, then the bang. The loudspeakers came to life for the first time in hours; the destroyer HMS *Antrim* was bombarding enemy positions on Fanning Head, joined soon after by HMS *Plymouth*. There was an easing of the tension in the public rooms as the crew sat up from their cushions and pillows and shook the sleep off; nervous laughter and the start again of chatter. The assault was under way, and even though all knew danger was still at hand, there was reassurance in their own side doing the firing; odd though they knew it was, men and women began to lay back down and close their eyes, more settled than they had been all night. 'We had another two or three hours before we were going to pick up, so I tried to sleep for a couple of hours,' said Reed. 'Lullabyed by the sound of *Antrim* shelling, bang, every two or three minutes.'

The binoculars trained on Fanning Head began to pick up flashes; out on the bridge wings, the sound of automatic fire and the crump of mortars became audible, punctuating the whoosh and crash of shells as the SAS and SBS attacked the garrison. It was just possible to make out a haze over the headland, the clouds of dust and dirt kicked up by the shelling. Faintly, from the south, there was more firing and explosions as the SAS laid down a diversionary attack on the Argentine forces at Goose Green. It remained quiet and tense on the bridge, but there was now an undercurrent of excitement. Kim Sabido had been allowed up with his tape recorder, and Burne, knowing perfectly well that there was no chance of his words being broadcast any time soon, talked him through what was happening: 'There were the guns going off and you could see the flashes of light, and Chris Burne gave me this running commentary. There was this atmosphere of excitement, all the fear and adrenaline that had been built up was now about to be released, and he talked me through everything very quietly, very calmly, exactly what was going on.' The landings were behind schedule, the delay caused by a faulty satellite system aboard *Fearless*; it was getting on for 4am before intermittent, terse situation reports started to come over the radio. Vaux recognised the clipped tones of his old friend Ewen Southby-Tailyour, and in the darkness, grins of relief were exchanged as codewords for successful landings were broadcast, as wave after wave of men got their feet on the islands they had spent weeks learning about and training for, as the landing crafts returned to the ships to take more in. All ears were cocked for word of *Canberra*'s lads, and here they were at last: 40 Commando and the Blues and Royals, second ashore after 2 Para. The bridge waited for what seemed like an age for 3 Para, way behind schedule as delays accumulated, and 45 Commando landed. At last, the word came: *Canberra*'s Paras were on their way. The intelligence had been spot-on; there had been no resistance, and islanders were coming out to greet the troops. There was no exhilaration on the bridge; they were too cautious for that. Satisfaction, certainly, that the first phase had gone according to plan and the astonishing feat of landing a formidable fighting force on enemy-held islands so far from home had been accomplished; relief, too, that the Argentines failed to detect the invasion force in the darkness. But there were no illusions about the day to come; this was only the start.

With the troops ashore, it was time for *Canberra* to go in. The shelling and gunfire on Fanning Head had ceased, and the night was quiet once more, as she weighed anchor at 5.20am, an hour before dawn, the rattle of the chains no longer mattering. Everybody was awake now, most unable

187

to see what was happening, listening intently for clues as the ship got under way, proceeding slowly and cautiously; in a matter of ten minutes, she entered San Carlos Water, where Scott-Masson and his officers took her towards the anchorage carefully. Down below the waterline, on H Deck, Don Cole was monitoring the load on the ship's electrical systems, listening to the rising whine of the generators as they clicked on and off according to the demands of the bridge as the huge liner was eased into position in waters that presented their own hazards. 'It ran through my mind that it's a shallow area, quite a narrow approach, the sort of place where there might be the risk of running aground,' he said. 'It was quite a challenge to get a ship that big into quite a confined area with all the other ships, but it was like being on standby for a difficult arrival navigationally at a port.' It took 35 minutes of manoeuvring before she anchored at 6.05am, as the sky started to lighten; landing craft still taking 3 Para ashore were just visible on the dark waters, and the profiles of hills around the anchorage started to emerge.

Canberra had never before arrived at a destination like this or in remotely similar circumstances, yet echoes of the polite routines of cruising persisted; breakfast was being served, albeit early, and by waiters who had abandoned uniforms and bow ties for layers of warm clothing as they bustled about the Pacific Restaurant with unaccustomed haste. This was not the day for a leisurely breakfast; their guests were running on adrenaline, and wanted to be in and out quickly, taking the chance to eat while they could before the sun rose and exposed the invasion fleet to the Argentines. The anxieties of the night had left military and P&O alike ravenous; the bacon and eggs seemed especially good, and the baskets of rolls that had kept Paddison and the other bakers busy – and glad to be occupied – for hours when others could only wait and worry were emptied as soon as they were presented. Everybody had been below, shut in, claustrophobic for long enough; they wanted sight of the land that had drawn them halfway around the world and jolted their lives out of the humdrum into uncertainty and threat.

Maybe it was the heightened perception of nerves strung tight, or maybe this really was the most breathtaking, exhilarating dawn they had witnessed; deep shades of blue gradually lightening as the horizon warmed to orange, the stars fading away into the clearest of skies burnished by the glowing promise of a glorious early winter's day ahead. The softly rippling waters of the anchorage were beginning to sparkle in the rising sun as this distant outpost of Britain revealed a little more of itself as each minute passed. It was disconcertingly familiar, nothing like the image they had in their minds of a storm-tossed, icy wasteland on this calm, cold, bracingly bright morning. Low hills of brown and green moorland ran up from the shoreline, the rough grass and tussocks of the survival lectures visible through binoculars, the slopes dotted with stumpy gorse bushes; bleak certainly, but so very like the places they lived or had grown up in or gone to on holiday. Comparisons flashed into everybody's mind's eye; Scott-Masson thought immediately of the isles off Scotland's west coast, Don Cole of the Lake District. For those from the north, it summoned to mind the Yorkshire moors, those from the south and west, Dartmoor or the Brecon Beacons. Instinctively, they grasped why the islanders clung so tenaciously to their lonely land so very far from the country to which they were unswervingly loyal; it was just like home. Close your eyes, and the cries of the seabirds wheeling overhead, alarmed by the intrusion into their normally tranquil habitat, might have been those of a harbour or estuary anywhere on Britain's coastline; listen carefully, and there, faintly in the distance, the barking of dogs kept as pets or to work the flocks of sheep, was the sound of anywhere in the countryside. All over *Canberra*, crew began to emerge, taking in the scenery from wherever they could find a vantage point, snapping the hills and each other with cameras they had popped down to their cabins to retrieve. Sue Wood and her husband, Graham, and a few of their friends made their way onto the forward part of the Promenade Deck, glad to see the sun after so many hours cooped up during the preceding days of storms and filthy weather. Cole made his way up from the switchboard on to an aft deck near the steering gear, the P&O medics out onto the Games Deck, just letting the daybreak soak into them, trying to take in that this disarmingly ordinary landscape had been the stuff of their nightmares, and that men were dying for control of it.

The reverie did not last long; all around were the ships they had come to know so well; *Norland*, *Stromness*, *Europic Ferry*, a constant traffic of landing craft growling between them and shore. No sooner had the sun risen than the noise of the seabirds was drowned out by the clatter of helicopters heading for *Canberra*, Sea Kings hovering and waiting their turn to come in over the flight deck to lift loads of ammunition, the downdraught of the rotors rippling the overalls of those securing the loads, and then the engines labouring as they took off for shore, the underslung nets swaying. The brilliantly clear morning was surveyed with wariness on the bridge; the night had favoured the fleet, but now day had broken, the Argentines could not possibly fail to realise that landings had taken place. Worse, it was perfect flying weather for the enemy's air force; no low cloud or fog to protect them now.

Watches were checked; on the cusp of winter this far south, if the sky remained as clear, there would be about nine hours of daylight, hours when air attacks could be pressed home. *Canberra*'s drills and preparations served her well for what she was there to do. Pontoons were quickly in place and gangways rigged; she was ready to offload 42 Commando and her huge tonnage of stores. Still, there were dilemmas, calculations and even gambles to be made; Reed found himself unsure whether to swing her lifeboats out, ready for embarkation if the worst happened, or keep them inboard, fearful that a missile strike could send splinters from them scything through *Canberra*, causing injuries or even deaths. 'We'd got three-quarter-inch pre-stressed steel, and no one had a clue what would happen if we were hit,' he recalled. 'It would either penetrate halfway, or it would explode on the outside and wouldn't go straight through. If it exploded on the side, there'd be a hell of a lot of shrapnel within about a hundred feet, which would include any lifeboats swung out. I just didn't know what to do, so I thought, "Sod it", and put half out and half in. We'll never know if it was the right decision.' The luckiest Marines on board were those detailed to man the GPMGs; outside, on the bridge wings, looking around the anchorage at the constant helicopter traffic and the stores being floated ashore on rafts from the landing ships, it was impossible not to believe that everything was going 3 Brigade's way. Immediately below, on the Captain's Deck, where the senior officers' cabins were, the men armed with Blowpipes felt the same. Down in the bars and public rooms, where the rest of 42 remained shut in awaiting orders to move, the mood was more fatalistic. Kevin Mountney had spent the night in the William Fawcett Room, on the Promenade Deck: 'I asked one of the Marines, "Do you think they'll come?", and he said, "Oh yes, they'll come".'

They came when the sun was high enough to lend the rusting, grubby *Canberra* the illusion she was still brilliant white, at least from the distance of the shore, where soldiers and islanders looked out at the rugged ships of the invasion fleet and shook their heads in disbelief that in its midst lay this vast liner lying at anchor as serenely as if she were sending off boats full of day-trippers on sight-seeing excursions, and not helicopters weighed down with the tools of war. It was 8.45, a little under three hours since she had anchored, and the outloading was going without any hitch. Crew with no role to play in it found a spot to loaf where they would not be in the way, chatting, smoking, taking pictures, when Burne came on the loudspeakers, his voice urgent; aircraft approaching the anchorage. Almost immediately, they caught a flash of silver out of the corner of their eyes, the sun catching the wings of a solitary plane rounding Fanning Head and swooping towards HMS *Argonaut* fast and low, with the grace and precision of an air show display, the sound of its engines abruptly eclipsed by bright flashes and a harsh chatter that rang across the water as its cannons opened up, followed a split-second later by the brilliant orange bursts of rockets being fired, straddling the warship and stitching a pattern in the rippling waves of the sound, as the aircraft made the tightest of turns and headed straight at *Canberra*.

'Open fire!', bellowed Burne. 'Open fire *now*!' Tracer hosed into the air from the GPMGs on the bridge wings, dazzling and deadly, bright and burning even against the luminous sky, the fire snaking up, chasing the attacking aircraft as the Marines clamped on the triggers, trying to keep their gunsights on it, feeling the percussive whump of a Blowpipe being fired just below them. Reed, on the bridge wing, went cold as the aircraft turned, began to run in and then altered course, peeling away and turning tail towards the headland. 'He hauled round and came straight for us, and I thought, "Oh, f**k", and all this tracer came up at him and must have caused absolute horror, because he picked up and sped away over the hill. He came straight to us and we banged him. I'm sure we scared the bastard, because I've never seen anything go like that.' The stern gunners were blasting away ineffectually at the diminishing dot in the sky as Reed and Philip Pickford charged to the rear of the bridge. Reed glanced down at his trembling hands, and then back up at Pickford, whom he had nicknamed Pickering. 'I said, "Pickering?", and he said, "Yes, my chief?", "Pickering, my hands are shaking", and he said, "Don't worry, my chief. So are mine". And we turned round and went back round the other side.'

It was over in seconds, so rapidly that those outside enjoying the morning hardly had time to realise what was happening; Sue Wood and her friends scrambling for safety away from the fo'c'sle as an officer shouted, 'Get inside, quick,' Morgan O'Connell realising the glint of sunlight was something flashing through the air and diving for cover; John Shirley registering the gunfire sounded like handfuls of stones hurled against a metal container. Of all the ships in the anchorage, *Canberra* had fired first of all; Burne's preternatural alertness and split-second reaction to the appearance of the aircraft had put *Canberra*'s pyrotechnic shield up before any of the other ships in the anchorage reacted to the incursion. It had worked; she had not been fired on, but the mood on the bridge was grave. The aircraft was a relatively lightly-armed twin-engined Pucara, used for ground attack, probably based on the islands; the likelihood was that it had been reconnoitring San Carlos. If the Argentines had been unsure during the night hours if landings were under way, they surely knew now, and would respond with faster, more heavily armed warplanes from the mainland. There was also concern about the woeful ineffectiveness of the Blowpipe fired; Vaux had raged as it spluttered impotently into the sea, not for a moment threatening the Pucara. All sensed that *Canberra*'s ordeal was just beginning; out in the middle of this calm, sunlit inlet, she felt dangerously vulnerable.

The next attack on the fleet, a few minutes later, they all heard but could not see as a lone aircraft targeted HMS *Argonaut*, just outside the anchorage, strafing her with cannon fire and rockets, wounding three men. The stream of helicopters ferrying between *Canberra* and the shore was now constant, shifting stores from the chacons on the overloaded Sun Deck as rapidly as possible before the next raids; they had a clear half hour and then Burne came over the loudspeakers. 'Planes are forming up to the north of the anchorage, stand by to take cover,' then seconds later, 'Take cover! Take cover!' The thunder of jet engines warned that this was altogether more formidable than the first attacker, and then they were on them, a flight of Mirage fighter-bombers screaming overhead, as the men and women below decks flung themselves face-down to the hardboard flooring, covering their heads with their arms, feeling the explosions as *Canberra* lurched from the impact of a blast in the water. The bursts of tracer pursued the fast jets hopelessly as the gun teams also fired flares from their Very pistols, filling the skies with flashes of colour, the din intensified by the noise of helicopters caught in the middle of loading dropping low to the waterline alongside the hull for cover, a jolting, shocking explosion in the air as one of the Mirages blew up in an orange fireball as a Sea Wolf missile from one of the warships caught it, a speck glimpsed hurtling away from the inferno as the pilot ejected, and then another bearing down on *Canberra* impossibly fast and terrifyingly close, the approaching howl of its engines drowning out everything else as those on the bridge watched horrified. 'This Mirage came straight down the nose at us, and I thought, "This is the finish for us, there's nothing we can do"', said Reed. 'There was nothing between me and him except a quarter-inch of aluminium, whatever he throws at us, it'll go through, but he just pulled up and flew away – he had nothing left underneath, all his weapons pods were empty.' Sabido said, 'He was so close and low that I was staring at the pilot, looking him right in the face, and then he just flew off.'

As abruptly as the Mirages had appeared, they faded away. It was the briefest of respites as the sheltering helicopters rose up from the side of the ship and carried on loading with new urgency; barely 15 minutes before 'Take cover! Take cover!', and the approaching rumble of the next wave, growing louder by the second, not yet seen, and then, all around, Mirages again, Skyhawk fighter-bombers as well, maybe four of them, maybe six, too fast to count as they flashed by suicidally low; the bridge could look down on them flying at the level of the Meridian Room, trying to dodge the hail of fire. Every British sailor and soldier in San Carlos was fighting off the threat from the air; tracer, flares, the blast of Blowpipes and Stinger missiles, the boom-boom-boom of Bofors guns, Marines and Paras blazing away from their positions ashore to protect the ships that had brought them here, even the light tanks of the Blues and Royals firing too, all chasing the kill, and in doing so disrupting the attacks. Even so, an airburst jarringly close to *Canberra*'s upper decks made everybody flinch; another blast in the water rocked her once more, kicking up the sea into cold spray slapping across the sweating faces of the men on the GPMGs, the guns an extension of themselves as they pursued the warplanes across the sky. Chris Sheppard, ordered to the bridge wings to relieve one of his comrades and haring up the staircases, eager to hit back, found him locked to the weapon, refusing to give it up, utterly consumed by battle, his sole object to shoot down the enemy, everything in him focussed on the aircraft in his sights, his speech chattering in time with the tracer. 'He wouldn't let me take the gun, he said, "You can f-f-f-f-f**k off," as he was firing it, he was so glued to it.'

Furiously determined though the defence teams were, there was a growing and uncomfortable realisation of *Canberra*'s helplessness if an attacker got through the shield of fire from sea and land. Lights in the sky had appeared to see off the first threat from a lone aircraft, but against successive waves of sophisticated, well-armed, fast fighter-bombers, half a dozen machine guns loaded with tracer, flares and Blowpipe missiles that apparently posed little threat to the warplanes streaking past felt hopelessly inadequate. Naval, military and P&O officers alike gave thanks for the choice of anchorage; the hills surrounding it meant that attacking pilots had only split-seconds to pick their target after swooping down, but if they chose *Canberra*, she would be lost, and there was nothing bigger, nor more instantly identifiable. All eyes of the fighting men and civilians ashore were on her: massive, white, absurdly out of place amid the spouts of water erupting all around. If they were unable to draw their gaze away, why should attacking pilots do otherwise? The bridge afforded no protection, and during the last raid, Burne had been outside with Vaux, the two men stumping up and down the bridge wing, urging the gunners on, flinching at the airbursts around them.

As the Mirages and Skyhawks screamed away, Burne turned to Vaux, his voice urgent. 'He said, "Nick, you've got to get your men off before we're sunk." I was absolutely convinced *Canberra* was going to be sunk, I couldn't see any reason why she wouldn't be, she was bigger than any other ship there, she was the obvious target and what made her so vulnerable was that she was stuffed with ammunition and explosives, so a direct hit could have blown the whole stern off.' Four fraught hours were to crawl by before 42 could leave, as communication problems and the logistics of getting the Marines off in an anchorage under attack were addressed. They came again; Dagger fighter-bombers now joining the Mirages and Skyhawks over the anchorage and the warships providing a defensive screen in Falkland Sound. A deadly trade-off was emerging; the hills that provided some protection from air attack also hampered radar detection of incoming attackers, and the casualties were mounting; *Antrim*, whose guns had offered a strange sort of comfort to frightened men and women aboard *Canberra* huddled down in emergency gear in the depths of night, had been hit. Eight men were injured, one of them blinded; a bomb had bounced off her fo'c'sle and exploded in the water alongside, and another was lodged unexploded deep inside her.

Canberra could only watch, wait, hope, carry on unloading, defend herself as best she could; a helicopter coming in fast and low to the water before rising up to the flight deck brought in additional Blowpipes. Her vulnerability gripped all of them, from the bridge a hundred and more feet above the sea, to the men in the engine room below the rippling waves. As another wave of aircraft came in, Vaux caught sight of Scott-Masson's expression, later writing, 'It was a mask of horror and outrage, as if some madman was trying to destroy his family.' Eleven decks below, watching the dials of the switchboard, Don Cole became aware of thuds and thumps that he could hear even through the ear defenders he wore against the noise of the engines, and then his nostrils began to twitch as the smell of battle seeped in: 'I smelt cordite, which I remembered from firing weapons when I was in the cadets, and that's what made me register that it's a bomb going off, and on the bridge people are probably ducking left and right, and here I am enclosed in this metal hole below the waterline, and I didn't like to think about that.' As the deck swayed under the impact of bomb bursts in the water, Cole's eyes were drawn to the desk and chair at the end of the switchboard where he sat to make notes: 'It's only six feet from the hull, and if anything comes through, it will be upon me, so I moved to the middle of the generator room. I didn't think about it all the time, but it just goes through your mind now and again.'

All over *Canberra*, men and women tried not to think about what might happen, distracting themselves as best they could, clinging to shreds of everyday normality, however incongruous amongst booms and blasts and the ship being buffeted, as if they might protect against the bomb or missile that could strike at any second. Susie West laughed in spite of herself as she heard one of the crew drawn in from the pool fuming about what was happening. 'He was very angry, and saying, "Just wait 'til I get back home, I'm going to tell my union rep about this", and I thought, "That's your priority?"' One of the engineers tried to take his mind off things by close scrutiny of one of W H Smith's dirty magazines. John Muxworthy came across a couple of cabin staff carrying on as usual, changing bedding and tidying. Sue and Graham Wood, luckier than most in having each other to cling to, held hands as they sheltered; in between raids, she managed to lose herself in one of Tom Sharpe's comic novels. Angela Devine was overwhelmed by the desire to take a shower and wash her hair. 'If I was going to die, I wanted to be clean, and Rosie said, "Go and have a shower, and if there's a red alert, I'll come and get you out", so I was in there for what seemed to be a long time and it was lovely, and I opened the door, wrapped in a towel and said, "That was fantastic". And of course, there'd been a red alert because they were happening all the time, and Rosie said, "Oh, we've had one, but I thought we'd give you time". I thought, "Some friend you are."' The few minutes' respite was soon forgotten as yet another wave of raiders swept in. 'I grabbed a tureen and put it on my head,' said Devine, 'And I sat in the stairwell, thinking, "I'm going to die".'

Disbelief slowed the reactions of some as they looked around in the midst of a waking nightmare. Kevin Mountney watched Marines diving to the deck of the William Fawcett Room and found himself unable to do likewise: 'I just froze, I didn't know what to do, and slowly got down onto my belly. It's that difference between a serviceman who's trained to do that, and a civilian who just doesn't know what to do.' For some, the sheer other-worldliness of what was happening led them into hazardous behaviour. Muxworthy said, 'I didn't have a lot to do, so I wandered round to the galley to see how the lads were, and they had the big doors opened up and all standing there goofing, and I lost my rag and told them all to get in.' A few lost their nerve, needing the comfort of friends as they came close to hysteria, clamping their hands to their ears, trying to shut it all out; Graham Harding heard rapid female footsteps and sobbing, and reflected, 'Poor girl. You didn't sign up for this.' Scott-Masson left the bridge and started to tour his ship, from bows to stern, from upper decks to lower, talking to the crew; it helped that he radiated calm and kept his head up as explosions went off. Those who listened intently to his broadcasts were cheered by seeing him, bolstered by his encouragement. He would walk round several more times, as did Burne, the two taking turns to boost morale which was, for now, holding up remarkably well.

Everybody took whatever shelter they could, however ineffective; Marines in one of the public rooms were compassionate enough not to further spook a pair of stewards sheltering under a flimsy table by pointing out that there was a box of grenades on it. John Shirley found himself flattened to the deck alongside Vaux, who observed drily that it all reminded him of a bad night in the Divis Flats, one of Belfast's most notoriously dangerous spots. In the hospital, Peter Mayner and Rosie Elsdon got underneath beds. Everywhere on a ship laden with ammunition and explosives held risks; Commander Tim Yarker, the RN Executive Officer, charged into the back room of the radio office and announced that he was taking it over as a reserve command position. Harding pointed out that there were 15 tons of mortar bombs stacked outside awaiting airlift. 'He disappeared and then rang through from the purser's department at the other end of the ship to say he'd set up his command position there.' John Ware had a fraught morning on the flight deck; he was attempting to get across to *Norland* to brief 2 Para about a new communications system for reporting casualties. 'Every time a helicopter came in, I went shooting up to try and get across, and no sooner had it come in, another Argentine aircraft would appear and the helicopter would take off, so I spent most of the day running up and down or lying flat on my face.' At least he could see what was going on; Vaux fretted for his men, still grouped by company below, more than ever itching to get their boots onto land. Like the crew, they could only wait and hope, even though they took the attacks more calmly. 'We'd all been given our ammo and we were in the Peacock Room waiting for the order to go,' said Bungy Williams. 'We were watching a video when this explosion went off and whole ship shook, and we all looked at each other. There was no point diving under a table, it wouldn't have done any good, so we just sat there and laughed about it.'

Abruptly, it stopped. No more explosions, the GPMGs ceasing firing as the sound of jets faded away over the hills, suddenly quiet enough to once again hear the seabirds. The warships' radar screens were clear of incoming formations of aircraft; nothing closing from 90 miles, 60 miles, 30 miles, as they had all morning. Maybe the Argentines were regrouping, or a change in tactics loomed; impossible to know, but it felt like a respite and *Canberra* seized it. As earlier that morning, the cruise ship instinct of feeding and watering those it carried reasserted itself; if the Argentines were being civilised enough to take a break for a bite to eat, then the ship would do likewise. At 11.45, the loudspeakers announced that lunch was being served. Ware was not going to get across to *Norland* any time soon, and headed down to the Pacific Restaurant; if the waiters had been harried at breakfast, they were jittery now, distracted and jumpy. Amid the trials of the morning, the galley had turned out a basic meal of hot stodge. 'They dished me up this plate of cottage pie and a few veg,' said Ware. 'And the guy on the table next to me said, "Well, this is alright, but not a patch on what we usually get, and where the hell's the wine?"'

Thoughts were also turning to having a drink amongst those on the bridge. The unexpected lull was, fortuitously, perfectly timed for pinkers, a large and deserved one after the morning that Scott-Masson and his ship had endured, and he retired to his cabin. That seemed like a very good idea to Reed. 'I thought I'll nip down and have one as well, and outside the door to the bridge was Dennis's steward and mine, and my chap's lying there with his lifejacket and escape kit on, and he says, "Sir?", and I said, "What's the matter?" and he said "Something's gone bang in your cabin". Oh Christ, that's all I need. So I pop down, open the door, and there's nothing wrong, so I went across to my grog locker, which is by the outer bulkhead, grabbed the whisky, poured myself a large glass and grabbed the ice flask, shook it, and it had shattered.' That was not what had gone bang. As he was about to take a drink, Reed noticed that next to his window, all the metalwork was buckled inwards. 'I shot outside, and there's this very sheepish Marine, and he said, "I tried to miss the window, sir", and there's this big dent in the bulkhead and the paint's all scarred and buggered, and I said, "What have you done?" He had a Blowpipe, and there's a disc at the back that pops off when it's fired, and he'd tracked this aircraft going past, fired, and the disc had gone straight into the bulkhead.'

Even though the air raids had halted for now, the mood on board grew grimmer as word spread of the casualties flown aboard during the course of the morning. The airlifts had begun in the worst possible manner; three dead aircrew of two Gazelle helicopters shot down by Argentine ground forces close to where 3 Para had watched in helpless despair, unable to warn the pilots that they were flying into an ambush because they were on a separate radio network. The helicopters plummeted into the sea; the injured and defenceless crew had been machine-gunned as they floundered in the water. Pickford was communicating with junior officers stationed around the ship; one, shaken by what he was seeing, called up to the bridge from the casualty receiving area. 'He was a first trip cadet not long out of school, and he said, "There are a lot of dead bodies piling up here", and I just said, "Stand by your post", and he said, OK, OK".' They were taken to Mayner for examination and death certificates to be issued. It was even more distressing than the day before; as he gingerly removed the flying helmet from one of the young men, part of his head came with it. The bandsmen bore the corpses to cold storage to join the victim of the Sea King crash.

The first wounded on board were the source of intense curiosity; three Argentine soldiers who had been part of the garrison attacked on Fanning Head. All had been shot in the legs, and one had part of a foot missing. So this was what the enemy looked like; in microcosm, it turned out to be an accurate picture of the Argentine army. Two were terrified teenage conscripts, little more than boys, underfed and filthy, trembling with cold and fright, who had resorted to slaughtering sheep for survival after spending days without being supplied with rations. The third was an altogether more dangerous customer: a tough, saturnine special forces lieutenant whose eyes burned with furious hatred at having been captured. He spoke perfect English and began issuing threats to destroy *Canberra*, which were laughed off since he was all but immobile; disconcertingly, though, the officer then clammed up and refused to speak further, waging a silent war of nerves with the surgical team, glaring from his bed, occasionally making them uncomfortable because they knew he understood everything being said around him. Burne was taking no chances in the face of threats, however remote; he ordered an armed guard into the hospital. The condition of the two younger men attracted the sympathy of the medics, one wag dubbing them Pinky and Perky after the children's television puppets. But nothing they did could settle them; their terror at being captured was plain, until somebody noticed both wore rosary beads and asked the Marines' Roman Catholic chaplain, Father Noel Mullin, to come to the hospital. 'Prior to this, they'd been lying in their beds rigid, the only thing moving was their eyes,' said Morgan O'Connell. 'They'd been told that if they were taken alive by the Brits, they'd be eaten alive, and here we'd dressed their wounds, we'd washed them, fed them, and now the chaplain came round with holy communion, and you could see them visibly relax. Just to see the power that went with the ministration of the chaplain to these poor, frightened, defeated 16- and 17-year-olds, that was an image that I will carry with me for the rest of my days.'

The first British serviceman flown aboard for treatment, from 2 Para, was hardly less angry than the Argentine lieutenant, but with himself; his war had ended before it began when he stumbled into a ditch in the darkness soon after landing, ricking his back so badly that he could hardly move. Hour by hour, more and more casualties were arriving from the warships that had been under attack all morning, among them *Antrim* and *Argonaut*. The Stadium, lent a ghostly aspect by the makeshift screens of white snow camouflage netting that now hung in place of velvet stage curtains, began to fill, the doctors and nurses raising their voices to be heard above the clatter of helicopters landing on the creaking steel plating of the flight deck above, the bandsmen lifting the stretchers bearing wounded with the utmost care onto the Heath Robinson casualty chute squeaking on its wooden runners as it descended. Blast wounds and shrapnel accounted for most of the injured, who often enough struggled to hear as well; the medics quickly spotted what they termed the '*Canberra* Sign', singed hair, which almost certainly meant eardrums burst by explosions. For now, the priority was to get the wounded aboard, assessed and stabilised; surgery would have to wait until nightfall when the air threat receded.

Canberra's unaccountable lunch hour was over; at about 1pm they came again, closing in fast from the sea, 60 miles, 30 miles, everyone clenched, counting off the seconds until 'Take cover! Take cover!', hitting the decks and covering up as the Mirages and Skyhawks screamed in and the waters of the anchorage seethed with blasts. The Argentines seemed to have regrouped and got the measure of the invasion fleet, coming in at a higher altitude; bombs straddled *Canberra*, sending waterspouts into the air and spray flailing across her decks. 'There was no doubt they were having a go at us,' said Reed. 'The bomb blasts were bloody close. We were lucky on the bridge, because it was intense and you're intent on what you're doing, but the engineers down below were ticking it off, cracks and bangs, they could hear the machine gun fire through the fabric of the ship.' Harding was ordered to ring down to the engine room every 15 minutes to let the crew shut in below the waterline know that the ship was intact. The casualties were still coming aboard, and the bandsmen worked tirelessly and courageously as raiders screamed overhead, sending crew and military personnel diving for the decks. Musician George Latham simply ignored the aircraft, neither flinching nor pausing as he carefully lowered a badly wounded man down the ramp to two of his comrades. In the hospital, Rosie Elsdon got onto beds and laid over wounded men – British or Argentine – to protect them. 'We'd got used to it a bit,' she said. 'You can't be in a panic for very long, you've got to get on with it. If you were busy with a patient, you couldn't take cover. We could hear everything, but not see anything, all the helicopters coming in really loudly and the firing and bombing, all the aeroplanes over the ship.' O'Connell said, 'We were all frightened, but as soon as we had casualties on board we had something to do, and that helped us manage our fear.'

So did Burne. Once *Canberra* anchored in San Carlos, he had operational control of her. 'Chris was fighting the ship,' said Reed. 'He was getting the information from *Fearless* through the naval signals team about where the raids were coming from, whereas Dennis was part of the team, waiting to see how we were needed, and ready to take over if necessary.' Burne's energetic lopes around the ship to lift morale won him much admiration. His broadcasts during the day did even more. 'That was his moment, and he rose to it superbly,' reflected Vaux. 'He was inspired and he got it absolutely right, and that was very important because morale could have faltered, and that stopped anything like that happening.' Burne adopted the unruffled tone of a gentleman cricket commentator in blazer and tie, no more put out by bombing than by sloppy fielding; the crew could visualise him raising a quizzical eyebrow at the damnable impudence of these people overhead, yet loftily refusing to be perturbed by them. It was a quintessential display of British coolness under fire. Muxworthy noted one of his addresses: 'Well, there's some more aircraft milling around out there, be ready to take cover when I tell you. I don't know about you, but I'm getting rather bored with these Argies. Ah well, here they come again. Take cover! Take cover!' Only once did the mask slip and the strain he was under show. In mid-afternoon, as another attack approached, Burne inadvertently kept the transmit button depressed as he awaited the incoming aircraft; the crew watched the loudspeakers and waited, listening to his breathing, tense and shallow; when he realised the microphone was open, he snapped back into ball-by-ball commentary and calmly informed them that the next lot of nuisances were about to arrive.

Burne's tone belied his bleak appreciation that *Canberra* was an instant away from disaster if any of the bombs plummeting into the water around her found their mark. The worst scenarios envisaged by naval planners when they had first grappled with the practicalities of requisitioning had been soberly precautionary. Blast, fire, the lethal storm of glass shards, evacuation; all had been pondered and prepared for, even as nobody quite believed they would happen, that the Argentines would pack up and go, the dispute returning to the desks of diplomats who would sort everything out. Drills had reinforced *Canberra*'s preparedness, more seriously than ever as she had sailed south from Ascension and braved the storm, even as naval officers calculated that if the worst happened, she was likely to settle in San Carlos Water allowing an evacuation. They might yet be proved correct, it could be possible; but the men from the ships that had taken hits, their faces contorted with agony as they were flown aboard riddled with shrapnel that had torn through their chests, groins and limbs bore witness to the grievous cost it would extract.

By early afternoon, 42 Commando's departure was imminent because of the danger *Canberra* was in; if, somehow, she made it through these desperate hours, the Navy would withdraw her to safety. 'Chris Burne said to me, "It's been decided we sail tonight, if we can survive",' said Vaux. She felt more vulnerable with each passing minute as the attacks continued, not least because the Marines were taking the Blowpipes and GPMGs with them; they were needed ashore. One by one, the guns were unbolted from the brackets at the bridge wings and stern. Her own defences had been puny enough; now they consisted of a single machine gun, hastily assembled from spare parts. The companies of men growing ever more impatient to be let out of the bars and public rooms where they had been penned in for hours were finally, and gratefully on the move, hefting packs and weapons and being barked into lines that snaked through E Deck towards the galley doors where the landing craft would come alongside. Crew were assigned to help keep the passageways clear, among them Sue Wood, who said, 'It was horrible to see them going, not knowing who would come back.' Bandsmen were at the sea doors to assist. Evenings touring the bars playing for sing-songs and Wood's performances during *Canberra*'s phony war had forged close bonds between them and the men preparing to go ashore. John Ware said, 'One of the Marines turned to one of my musicians and said, "You know, I'm glad you're going to be there as a medic, because if anything happens to me, I'm glad to know you'll be looking after me".'

There were other farewells, no less touching. Vaux was taken aback when Geoffrey, the camp steward from the Crow's Nest, approached him. 'He actually drew me aside and said, "I want you to know that we're all hoping you come back safely", and it was quite moving, I never thought he'd have said that.' Another wave of raiders had swept overhead minutes before four landing craft headed out towards *Canberra* at about 2pm, reinforcing the urgency of the disembarkation. There were last-minute scurries. Sheppard said, 'Suddenly, the company commander came in and said, "We're going", and some shit-for-brain took my rifle, so I'm the last man to leave because I'm trying to find it. Of course, I found a rifle, and when I'm above the landing craft, I shouted out, "Which arsehole's got rifle number eight?", and one of the lads in the section shouted, "I've got it", and I went, "You wanker".'

In the sheltered waters of the anchorage, getting the Marines off *Canberra* progressed swiftly and smoothly, as a constant stream of helicopters shifted ammunition and supplies ashore. There was an unexpected, imposing figure aboard with Vaux. 'To my amazement, Tom Seccombe was standing in the back of the landing craft with the coxswain. I said to him, "You shouldn't be here, you should be having a gin and tonic on board the *Canberra*", to which he replied, "Bloody sight safer here".' As he neared shore, Vaux looked back to the ship, so bright, so huge, so surely unmissable the longer this ferocious day continued. 'I thought, "Thank God she's going to sail to safety tonight."' As the Marines headed for shore, Scott-Masson fired off a telex to P&O in London that displayed a certain sang-froid under trying circumstances, as he informed the company that troops had left *Canberra* in the same terms he might use to tell it that a boat full of day trippers had gone sightseeing. It read, 'Have survived our first but prolonged air attacks and all sips (sic) company still in good heart having delivered their passengers as required. Deployment of uncertain length and will give more details when known. Dennis.'

Nightfall was on everybody's minds; there was no more than two hours' daylight left until the relative protection of darkness. It could not come soon enough; the threat from the air weighed ever more oppressively as a story of horror unfolded from naval signals, the distant sound of explosions and a plume of oily black smoke coiling upwards from beyond the hills. *Ardent*, which had watched over *Canberra* tirelessly on the way south from Ascension in the jumpy days after *Sheffield* was hit, which had streaked past on sports day with a flourish and a firepower demonstration just to lift everybody's spirits before they entered the danger zone, was in flames, fatally damaged, 22 of her crew dead, as many more injured, one officer missing, after coming under repeated attack in Falkland Sound. She had played a key role in the success of the landings, first bombarding Goose Green – and surviving two air attacks unscathed – then patrolling the sound, where she was fatally exposed. Wave after wave of warplanes swooped down on her, as a fault in her Sea Cat missile system left her unable to defend herself; bombed twice in the first raid, the explosion lifting her stern, her horrified captain, Commander Alan West, watched as the missile launcher thrown into the air by the blast plummeted down to snuff out the life of one of his officers, seeing also a helicopter pilot and his observer killed as they tried to engage the attacking aircraft with machine guns. Two more bombs hit her as she tried to steam towards the protection of other ships, killing the men trying to fight the fires already raging aft. The blasts threw three men into the sea; two of them were plucked to safety by Rick Jolly aboard a medical evacuation helicopter, putting his own life at risk in an act of astonishing bravery by descending on a winch line which he was neither trained nor equipped to use, to haul them from the icy waters; a third, the ship's doctor, Lieutenant Stephen Rideout, flung overboard as he treated a wounded man, was missing. *Ardent* was doomed; West ordered his surviving 160 crew to abandon ship. They struggled into one-piece survival suits as the frigate *Yarmouth* came alongside, bringing her stern against the bows, and scrambled across to safety. The burned-out shell of their ship remained afloat for less than 24 hours before sinking. *Ardent*'s fate stretched nerves aboard *Canberra* even further because of the closeness between the two ships; if she had been unable to defend herself with the gunnery she displayed on that sunlit Sunday morning, what chance did they have with a single machine gun? Her casualties were already being flown aboard; her survivors would follow and Rudderham began preparing for them, organising food, drinks and fresh clothes.

The Argentines were still coming relentlessly, the planes tearing across the sky. The frigate *Argonaut* was the next casualty, an unexploded bomb putting her steering out of action, though her weapons systems remained intact and she continued fighting. The sky was just beginning to darken at about 3.30 when another wave approached; once more, men and women flung themselves to the deck, once more the troops ashore and the warships sent up a storm of fire, watching as the waters of San Carlos boiled and erupted, holding their breath until they realised that *Canberra* had been hit by nothing worse than spray as the roar of the attackers' engines faded. The bridge waited; Burne monitored the signals as the fading light gradually turned the hills to silhouettes once more. Aboard the warships out in the sound, the radar screens remained blank; nothing yet, still nothing as half an hour passed, then an hour as the nightfall all aboard *Canberra* had willed to arrive more fervently than they had wished for the dawn what seemed like an age ago descended, bringing with it the likelihood that the raids would cease. They had; it was over after nine hours, her only scar the buckled metalwork next to Reed's cabin window. An overwhelming sense of relief and release washed through the ship; crew found themselves suddenly weak, shaky, tearful as the tension of the daylight hours ebbed away and the realisation of what they had endured and survived hit them. 'We were all wearing thin by the time it stopped,' reflected Graham Harding. 'The longer we were there, the more likely it was that something would hit us either by intention or accident. If the decision hadn't been made to withdraw, the effect on morale would have been pretty bad; another day or two of that and a lot of people would have cracked, and quite understandably because we weren't supposed to have been anywhere near it.'

The plight of *Ardent*'s survivors arriving aboard landing crafts that ferried them from *Yarmouth* about an hour after the final raid snapped the crew out of thinking about themselves. Everybody wanted to help the shocked, fire-blackened seamen reeking of smoke, many of them grimacing with the pain of injuries or burns on their hands and faces. Some were in a daze; a tall officer peered intently at the stripes on Reed's shoulder, and said, 'Oh, you must be one of me,' before being guided gently aboard. The Meridian Room had witnessed men preparing for war, listening to lurid survival lectures or their commanders rallying them on the eve of battle; now it saw the victims of it, seamen in baggy bright orange survival suits slumping down on the pink sofas and chairs, utterly spent. Most were consumed by fury at the loss of their ship; a few so traumatised by what they had witnessed that it had reduced them to blank, staring silence. West strode about the room thanking his men, doing his utmost to lift their spirits as Rudderham's staff dispensed tots of rum, cans of beer and cigarettes. Paddison and one of the cooks opened a pantry nearby and started supplying hot drinks, sandwiches, toast. Accommodation was being arranged, baths and showers organised, clean boiler suits or slops, seamen's working clothes issued. The walking wounded were escorted up to the hospital, where Susie West was working in the minor injuries unit: 'They were both shocked and relieved, and in some ways couldn't believe their luck. One chap had been in a compartment when it exploded, and I checked him all over and the worst injury he'd got was a ballpoint pen that had been in his pocket that had got driven into his thigh, which was amazingly lucky. There was somebody else who had shrapnel go straight through his chest in front of his larynx, and he would have been a dead man if it had gone a fraction into his larynx.' Amid the shock, and the pain of the loss of 22 men, a glimmer of good news; *Ardent*'s doctor had been rescued from the sea unharmed and was gratefully downing a very large drink in the wardroom of one of the warships.

Burne came over the loudspeakers once more: no cricket commentary this time.

'We are marked by courage, good humour and sadness. One of the sadnesses is that we should have on board at the moment the ship's company, the gallant ship's company of HMS *Ardent* and we are aware of the fact that some of them are injured and others are lost, and in fact there's been a bitter air battle going on during the day out in the Falkland Sound and sitting here watching the naval Frigates do it have made me at least proud to be a Naval Officer. On top of that, one must say it is tremendous to be here with the P&O, and the way the P&O crew have worked, and worked with good humour despite it all is something which I will forever remember . . . So we look forward to tomorrow with the expectation and hope that it won't be as much of an experience as it's been today, but I can't promise anything, so all I can say is thank you for all that you've all done today, and I know you will do the same again tomorrow.'

Aboard *Hermes*, where Admiral Sandy Woodward and his staff were taking stock of the day, one thing was absolutely clear; *Canberra* and the other transport ships must be got out of San Carlos, which was rapidly becoming known as 'Bomb Alley', before dawn on the 22nd. Woodward later wrote, 'Everyone was dumbfounded as to how the Args had come to miss the *Canberra*, the Great White Whale, as she came to be called. She had sat, gleaming white, bang in the middle of the bay all day and never been hit by anything. The fact was, the Args had screwed up this operation very badly indeed.' He and his officers believed that the Argentine pilots had targeted the warships and not the transports; after the war, the pilots themselves insisted that was the case.

That was hard to swallow for those who had watched helplessly as warplanes came straight at them at least twice, had lurched with the ship as she was rocked by bombs that straddled her, seen rockets stitching explosions in the sea close by, and flinched at airbursts. Years afterwards, Reed talked to some of the pilots who had been over San Carlos: 'One said, "We were in so fast and out so fast, all we could see were targets; it didn't matter how big it was, what colour it was, if we found something in our way, we tried to get it", and they tried to get us. There was no doubt they were attacking us.' Others, though, were not quite as certain, never able to answer definitively the question of whether one or more aircraft homed in on *Canberra* and launched an attack that missed. Scott-Masson believed she had been attacked; his deputy, Michael Bradford, did not. Burne, the shrewd senior naval officer, said, 'I think they initially concentrated on the warships. They thought that if they got the warships, they could polish off the others fairly easily afterwards. But it was all very confused.' The confusion of those hours of air war makes it impossible to determine which, if any, of the raids was directed specifically at *Canberra*; that she was freakishly lucky to survive the day intact is beyond question. Bombs certainly crashed into the water around her as she lay at anchor but the anchorage and the curtain of fire every British sailor and soldier within it threw up were her salvation. The hills surrounding San Carlos hampered the pilots, and the flak coming at them disrupted their aim. That compromised the raids, as did the pilots flying so low that many of the bombs they dropped failed to detonate because they did not have sufficient time in the air to fuse themselves once released. If Woodward was right and the Argentines had blundered on the first day, they would not make the same mistakes on a second. *Canberra* and the other transports were not going to be around to find out; he ordered her, *Norland* and *Europic Ferry* to sail for the relative safety of the open sea no later than 1.30am.

The order was received at 7pm, and threw *Canberra* into a round of feverish activity that occupied the next four hours. Before leaving San Carlos, she was to offload as many stores as possible, two surgical support teams, and the rear elements of 42 Commando who had expected to stay on board for the next few days until called ashore. Crew who were weary to their bones after 24 hours of strain roused themselves, volunteering to help even if off duty and desperate for sleep, humping stores around as landing craft chugged out of the darkness to the sea doors. Officers gave thanks for the presence of *Ardent's* men, desperate for something, anything, to do that made them feel useful, who pitched in energetically. A human chain formed half *Canberra's* length, from the forward hatch to the galley doors, as box after box was passed hand to hand, man to woman, cook to cleaner, uniform to boiler suit, then down into the darkened landing craft bobbing gently alongside. It was heavy, exhausting work, and as the hours passed, obvious that vast amounts of the supplies aboard could not be unloaded in time. 'It was a total f**k-up,' said Reed. 'There was stacks of stuff that needed to go ashore, and then we got this message saying, "Unload two surgical support teams and bugger off". We were still stuffed with stores, and not being able to get them off caused all sorts of problems for the Marines, in particular.' *Canberra* was now to sail by midnight; up on the Captain's Deck, Scott-Masson went into Norman Pound's cabin and asked if she could be ready to sail in an hour. 'We can be ready to sail in ten minutes if you want,' he replied. It seemed like an age since she had arrived in San Carlos; at 10.42pm, she weighed anchor and set sail for an area of sea 150 miles north-east of Port Stanley under the escort of the damaged *Antrim*. It was another black night, and as she headed out into Falkland Sound, there, in the distance, the only light anywhere: the flames of *Ardent* ablaze on the sea.

Her survivors had fanned out through *Canberra*, offering to help wherever they could, from the engine room to the naval signals office. Pickford had been joined on the bridge by West: 'He said it was the most peaceful place to be, and he liked being on a bridge. I had a brief conversation with him, but he was preoccupied writing letters to the families of the men who had died; it was very poignant.' Her wounded were now being settled for the night; those who had needed surgery had been operated on. Rosie Elsdon began an exhausting routine of eight hours on duty and eight hours off. It was her first sight of the men from *Ardent*. 'They were totally shocked, they'd lost their home, their friends, they were just numb, physically and mentally. It had been hard to know how badly injured they were sometimes, because if they'd been in the water all the blood had gone, so you had to be really careful in assessing each person.' Amid the training of the weeks before, nobody had introduced Elsdon to the system of painkillers being used; a small syringe attached to every patient that gradually increased the dose until they were comfortable; 'This was something I'd never come across in my life, and I remember hoping that I could cope with it well and do my best for everybody.'

Morgan O'Connell was also on duty that night, and took an unorthodox approach to settling the patients when he found they had been prescribed sedatives.

'I didn't think this was entirely appropriate. Twenty-four hours previously they had been fit healthy Marines and Paras, and so I went down to the chief bar steward with my prescription pad and wrote, "One bottle of gin, one bottle of brandy, one bottle of whisky and a crate of beer". I took it and put it on top of the drug cupboard and said to the nurse in charge, "All those written up for night sedation unless it's contra-indicated, then give them a choice of the drug of their knowledge," as opposed to the valium or mogadon they had been prescribed. She thought I had gone mad, and I said, "No, you can share a beer or share your whisky, but you can't share a mogadon or your valium", and that's what I was

211

encouraging people to do, to share because that's the natural process in the military in a small group. Even when you're injured you want to be with your mates and share, and perhaps the General Medical Council might have something to say about that, but that's what I chose to do at that time and I would do the same again.'

Canberra was accustomed to the clinking of glasses in The Stadium, and so it happened again at the end of this day that marked all who had lived through it ever after. Except now, it was not the wealthy toasting their own health, but the wounded their own survival, and friends who had not been so lucky.

CHAPTER TWELVE

Rendezvous at the End of the Earth

IT WAS NOT only the chill air of dusk rushing in through the open sea doors that made 200 men shiver as they packed tightly, but in the most orderly of rows, into *Canberra*'s main entrance on D Deck; it was the four stretchers, each shrouded in the Blue Ensign, bearing the bodies of the airmen who had died in the preceding two days. Few, if any, of the congregation had witnessed a burial at sea before; in the 1980s, they were about to participate in a solemn service hardly changed since Nelson's time. This was where *Canberra* welcomed passengers as they embarked at Southampton, and bade them farewell at the end of their cruise; never before had she said goodbyes like this. Earlier that day, in the makeshift mortuary, Sgt Bugler John Tansey from the Marines band had braced himself and prepared the bodies for burial, weighting each at the feet with iron, then sewing up a canvas shroud, the final stitch of the stout sailmaker's needle being forced through the big toe to ensure it remained in place. The men standing for the service represented all those aboard; P&O, Royal Navy, Royal Marines. There was not enough space for the survivors of *Ardent*, so they mustered, silent, in their white boiler suits on the flight deck. At 4pm precisely, Father Noel Mullin began the short service; from its start, men bowed their heads to hide their tears. Readings were given from the Bible and then, as it had done so often in these long weeks, the band played 'For Those in Peril on the Sea', the hymn faint but audible to *Ardent*'s men on deck, who, only a day after 22 of their friends had been lost, wept for them as well as the four men going to their rest. Two of the band's buglers played 'Last Post' over the airmen and then the

Royal Marine pallbearers stepped forward. One by one, steadily, carefully, the stretchers were tilted at the doors; one by one, the Blue Ensigns flapped emptily as the men they honoured slipped away. There were no words as the congregation dispersed.

The open sea greeted *Canberra*'s crew that morning; most had managed to sleep, knowing that every mile diminished the threat from Argentine warplanes. Now they knew how savagely different reality was, as the ship shivered under the impact of explosions close by, the suffering of the wounded flown aboard, and the stories from *Ardent*'s crew of seeing men for the last time as they attempted to tackle the raging, uncontrollable fires *Canberra* had glimpsed still burning on the sea. The survivors' determination to make themselves useful quickly fostered a mutual regard with the crew akin to that which had sprung up with the Marines and Paras. She saluted *Ardent*'s lost on Sunday the 23rd, when at West's request, a service of remembrance and thanksgiving was held, every seat filled. It was a pause for reflection during a relentlessly busy day; after *Canberra* had caught her breath on the 22nd, an endless succession of airlifts began to offload the huge amounts of stores there had been too little time to shift before the dash for safety. Hour after hour, the helicopters continued, lifting compo rations and ammunition, as well as men, back to the islands, among them three reporters, Patrick Bishop, Kim Sabido, and John Shirley, who had come back aboard late on D Day to file their dispatches. They worked all night and grabbed a few hours' sleep, waking to find that land was nowhere in sight, as appalled to be so far distant from the Falklands as the crew were grateful. Shirley's first encounter with an islander had wrong-footed him after a morning of air raids and the tension of the landings. An elderly farm labourer proffered a Queen's silver jubilee mug full of soup. 'You a reporter?' he asked. Shirley said he was. 'Tell me,' said the old man, 'Did Leeds United get relegated?'

More pressing matters occupied most minds. On the hour, every hour, the announcement 'This is London,' followed by the lilting theme of 'Lillibulero', was to be heard from behind cabin doors from upper decks to lower as radios were switched on and turned up for the latest bulletin from the BBC World Service; the news made them gladder than ever to be away from Bomb Alley. As *Canberra* commemorated *Ardent*, the frigate *Antelope* was ordered into San Carlos to replace her. Within four hours, she was under unrelenting attack; a Skyhawk came screaming over the hill and collided with her mast, surviving to make its escape; a second was shot down, instants after one of its bombs skipped off the sea and drove into the ship, failing to explode and lodging above the engine room. A second wave of Skyhawks came straight for *Antelope* and put a bomb into her port side; again, it failed to explode, getting stuck in a forward cabin. Further attacks were repulsed, and Royal Engineers came on board to defuse the bombs, noting with weary resignation that they were British-made 1,000-pounders. The operation went horribly wrong. A massive explosion tore open the ship's side, killing two men, ripping an arm off a third, and sparking an inferno. *Antelope*'s fate was to mirror *Ardent*'s; there was no option but to abandon ship as the Marines dug in ashore watched and willed them to make it in time, close enough to hear the frantic shouts of the evacuation. They did, but only just; minutes after the last man was taken off, the fire reached the Sea Cat missile magazine, and the blast broke *Antelope* in half. Once again, a frigate destroyed and ablaze lit up the night before what was left of her sank.

The World Service broadcast news of *Antelope*'s loss on the Monday; depressing enough to hear, but then, as the bulletin continued, everyone listening in their cabins stared at the radio in bewilderment. Argentine radio and television were reporting that *Canberra* had been hit and was sinking, said the newsreader. The reports were unconfirmed. The moment of incredulity quickly passed, crowded out by concern: what must their loved ones at home be thinking? On the bridge, there was a debate about what could be read into the Argentine claim. Was it simply propaganda, or was it conceivable that they had mistaken a 3,250-ton frigate painted grey for a 45,000-ton liner towering above the water, whose most immediately identifiable characteristic was her white paintwork? Perhaps, in the few seconds amid the hail of fire over the anchorage, now more daunting than ever because Rapier missile batteries were operating from the shore, they had, especially if they were not familiar with *Canberra*. Did they really believe that she had lingered in San Carlos Water for two days after the landings? Burne thought so. '*Antelope* was in the berth *Canberra* had occupied,' he said. 'One of the aircraft dropped his bomb into *Antelope*, reported that he'd hit his target and was promptly shot down by a Sea Harrier before he could get very far. Almost immediately, the Argentinians broadcast on national radio that *Canberra* had been hit and badly damaged. There's no doubt in my mind that that attack was aimed at *Canberra*.'

Back in Britain, the Ministry of Defence woke up to the demoralising effect of the claims on a country that had cheered *Canberra* away with such emotion, and refuted them. By then, however, relatives and friends had suffered hours of anxiety. Martin Reed's mother, Pat, sang in a choir at HMS *Vernon*, a shore base in Portsmouth, where a padre heard the bulletin and realised how harrowing it must be for her. He jumped on his bicycle and pedalled the two-and-a-half miles to her home as fast as he could. 'She was just about to go down the road to see a friend when the doorbell rang,' said Reed. 'She opened the door, and there was a Naval padre, and of course her heart sank, and he said, "Don't worry, I've checked and he's fine".' Mrs Reed was one of the lucky ones, plugged in to the well-established Navy support system for families, which could quickly soothe fears caused by propaganda or erroneous reports. No such network existed for the families of P&O crew, beyond the weekly newsletter, which was hopelessly out-of-date by the time it arrived, only recapping what families knew from the news and unable to tell them what *Canberra*'s future movements were.

In Somerset, Anne-Marie Scott-Masson's telephone began ringing constantly. Wives of the ship's officers trusted her to keep them informed, and a round of calls began in which news was passed on and cascaded down to crew's families. It could be frustrating; operational details of *Canberra*'s role had to remain confidential, even if they would have calmed nerves. 'I've never had such a huge telephone bill in my life, but it was important,' she said. 'I had a son in the army and he did hear things pretty promptly and telephoned me. I heard at 6am that *Canberra* had been hit, and it was 12 or 1 before it was put out that it was Argentinian boasting and not true. I actually heard before that, but wasn't able to say so to the wives who were ringing me, I could only just say, "Keep calm, it may not be true". I couldn't tell them what I knew.' Much of the information she was receiving was coming from P&O's general manager (fleet), John Turner, who had established informal lines of communication with the Navy. Even so, there were some disturbing moments; on at least two more occasions, the BBC reported claims from Buenos Aires that *Canberra* had been attacked and hit. 'I heard one on the car radio driving back from an engagement I'd been at in London,' said Turner. 'It was about midnight and I spent most of that night trying to find out what the real story was so I could tell the crucial people, the families, that all was well.'

Families were not alone in becoming restive; so was P&O, smarting that after answering the call to join the task force and allowing its flagship to be put in the most extreme danger, it was now being fobbed off. Relations with the Department of Trade (DoT) and the MoD over *Canberra*'s requisitioning had deteriorated to the point of animosity as negotiations became bogged down in a prolonged wrangle over what the government should be paying for her. The day before she sailed from Southampton, an invoice for £750,000 in provisional compensation for the period from 7 April to 6 May had been submitted; it was paid within a month, but the arguing was only just beginning.

On 26 April, the chairman of P&O Cruises, Rodney Leach, sent a confidential memo to his most senior staff in which his annoyance with the government side was plain. 'Delays to date are totally reprehensible, considering that a normal commercial deal would have been struck in a few hours,' he wrote, going on to emphasise that officials should be reminded of the willingness that the company had displayed. The root of the problem lay in the archaic, and essentially obsolete, legislation that appeared to provide the only framework for settling a formula for reimbursement; nobody had blown the dust off the Compensation

217

(Defence) Act 1939 since the end of the Second World War. Civil servants at the DoT could find no trace of it being used in the intervening years, and at one point informed P&O that they believed it was no longer on the statute book. Nevertheless, in the spirit of compromise and improvisation that characterised everything about sending *Canberra* to war, it was used as a basis for negotiation in the absence of anything else. The government effectively argued that under the act, it should only be paying a charter rate for *Canberra*; P&O's position was that it should also be recompensed for loss of earnings. As it became clear that the Falklands crisis was not going to be resolved quickly, *Canberra*'s cruising programme for June was cancelled, as May's had been; if July and August went the same way, as seemed likely, the entire summer's income from her would be lost. Similar concerns applied to SS *Uganda*, and to a lesser extent, *Norland* and *Elk*. 'It would be helpful if MoD could stop arguing naively about small change,' observed Leach acidly, before concluding, 'Please let me know when the first meeting with MoD has been arranged and be sure they are aware of justifiable P&O impatience and concern that their performance in this matter to date is below the standard we would expect. They may be dealing with taxpayers' money. We are responsible for shareholders' assets and for our employees' continuity of jobs.'

There appeared to be a wilful refusal on the government's part to recognise the nature of operating a cruise liner. *Canberra* was not a workhorse cargo ship, but a floating holiday destination, with multiple sources of income from the passengers on board and ancillary costs to be met for their comfort and enjoyment. P&O was already paying compensation to contractors whose summer of work had vanished and for whom it was proving impossible to find other employment. Hairdressers who primped up blue rinses, photographers who took happy snaps of glittering evenings, croupiers who span the roulette wheel, chaperones who escorted the nervous ashore; all of them were entitled to their lost earnings. The cost of replacing *Canberra* was still being argued over, forcing the company to take out additional war risk insurance at Lloyd's for her and *Elk*, at a hefty combined premium of £528,000. Other costs were mounting too. Company accountants leading orderly lives in their offices at St Botolph Street could only wonder what was going on aboard as they totted up the invoices from the Naafi for additional alcohol supplied by ship or airlift, having no concept of the Marines' and Paras' fondness for beer, nor their unswerving devotion to outwitting restrictions on how much they could drink; by the end of the first week in June, supplementary bar stores since leaving Southampton ran to £16,094.

As May began, and *Canberra* prepared to sail south from Ascension, the chairman of P&O, the Earl of Inchcape, wrote to the Secretary of State for Trade, Lord Cockfield, saying, 'We have become increasingly anxious about our inability to reach firm agreements with your officials on a number of pressing commercial and legal matters.' Those matters were to be addressed over lunch between the noble lords two days before *Canberra* anchored in Bomb Alley, the unspoken understanding being that the old boys' network would reach a gentlemanly agreement. It did, Inchcape setting out a series of headline costs that P&O was incurring in the service of the country. The company was £4m out of pocket so far from the loss of the £8m that its four ships under requisition earned every month. Insurance premiums for them already ran to £1.7m, and a further round would be due in June. Now he came to *Canberra*, this irreplaceable, iconic liner born of a lost age, reinvented as its most profitable cruise ship. For every 30 days under requisition, she would cost Britain £3,248,000. P&O eventually got what it wanted, though not quickly, even given Inchcape and Cockfield's amicable parting. Negotiations dragged on long after the war was over, not concluding until the autumn of 1983.

There was still no contact between *Canberra* and P&O, save the terse daily signal from Scott-Masson, 'All fine and well,' as she remained on station north-east of the Falklands, ploughing up and down a sector of sea, uncertain as to her next deployment. It was the Naval signals that provided clues to what it would be, and Burne, shrewdly attuned to the movements of the task force and the units it carried, who put them together and decided a course of action. The signals system was cumbersome; the

Navy was sending them encrypted to Northwood, where they were re-encrypted and flashed back to *Canberra* via her satellite system in a form she could decipher, often resulting in a delay of up to 36 hours. Burne's judgement was that *Canberra* would be ordered to South Georgia to rendezvous with *Queen Elizabeth II* and take 5 Brigade aboard to bring them back to the Falklands; he backed it, and was proved exactly right. *Norland* would be needed as well; with her in company, *Canberra* set a course farther south than she had ever ventured. Twenty-four hours later, the signal duly arrived to make for South Georgia; Burne could not resist just a touch of one-upmanship. 'Old clever clogs took very great pleasure in sending a signal back saying, "I'm halfway there",' said Muxworthy. The P&O officers were no less susceptible to putting one over their rivals aboard the Cunard liner when she signalled a delay because of the weather and sea state. 'We got this message from the *QE2* saying, "Encountering thick fog and icebergs, speed reduced, will be late at rendezvous",' said Reed. 'Our reply was, "Encountering thick fog and icebergs, speed 27 knots, will be on time".' She was making nothing like that speed, since *Norland* could not have kept pace, but nevertheless, the two ships were ploughing across the 800 miles of ocean as rapidly as was practical. 'The message said, "Proceed to South Georgia with all dispatch",' added Reed. 'I'd never seen that before, I'd read it in books, but never seen it, and it means don't wait for anything.'

The urgency of their task in bringing reinforcements became plain in the hours after sailing in the middle of the afternoon on Tuesday 25 May. Their radios that evening began to relay the outlines of the most brutal day yet for the task force; one with shocking resonance for *Canberra* because the first Merchant Navy lives were taken, and uncomfortably close to where she had just been.

This was Argentina's National Day, and the task force was braced for a show of strength against it; pride, and the egos of the junta, would demand no less. It manifested itself to the north of Falkland Sound, where the frigate *Broadsword* and destroyer *Coventry* were standing by to intercept attacks heading for San Carlos. Both were in exposed positions but the morning had sent morale soaring; two Mirages were shot down as they ran for home after ineffectual raids on the anchorage. Then, at about 2pm, the Argentine Air Force exacted its revenge. A co-ordinated attack by Skyhawks and Super Etendards roared in from the west, not against the landing ground this time, but aimed at the two ships. *Broadsword* was hit first, a bomb bouncing off the sea and slamming into her just above the waterline on the starboard side, tearing upwards through the ship and punching its way out through the flight deck, across which it skeetered and plunged overboard without exploding. It was a miraculous escape. No such luck was with *Coventry*, as a second pair of Skyhawks bore down. Three of their four 1,000-pound bombs hit her and went off, the devastating blasts killing 19 men and spelling *Coventry*'s end. Her captain, David Hart-Dyke, momentarily rendered unconscious, came round to the most hellish of sights. 'All I could see around me were people on fire, like candles burning,' he recalled. His ship was already capsizing, consumed by the raging inferno, as helicopters scrambled to rescue the survivors clambering down the hull already growing red-hot from the intensity of the blaze; she remained afloat, upside down, until sinking the following day.

Only ten minutes or so after *Coventry* keeled over, the main carrier group, 70 miles north-east of the islands, came under attack. Super Etendards fired two Exocets, which were picked up by the ships. Rockets containing chaff, metal fragments to disrupt the missiles' guidance systems, were fired; they worked, one veered away – but then it locked on to a new target, the *Atlantic Conveyor*, which had carried Harriers down to the task force and still had Chinook and Wessex helicopters on her flight deck, as well as vast quantities of stores below, hitting her on the port side aft. It has never been clear if the warhead exploded, nor what happened to the second missile fired; nevertheless, as with *Sheffield*, a single Exocet proved fatal, starting fires that spread through the ship. As darkness fell, and she was buffeted by a heavy swell, the 160 men aboard, Merchant Navy, Royal Navy and RAF alike, fought a desperate battle to bring the flames under control and save the cargo they knew was so essential to the troops ashore.

Their bravery was in vain; an hour and a half after she was hit, the order came to abandon ship. *Atlantic Conveyor*'s master was Captain Ian North, a much admired 57-year-old veteran of the Second World War, whose bushy beard earned him the affectionate nickname 'Captain Bird's Eye'. He was the last to leave, and reached a liferaft on the black, heaving, bitterly cold sea, only to find it already dangerously overcrowded. He swam away into the darkness in search of another, and vanished. Captain North was one of 12 men dead, his ship the first British merchant vessel sunk by enemy action since World War Two.

She had been only 60 miles from *Canberra*'s position; suddenly, the vastness of the open sea, seemingly so safe after being shut in at San Carlos, once again became as treacherous as it had been during the voyage from Ascension, the spectre of the Exocet returning to haunt the dark hours when lights were turned out. All she had to defend herself was a solitary machine gun on the starboard bridge wing. Reed was in charge of it, and called for volunteers. He got 50, like the *Ardent*'s men all eager to feel they were doing something to take on the Argentines, however futile they knew a single GPMG was against warplanes capable of sinking well-armed warships He set about training them. This irritated Scott-Masson, his pinkers interrupted by prolonged bursts of fire in an open sea and empty sky. 'Dennis got very annoyed,' said Reed, 'And he came steaming in, saying, "All this bloody noise".' It was a momentary flare-up, an indication of how much was on his mind; new, unfamiliar dangers surrounded his ship in addition to whatever threat the Argentines presented. The liner whose every year was spent following the sun so its passengers arrived home tanned with their elderly bones warmed was heading towards the Antarctic, keeping Scott-Masson and his officers on their mettle. 'We had to go through and around a number of icebergs and growlers,' he said. 'Those are the bits that come off icebergs, which are dangerous because you can't see them, and if you hit them at speed, they'll rip a hole in the bottom of the ship.'

The night brought lurking, silent hazards that had the bridge on edge; Scott-Masson slowed *Canberra* to a crawling five knots after icebergs were sighted in poor visibility and posted lookouts on the bridge wings as he took her onward cautiously. The men scanning the numbingly cold darkness for threats looming out of the winter sea were blue and shaking by the time they were relieved. Daylight was hardly warmer; layers of clothing were needed not just for lifeboat drills; men and women muffled up before going on deck, putting on gloves and hats, zipping jackets right up to the scarves they wore, feeling the bite of the air on their faces. The hot, hearty stews the galley was turning out were a boon in this clear, sharp weather, which was beginning to layer *Canberra*'s upperworks with frost. The vegetables looked distinctly past their best and oddly shaped, the rotting bits having been carved away in the galley, but what was left was served by waiters who presented them with as much poise as they could. The occasional blackened potato reported with such disdain by Max Hastings on the voyage south was becoming the norm. She was running worryingly low on fresh food; down on H Deck, the chilled compartments forward of the engine room for vegetables, salads, fruit and eggs were all depleted. What was left of the last substantial loadings, at Ascension, mouldered; airlifts since then had helped, but *Canberra* was in desperate need of supplies, especially for the 2,000 troops about to come on board. Still, Rudderham and Muxworthy were not unduly concerned; *QE2* would be able to help. She had been at sea for less than two weeks, fully laden with stores; the rendezvous could not have been more timely.

Sunrise on Thursday the 27th brought to life a picture the crew had carried in their minds since Southampton; a barren, rocky, frozen land of mountains, their peaks clad in snow, a harsh and inhospitable landscape at the end of the world. They thought the Falklands would be like this, and had been disconcerted at how familiar those hills and moorland had seemed; this was the scenery of their imaginings, even though 800 miles south. As they had six days before, everyone who could get on deck took the opportunity; harsh though it was, there was a majestic, unspoilt beauty to this forbidding place that belonged to the seabirds crying overhead and the marine life, customarily empty but for a handful of scientists studying the Antarctic until this remote outpost of Britain had been drawn into the unlikeliest of conflicts. The crew lined the rails, their breath condensing as they talked, fascinated and a little apprehensive, watching slab-like growlers pitching heavily in the wake, the waters full of rapid, agile, unfamiliar motion that they took a few moments to recognise as penguins scattering away from the bow-wave.

The patrol vessel *Endurance* was waiting, and after rendezvousing, *Canberra* sailed on for her anchorage at East Cumberland Bay, Grytviken, on the northern side of South Georgia, where whalers had once arrived grateful for the shelter of the mountains after the storms of the South Atlantic. A cluster of rusting, derelict buildings was the only monument to a trade that had once thrived on this lonely isle. There was a monument to this war, too: one of Argentina's four submarines, the *Santa Fe*, listing and crippled after being attacked by British helicopters more than a month before, on 25 April. The gleaming white of the mountains emphasised how grubby *Canberra* had become, now as rusty and salt-encrusted as the trawler *Cordella*, converted for minesweeping, making its way towards her across the still waters in readiness for transferring troops and their equipment. She was soon to be joined the tug, *Typhoon*, the small ships dwarfed by *Canberra*'s bulk, but all three bearing the scars of the campaign. Now, there was nothing to do but wait.

It was nearly seven hours after *Canberra* anchored before the *QE2* emerged out of the night and made her leisurely way into the anchorage as Naval and P&O officers alike fretted over the delay in her arrival. The signal that had brought them to South Georgia had emphasised the urgency of their task and they were anxious to get started. No such impatience seemed apparent across the bay, even as all aboard *Canberra* registered how extraordinary a rendezvous this was; two great liners, if glimpsed together, usually at Southampton, here in this frozen wilderness. To the annoyance of Burne and Scott-Masson, *QE2* anchored nearly half-a-mile away, which would increase the time it took to transfer the troops. Before she did so, Reed was heading across in one of *Canberra*'s boats to get the operation underway, only to spend 40 minutes shivering alongside waiting for the sea doors to be opened. A similarly unhurried approach to offloading 5 Brigade was greeted with annoyance aboard *Canberra* when *QE2* signalled that her embarked military force considered it would be bad for morale for the transfers to begin that night. Burne's reply was blunt; nonsense, get on with it. This was not a good start; matters were about to get very much worse.

Muxworthy headed across the anchorage to see his opposite number, armed with a detailed list of the supplies *Canberra* was short of. 'I told him I needed everything he'd got, beer, food, a fully itemised list. And he said no. I said, "Excuse me, we're going back in, you're buggering off back home, give me everything you've got." We ended up having a bloody barney, he was making out things might change and they might get different orders. I said, "You're offloading all your troops to *Canberra*, we're short of food, and that means they'll be short of food," but he wouldn't do it.' There was a steadfast insistence from *QE2* that she needed the supplies she carried. The 36-hour delay in signals between Northwood and the South Atlantic was more frustrating than ever; there simply would not be time to get an order to *QE2* to hand over food. 'It was very, very strange, and we were very, very angry,' said Reed. 'We were very short of fresh vegetables and eggs. We had enough for one egg per bloke between then and going to war.' Scott-Masson and Burne were seething. Weeks later, there would be a bitter, infuriating coda to the argument that unfolded in that bleak, freezing anchorage. *Canberra* followed *QE2* into dry dock at Southampton for refitting. All around was the detritus she had left: tons upon tons of rotting, stinking food, taken on a 16,000-mile round voyage and never used.

The transfer of troops went ahead in an acrimonious atmosphere; the *QE2* refused to use her boats to help with the cross-decking. The animosity felt towards her by those on board *Canberra* was aggravated by the realisation that this quiet anchorage was the nearest that *QE2* would come to the Falklands and the dangers of Bomb Alley. It became clear that she had been ordered back to Britain; buzzes swirled that she was mechanically unsound, and the chance of breakdown could not be taken, or that she was too big for San Carlos Water. The truth was simpler: the War Cabinet had ruled that she must not be put at risk. If the Argentines damaged or sank a ship bearing the name of the sovereign, the propaganda coup would be immense. *Canberra* did not yet know for sure, but the suspicion that she might have to brave air attacks once again as 5 Brigade was offloaded began to weigh heavily. The crew tried not to think about it; busying themselves with work, and sticking close to friends. Susie West and Angela Devine decided to have a dinner party for six, improvising with one of *Canberra*'s characteristic accoutrements, a champagne ice bucket. With a little ingenuity and a hotplate, it became a slow cooker; all agreed the resulting hotpot was the best meal they had eaten since Southampton, even if it lacked carrots because none could be found.

Getting the 1st Welsh Guards and the 2nd Scots Guards aboard seemed to take an age; the other unit that had come south with *QE2*, the Gurkhas, were transferring to *Norland* much more quickly. This was a very different loading to the Marines and Paras coming briskly aboard with all their kit on their backs; the Guards appeared to have brought everything they possessed with them. They seemed to have more suitcases than cruise passengers with different outfits for every evening of a world voyage. 'I've never seen so much crap in all my life,' said Reed. 'They had suitcases and God knows what, they'd brought the mess silver as well, and the officers had brought their evening wear; most extraordinary, and it just didn't link up with what we were doing.' The sense that Guards equipped with silverware and dinner suits had an imperfect grasp of what awaited in the Falklands was reinforced when a group of men started to manoeuvre a box the size of a desk towards the trawler waiting to take them across to *Canberra*. 'This Royal Marine sergeant who was in charge of cross-decking asked what it was,' said Don Cole. 'And this Hooray Henry type officer said it was a disco unit, and the sergeant went mad. He said, "What the f**king hell do you think you're into here, you've come to fight a war, you're not bringing a disco unit with you. Chuck it over the side".'

The loading continued all night and into the 28th, the trawlers *Pict* and *Farnella* joining the operation to shuttle the Guards from one liner, still pristine in royal blue and white, to the other, scarred and scruffy. It was impossible to shrug off the sense that *QE2* felt she was altogether too grand for all this sort of thing. Muxworthy wrote that as the battered workhorse from Hull, *Cordella* first went alongside, an imperious voice from the bridge far above inquired as to her identity.

'Which one are you?'

'HMS *Cordella*,' came the cheerily sardonic reply.

'Which one are *you?*'

Canberra's passageways once again filled with men in uniform trying to find their way to their cabins, sorting out which of the berths to take, getting lost, finding the bars, eyeing up the women and being eyed up by the stewards. The Guards set about preparing to defend the ship, which made the crew feel a lot more secure. The Welsh built sangars from sandbags filled with the South Georgia shale on top of the chacons on the Sun Deck, equipping each with a heavy machine gun; the Scots mounted 20 GPMGs along each side of the Promenade Deck. From having a solitary gun to defend herself, *Canberra* now had 50 with trained soldiers on each; if the Argentine Air Force came calling, she would put up a withering hail of fire to see it off.

Darkness was falling by the time the last Guardsman was aboard. The wounded men who had recovered sufficiently to be moved were transferred to *QE2*; they at least would be well fed and comfortable on their way home. Another group was going too, albeit reluctantly; *Ardent*'s men. Not one among them wanted to leave; even though their ship was lost, being aboard *Canberra* made them feel they were doing something towards winning this war. A particularly strong bond had developed between them and the band, fellow Royal Navy men, who not only looked after those with minor injuries, but had provided a sympathetic ear whilst they talked through the trauma of losing so many old friends. The patrol vessel *Leeds Castle* came alongside to take them across to *QE2*; one by one, they climbed down onto her flight deck and stood, gazing up at new friends who had shown such kindness. Everybody wanted to wave them off, and they came to the rails at the port side; virtually all the crew, the

Naval party, some of the newly-arrived Guards. 'All of a sudden, a group of my chaps appeared with their instruments and started playing, just completely spontaneous, all kinds of tunes,' said John Ware. More and more appeared, until the full band was there on the Promenade Deck and struck up; 'Rule Britannia', 'Heart of Oak', 'A Life on the Ocean Wave', 'Hootenanny'. The music drew the rest of the Guards on deck, and for a few moments on a cruelly cold night at the ends of the earth, this forgotten stretch of water was like Southampton the evening *Canberra* had left; patriotic tunes and the cheers of thousands, here echoing back from the snowy mountains. *Ardent*'s men were not to be outdone. They started the chant heard at rugby grounds everywhere, 'Oggie, Oggie, Oggie!' Everyone caught it instantly and roared back, 'Oi, Oi, Oi!' And then the survivors simply applauded the ship, its company, its band, as the men and women at the rails cheered them. Gradually, the noise died down as *Leeds Castle* slipped away, her passengers looking back at *Canberra*, the men at the rails watching them go until the white of their boiler suits faded into the darkness.

She was under way for the Falklands by 9pm, having bid a none-too-fond farewell to *QE2*, watchfully making her way back out to sea through the growlers. The uneasiness amongst the officers about the readiness of units who had been about to take a mobile disco to war resurfaced even more powerfully, when the suggestion was made of a meeting the following morning. 'We sent the message that the senior officers needed to meet the Naval and P&O staff so that we can make sure everything is tickety boo at 11.30 in the deputy captain's cabin,' said Reed. 'And the message came back, "I'm terribly sorry, but I usually take sherry with my officers at this time". I was absolutely stumped, I really couldn't believe it. What planet are they on? The Beagle went bonkers.' There were other clues; they had only recently come off ceremonial duties and plainly their levels of fitness, alertness and motivation did not even approach that of the Marines and Paras. The crew found them somehow harder to like; some were borderline rude, and there was no attempt to moderate language around the women. 'I was really surprised at their manners,' said

Sue Wood. 'It struck me that there was a lot of swearing, and I thought, "Gosh, you never heard that from our lads".'

The troops seemed astonished at having to practise lifeboat drills, and their commanders were studiedly bored, leading both Naval and P&O officers to conclude that little in the way of emergency preparations had been done aboard *QE2*. That worried them. 'We were very concerned about how the troops would behave if we were badly attacked,' said Reed. 'The first time, we only had 42 Commando on board and they were well trained and knew what they were doing, but to abandon the ship with this lot would have been atrocious, it really didn't bear thinking about.' Then, to the alarm of officers who fretted endlessly about the risk of fire, a Guardsman was found cooking over the open flame of his hexamine stove for heating rations in the field on the floor of his cabin. An aghast Tim Yarker came over the loudspeakers, the words tumbling out in incredulity as his voice rose in disbelief at this degree of bone-headed stupidity. 'I have had the most amazing report, I can't believe it, this is incredible, somebody was caught with a primus stove alight in their cabin earlier on – this is impossible – we've got the Argentinians to set this thing on fire, not you. If anybody does that again there will be quite severe repercussions. The ship has a quite sufficient fire system but it is not designed to cope with people cooking up on primus stoves, camp fires or what you will in your cabins. Don't do it again.' It struck the P&O crew that they had been exceptionally fortunate in the soldiers they had brought south and their officers, who were disciplined and focussed, giving much thought to how they worked with the ship's company. 'This lot were different,' said Reed. 'Strange, a very different mentality to what we'd been used to. We never got to know any of them, though they weren't on board for very long.'

The starkest reminder that winter was arriving came with a ferocious storm that blew up within hours of leaving South Georgia; the Roaring Forties had been bad enough, but this was worse. If she had ever encountered more violent weather, nobody could recall when, as the dark sky bore down and the foam-flecked ocean reared up. 'It was very unpleasant indeed, force 12 winds, a very heavy swell and we had to reduce speed,' recalled Scott-Masson. He brought her down to 12 knots in the middle of the night as she heaved and pitched crazily; nobody was allowed on the fo'c'sle as the waves lashed across her and the bows rose and fell precipitously. All was misery below; the Guardsmen, whose voyage south had been relatively calm, were plagued by seasickness, the passageways, toilets and cabins reeked of it as *Canberra* groaned and creaked and shuddered under the buffeting of mountainous seas, furniture clattering about, the soldiers' berths in chaos as everything they had tumbled from wherever it was stowed. The restaurants were empty; nobody could face food in this. Then, a couple of almighty crashes, setting nerves jangling and people exchanging wide-eyed glances of alarm. She was flexing so much under the impact of the slamming waves that two of the huge plate-glass windows in the Meridian Room had shattered, the spray pouring in as crew rushed to clear up the splinters and cover over the gaping holes with blackout canvas. Nobody slept.

The storm was mercifully short-lived, and began to abate as daylight approached on Sunday the 30th. With the new day came bittersweet news from the World Service: 2 Para had won a long, hard and bloody battle against Argentine forces entrenched at Goose Green and Darwin. It had come at the cost of 17 British lives, and the names being read out in the bulletins jolted the P&O and naval officers who had drunk in the Crow's Nest during the phony war. Lt Col 'H' Jones, commanding officer of 2 Para, had been killed on the morning of the 28th as he charged an enemy position in an act of selfless, reckless bravery that broke a deadly impasse, freeing his men from being pinned down and allowing them to press on to a victory that proved crucial in the course of the war. He was being hailed a national hero, the tributes being led by Margaret Thatcher, who described him as 'this valiant and courageous officer, who was loved by his men'. A posthumous VC would be awarded; the man who passed his few evenings paused at Ascension aboard *Canberra* debating military history with Hew Pike, Max Hastings and Robert Fox had written himself into it.

The news of the fighting and deaths as arrival off the Falklands loomed played on nerves; it looked increasingly likely that *Canberra* would once again have to go into Bomb Alley. The ship's company lay awake remembering ten days before, the fear, the helplessness, the prayers that they would survive. 'Perhaps we were too sensitive,' said Reed. 'We were very hyper because we knew what we'd done, and we also knew how lucky we'd been to get out once. Now we were going to have to be lucky twice, and it was going to be a bit scary.' Everybody felt the same. 'We were pretty quiet about it,' said Angela Devine. 'I mean, how could we get away with it twice?' Even at the highest level on board, there was trepidation; Argentina's crowing that it had attacked *Canberra* on the day *Antelope* was stricken meant that the junta had her in its sights. There had been enough information on the World Service to indicate that she carried reinforcements for the Marines and Paras forging inland from the beaches, and that made her a prime target. Good fortune had been with her on May 21; if the warplanes sighted *Canberra* in the anchorage again, they would certainly press home an attack.

'Everyone was getting a bit tired,' said Burne, who took some comfort from the military progress. 'We knew by that time that the campaign was going more or less in the right direction, and there were a lot of ships in San Carlos.' Scott-Masson reflected in a subsequent lecture on taking *Canberra* to war: 'We were to go back into San Carlos, and you can imagine we weren't exactly excited about that prospect.' Privately, he was enraged at his crew being put at risk again because of what he saw as the failure of the *QE2* to play her part in liberating the Falklands; he could not have known that the War Cabinet had ordered her home. His wife said, 'He was furious that he had to go back again, and that's when I got most calls from the wives. He had some pretty unrepeatable things to say about that ship.' The *QE2*, sailing sedately for Britain without suffering a moment's threat, became the focus of resentment and anger, the lightning rod for anxiety. 'There was a good deal of acrimony there,' said Reed. It intensified when one of the long-retired armchair generals heard regularly on the BBC offering supposedly expert opinions on the conduct of the war blithely announced that *QE2* had to be protected because she was the flagship of

the Merchant Navy, but *Canberra* was politically expendable, a pronounce-
ment that caused consternation on board as well as back home, where Mrs
Scott-Masson's phone began ringing yet again. He was partially correct,
in that the government was not prepared to risk the Cunard ship, but wide
of the mark in suggesting that it considered *Canberra* anything other than
a vital component of the task force that must be protected at all costs.
'Where he got that from, God alone knows,' said Reed. 'It didn't go down
too well with the ship's company. It's not the sort of thing you want to
hear, that you're expendable, and it put a great dent in morale. That didn't
last long, because we knew what we were doing, we knew we were okay,
but it's not the sort of thing you want the people sitting at home to hear
either.'

It left the ship's company more jittery than ever about going back in
before daybreak on Wednesday 2 June, after rendezvousing with the main
carrier group north of the Falklands. There was some reassurance to be
taken from the sight of Sea Harriers patrolling the skies from *Invincible*,
but even so, precautions had to be taken. Everyone berthed in Exocet Alley
or below was moved up several decks, even if that meant overcrowding.
Once more, the troops were dispersed by company around the bars and
public rooms, settling as best they could; the crew did likewise, clad in
bulky layers, clutching lifejackets, hats and gas masks, making themselves
as comfortable as possible with cushions and pillows, joking wearily about
here we go again. In her cabin, Susie West, sweltering under multiple
woollens and sweatshirts, was drifting in and out of an uneasy sleep when
she was jerked wide awake by a metallic bang from the bulkhead close to
her head. This had to be it. She leapt up, heart racing, grabbed her torch,
and got out into the passageway. Nothing, no alarms, nobody rushing for
the boats, no smoke; just the overpowering smell of orange juice from a
half-gallon can that had exploded.

The bridge was as hushed and dark as it had been on 21 May as *Canberra*
headed into Falkland Sound shortly after 5am; no need to worry about
Fanning Head this time as she sailed slowly into San Carlos Water, the
now familiar low hills beginning to be discernible against the sky. She was

making for a different point in the anchorage, much closer to San Carlos Settlement, in what was for her, very shallow water. Scott-Masson needed all his concentration as he and his officers eased her in so slowly that her bulk hardly disturbed the calm sea. Little by little, she reached her allotted position and anchored at 6.17am, the P&O officers blowing their cheeks out in relief at having completed this tricky manoeuvre. 'So again with fingers and everything else crossed we went further in this time, which was navigationally pretty hair-raising for this ship as there wasn't much room and there were a lot of ships in there, certainly quite a frightening experience trying to get the ship in there and anchored,' Scott-Masson recalled. It was days later that he and his officers learned that their position was a direct consequence of the Naval planners' calculations that if she sank, her upper decks would remain out of the water. 'It was quite sensible thinking,' said Reed, 'But it did cause us a bit of a shudder.'

The anchorage was far busier than it had been the last time, now full of ships, her old friend *Norland* amongst them, already busy landing the Gurkhas, but the most welcome of all was *Plymouth*, the frigate circling protectively. There was no glorious dawn today, but as the sky lightened, the crew's spirits lifted. The hills were indistinct, shrouded by fog. Perfect, couldn't be better; men and women whose working lives were spent under sunny clear skies rejoiced at the gloomy dampness that enveloped their ship. It was the worst possible weather for flying, so bad that even the British helicopters were having problems operating over the anchorage; and that meant the Argentines would stay away. Even so, all aboard attacked the task of offloading the Guards and their equipment with manic energy; they wanted to get everybody off and get out. Foggy or not, everybody had an eye to the sky, willing it not to clear, and their ears cocked to the loudspeakers; Burne had been much admired for the way he had kept them informed on 21 May, but they did not want to hear another ball-by-ball account of incoming air raids again today.

The weather, though, was as much enemy as friend; the longer it hampered helicopters airlifting supplies to the Marines in forward positions, the longer *Canberra* would have to stay. And the sheer volume of kit that the Guards had brought aboard was posing problems. Compared to the brisk, efficient men of 3 Brigade, they seemed sluggish and untroubled by any sense of urgency, even here with troops dug in ashore and alert to any threat, more preoccupied with their luggage than cruise passengers ever had been. The crew started silently cursing them. 'Getting these happy chappies off was just murder,' said Reed. 'They were so slow and wanted all their suitcases. There were tons of these things, and to explain to the deck crew that moving suitcases was good for the war effort was not the easiest thing.' She was also doing her best for the islanders; the unlikely presence of a liner still with supplies taken on for cruising made her the first place to look for anything off the supply list of military men fighting a war. The first signal received after she anchored was to aid the residents of Goose Green, freed after being imprisoned in a hall by the Argentines. The women were in desperate need of tampons; could *Canberra* help? They were sent on the first available helicopter.

The hours were ticking by and the piles of suitcases did not appear to be getting any smaller. The troops themselves seemed to be proceeding at a crawl; landing craft alongside the galley doors took forever to fill up as the Guards boarded at a stately pace. In an effort to speed up the operation, four of *Canberra*'s own passenger boats were lowered, full of men, and Reed took them ashore to the jetty at San Carlos, getting the men off and then sending the boats back for another load. At last, after all these weeks, somebody from *Canberra* finally set foot on the islands. Reed found himself alone, cold, and unable to get through to the ship on his radio, and guessed that the slow loading would mean a long wait before the boats returned. 'So I thought I'd go up through 40 Commando, who'd been my great chums; I'd been ashore training with them in Ascension, thought I'd stop off and have a quick mug of tea.' He found them grim and unreceptive; seven days earlier, the Argentines had bombed their positions on the beachhead. One Marine and a sapper attached to the commando had been killed. Now, as 5 Brigade arrived, men eager for action had been ordered to remain in their positions and hold the anchorage, a consequence of intelligence reports that the Argentines were planning an assault on it using paratroopers, whilst the Welsh Guards headed for the Sussex Mountains as part of the plan to retake Stanley, an operation the Marines were desperately keen to be involved in. 'They wouldn't talk to me,' said Reed. 'They were all just very stony-faced. These were my mates, and they'd just turn and walk away.'

From *Canberra*'s point of view, the weather began to deteriorate alarmingly by mid-afternoon; the fog cleared, the sun came out, and the clearest of winter days developed. The helicopters were up, but so far, not the Argentine Air Force. People checked their watches constantly, counting down to nightfall; maybe an hour-and-a-half, maybe less if some cloud came over. Nothing, still nothing; no 'Air threat red', no 'Take cover! Take cover!' as the radar operators aboard the warships stayed glued to their screens for Mirages, Skyhawks or Super Etendards approaching fast over the sea. *Canberra*'s men and women kept up a furious pace, racing the clock to complete the task, once more forming a human chain from the upper deck to the galley doors to pass what had become 'these f**king suitcases' hand-to-hand to get them into landing craft. Gradually, the light began to go, and with it, the nerves eased, even as the work continued. Finally, the last Guardsman was away, but not all the luggage: 450 suitcases remained. So did substantial amounts of stores for the Marines, the consequence of the fog that had grounded the helicopters. *Canberra* was going to have to stay the night, and carry on in the morning. At 6pm, her crew watched quietly and enviously as *Norland*, her unloading complete, weighed anchor and sailed for the open sea.

Even here, even under these circumstances, with another day of potential danger in prospect, *Canberra*'s flair for entertaining was not quite forgotten. It was John Muxworthy's 40th birthday, and Reed threw him a party in his cabin; there were 20 guests and champagne cocktails. 'We didn't get smashed, because that really wouldn't have been sensible,' said Muxworthy. 'But it was good to take the tension off for a while. There was an alert, but we thought, "Sod it". I wrote in my notebook at the time, "Glad to be 40, but not sure I'm going to make it any further" because it was a hairy time.' Elsewhere, the ship was quiet, its people subdued, trying and failing to sleep, counting down the hours until dawn.

When it came, they shook their heads in despair. It was as bright and beautiful as 21 May; unimprovable flying weather. Their luck had surely run out, despite the watchful presence of *Plymouth* and the Rapier anti-aircraft batteries all around the anchorage. The Guardsmen had taken the machine guns with them but, oddly, not the ammunition. Belts of it littered the Promenade Deck, 100,000 rounds, just dumped and left. She was back to the solitary GPMG on the bridge wing and her volunteers to man it. In came the clatter of the helicopters as the humping of stores continued, one after another, queuing up as so often before, gunning their engines and wheeling away over the hills and moorland. There was less resentment now, because the loading was no longer of suitcases, but supplies for the troops they knew and admired from the long voyage south. This felt like doing something to help the war those men were fighting, not having to act as porters.

The morning wore on; no alerts yet. They grabbed a quick bite of lunch, and Scott-Masson retired for pinkers; nothing disturbed the interlude. The countdown to darkness began as the pilots kept up the pace of landings and take-offs; still nothing in the sky apart from helicopters, no warnings from the loudspeakers. The nervous anticipation was as draining as the lifting and shifting. 'I lived on a diet of adrenaline and cheese-and-onion sandwiches,' said Reed. 'So by the end of the day you were absolutely whacked.' The approach of winter made each day progressively shorter; clouds came up and started to darken the sky half an hour earlier than yesterday as the hills over which no threat had materialised began to fade away, the final helicopter was waved off and *Canberra* blacked herself out with a smooth efficiency that had seemed impossible just a few weeks earlier. The warplanes had not come; for two days they had ignored the anchorage, and at 6pm, she was to weigh anchor. *Canberra* made her way out of San Carlos as carefully as she had come in, gradually and slowly, in company with *Plymouth*, then out into the sound, black and quiet, once more bound for a sector of sea 130 miles north-east of Stanley. On the bridge, in the hospital, in the restaurants, in the Pig and Whistle, down in the engine room, they looked at one other: my God, we got away with it.

CHAPTER THIRTEEN

All-Bran and Peat

SHE FELT EERILY empty and detached from the task force, steaming aimlessly in the middle of nowhere. Her passageways were quiet, her public rooms deserted, the bars silent. No queues formed at the shop, no feet thudded around the Promenade Deck save for the occasional runner from amongst the crew who rattled around the ship, unsettled by the silence as they passed through deck upon deck of unoccupied cabins. Their lives were bound up with crowds and chatter, of cruise passengers, and latterly of soldiers. Now they were alone with their thoughts, a little more than 600 people, sailing in circles 200 miles east of the Falklands with no role to play and no end in sight to this voyage to war. The officers of the watch waited for the next signal, hoping it would be the one that sent them home. Canberra was in the TRALA, the Tug Repair and Logistics Area, a stretch of ocean where merchant ships had been sent to reduce their vulnerability to attacks around the islands, under the protection of the destroyer *Glamorgan*. Her days grew monotonous; outward on the same bearings, back again, so predictable that seabirds began landing aboard, soon waddling into the wheelhouse from the bridge wings in search of crumbled biscuits that the crew scattered for them.

The pointless days did not even offer the consolation of feeling safe from long-range aircraft. 'There were the Hercules and the Canberras of the Argentine Air Force that were capable of actually getting that far,' said Scott-Masson. 'And of course there were always these submarines and nobody ever knew whether they were or weren't there, so you were always feeling slightly tense. Of course boredom was the other thing, we were just steaming round and round in a box, occasionally doing a VERTREP or dashing back into the carrier force to supply them with some stores.' After being so closely involved in the landings, the ship's company had become bystanders in the war, even though they knew the general outline of its progress from the World Service and newsletters issued by *Glamorgan* to the ships awaiting their next task. Occasional visitors from the islands hitching a lift on helicopters coming aboard to transfer yet more stores were pressed for whatever snippets they had. From them, they gleaned that the Marines and Paras were yomping and tabbing across the bleak moors and mountains of East Falkland in worsening weather in preparation for the assault on Port Stanley, the gruelling 50-mile forced march at least in part a consequence of the loss of helicopters destroyed when *Atlantic Conveyor* was attacked. Amongst the visitors was John Shirley, who came aboard to file dispatches, bathe, perhaps sleep overnight, and then stock up on whisky and cigarettes to take back for 42 Commando.

The military arrived as well, including a couple of young lieutenants from 40 Commando who needed to use the satellite, announcing themselves with the rank smell of men who had been in the field for weeks. When they were done, Reed took them down a deck to his cabin and ran a bath, only to find them reluctant to return clean whilst their men were enduring the filth of living dug in to defensive positions. 'I said, "The bath's full, and when you've had yours, your mate can have another one and you don't have to use the same water. There's the whisky and the glasses." They said, "We can't do that, they'll think we're strange when we get back ashore." I said, "Bollocks, what do they teach you? Eat when you can, drink when you can, clean up when you can".'

Food came aboard, though the vegetables were hardly better than what she already had after weeks in stores ships. That was only to be expected; completely unexpected was the arrival of tons of mail from well-wishers back in Britain, hundreds upon hundreds of sacks brought by helicopter, the letters addressed simply to 'A Soldier' or 'A Sailor'. Muxworthy noted 4,000 in one airlift alone. Plainly, nobody in the Navy had a clue how to deal with all this post; equally plainly, as with the request for tampons, anything out of the ordinary had been chucked *Canberra*'s way. A cruise ship well used to dealing politely and efficiently with the public would surely know what to do. There was an amount of head-scratching and debate after the first sackfuls were humped two decks down from the landing pad to the Bureau, emptied and the untidy piles sorted and opened; the sheer volume made answering each, even with a standard printed reply, impossible. There were simply not enough envelopes or stamps on board. They came from all over the country, all ages and all social strata; letters from junior school children in their neatest joined-up handwriting, with carefully crayoned drawings of aircraft or ships and letters from the elderly whose spidery words could be difficult to make out. Young and old alike wrote the same thing: good luck and come home safe, soon. They were touching in their sincerity, and some form of reply had to be made. Burne came up with the solution, sending a message over the satellite to the BBC and national newspapers, asking that the thanks of everybody in the task force for the good wishes be broadcast and published.

Sunday 6 June broke the monotony of ploughing ceaselessly through the TRALA, as an excited buzz spread through the ship when a Sea King piloted by Prince Andrew, serving with 820 Squadron on *Invincible*, landed on board as part of the continuing airlift, remaining for half an hour as crew scurried to grab their cameras. Scott-Masson noted his arrival in a lengthy letter to John Turner later that day outlining *Canberra*'s activities on 21 May and afterward. 'It was indeed an exciting day and, in retrospect, I can only say it was a miracle we survived unscathed. The ship's company and all concerned were quite magnificent in their stoical acceptance of the inevitable and good humour prevailed, if somewhat tinged with apprehension.' *Norland* was on her way to Montevideo with 1,400 Argentines captured at Goose Green, and Scott-Masson made it clear that he did not want *Canberra* to perform a similar task: 'It is my sincere hope, however, that we are not used in the prisoner-of-war role for the ship is entirely unsuitable for this purpose. Anyway, all of this is just speculation, and we have learnt the hard way not to speculate.' That evening, the ship's company gathered in the William Fawcett Room for a concert by the band; afterwards, in lieu of his usual broadcast, Scott-Masson addressed them, cautioning that there were no signs of *Canberra* being allowed to sail home yet. The mood was brighter, only to be downcast later that evening by a bulletin from the BBC, which reported that 5 Brigade had gone ashore successfully – a news blackout having delayed the announcement for four days – thanks to *QE2*, which had transferred the troops to what were termed 'small ships' for the landings. Two tense, relentlessly busy days filled with the constant fear of air attacks had been dismissed in a single, inaccurate sentence.

Scott-Masson seethed for the next 24 hours, contacted the captain of *Norland*, Don Ellerby, and then on 8 June composed another letter to Turner in his firm hand on behalf of both ships.

'I would ask you, if MoD permit, to put the record straight in the UK. At present, all the ballyhoo on the radio and in the press is about *QE2*, not helped by a broadcast by their captain not notable for its integrity. *Canberra*, together with *Norland*, landed both 3 Brigade and 5 Brigade. The *QE2* never went near the Falkland Islands and was not in much danger nor called upon to perform as our two ships did. I write to you about this for the sake of the ships' companies of both this ship and *Norland*, who are highly incensed at the inaccurate reporting.'

QE2's capacity to irritate was undiminished when she arrived back in Britain three days later, amid much hullabaloo with Queen Elizabeth, the Queen Mother sailing aboard the royal yacht *Britannia* to greet her. One of her officers, asked by a reporter about *Canberra*'s role in the South Atlantic, answered with haughty superciliousness: 'If you've got a dirty job to do you always send a Ford, you never use the Rolls-Royce.'

On the day Scott-Masson set down his annoyance, there were two reminders that this war was far from over, both felt deeply aboard *Canberra* because of her connection to their victims. The first was an attack on

Plymouth, which had watched over her only a few days before, bombed in Falkland Sound, leaving five of her crew injured. Much worse was to follow. A series of logistical difficulties and communications breakdowns had culminated in 350 Welsh Guards being transported by the landing ship *Sir Galahad* from San Carlos to Fitzroy, in readiness for the assault on Stanley. Unloading them was beset by delays and hampered by the unwillingness of their officers to get the men off and embark on a five-mile march to Bluff Cove, their allotted destination. Hours passed, more than long enough for Argentine spotters ten miles distant on Mount Harriet to alert their commanders and warplanes to take off from the mainland. *Sir Tristram*, also in the undefended anchorage, was bombed first, killing two crewmen. The horror of what happened seconds later aboard *Sir Galahad* resulted in the war's greatest British loss of life. A bomb landed among the guardsmen on the open tank and vehicle deck, where there were also twenty tons of ammunition and a large quantity of petrol. The ship became an inferno; 47 died, 39 of them Guardsmen. A further 115 were wounded, 40 seriously, many suffering grievous burns. A frantic rescue operation using boats and helicopters got the dying and injured to shore as smoke belched out and ammunition below decks exploded; eventually, it became clear there was no more to be done and *Sir Galahad* was left to burn herself out. She would subsequently be towed out to sea and sunk, a war grave for the men whose remains were left aboard.

It became colder, and thoughts turned to its effects on both the ship and troops ashore. 'I did rounds every morning with the bosun at 7am, and I stepped onto the flight deck and went arse over tea kettle on the ice,' said Reed. The decks were growing dangerously glassy as spray swept over *Canberra* by stiff winds froze. He had a picture in mind of the battleship his father served on during the Second World War, its upperworks encased in ice, and began to worry. It built up with alarming rapidity during nights now almost as bitter as those in South Georgia. Clearing it with scrapers was a mammoth job that took hours. A thickening sheet of ice across *Canberra* posed risks not just to people slipping and falling, but threatened the ship, adding additional weight to the heavy load she still carried;

thousands of tons of stores, including compo rations, were still on board despite the continuing airlifts. A signal went back to the technical support team in Southampton asking about the effects of ice build-up; the reply was that anything more than two-and-a-half inches could affect stability. 'I thought two-and-a-half inches wasn't very much at all, so it was a perpetual worry,' said Reed. 'We were already 13 inches deeper than standard, so the extra top weight would have been incredible, and it was getting bloody cold.' He and Rudderham started discussing the possibility that the onset of winter might halt the land campaign and bring substantial numbers of troops back on board. They sketched out a plan to use bars and public rooms for men suffering from exposure, a distinct possibility given the reports of the atrocious conditions ashore they heard from visitors. Snow and sleet driven by bitter winds flayed the troops marching across country. Men were being rendered unfit for action by frostbite, or a condition all thought belonged to the First World War, not 1982, trench foot, sores and decaying flesh caused by prolonged exposure to damp.

Canberra's medical team would be confronted by numerous cases of trench foot within days, but for now the demands on its doctors and nurses had eased; ploughing up and down the TRALA was boring, but it at least gave them a respite after the hectic and draining period that followed 21 May. They still had 18 Argentine casualties aboard; the British wounded were either being treated in the field hospital at Ajax Bay, or aboard SS *Uganda*, now fully operational as a hospital ship. Some had been transferred to *Canberra* for post-operative care to free beds before being taken aboard *QE2* for the voyage home. The contrast between the recoveries made by the British and Argentines had struck everybody; properly fed and clothed soldiers and sailors had made rapid progress, whereas the malnourished and badly equipped conscripts struggled to improve. Putting into practice the lessons learned on the voyage south about treating gunshot and shrapnel wounds proved less than straight - forward, as Rosie Elsdon found when she attempted to remove pads that had been put in as part of delayed primary suturing.

'This first chap, I gave him the painkillers and tried to soak it out, and it was really difficult because the pack was rock hard and you couldn't actually soak it out. I tried a bit, and it was really painful. I looked at him and said, "This isn't going to work, is it?" and he said, "No, I don't think so." I said, "You're going to theatre this morning to have this stitched up, and I think it's better that all these packs are taken out under anaesthetic." And so I took the decision not to try to take any more of these packs out of these poor chaps, because it was just too painful. I was really worried about it, and I went off duty and couldn't sleep. One of the doctors came down to the hospital later on and said, "You did absolutely the right thing".'

She was also losing sleep over the emotional suffering of her patients. It was apparent from their withdrawn silence, sitting up in bed lost in contemplating injuries that would change their lives forever, as in the case of Chief Petty Officer Terry Bullingham, blinded by shrapnel when *Antrim* was hit. Elsdon read him a letter from his wife that arrived several days later; Reed also sat with him. Drawing these wounded men out was difficult. 'It helped to try to have a little chat while you were doing something, changing dressings or giving them a wash,' said Elsdon. 'If you're helping them to eat, or doing something, then you can have a conversation. The fact that they weren't alone helped. As they got better, they would sit and have a cigarette or a chat with other people who'd been injured, and that was one of the most helpful things, to realise that they weren't in it alone.' The nights brought her a regular visitor, a traumatised Naval man who seemed able to cope during daylight, but needed to talk when darkness fell, returning again and again to the dimly lit ward with its ghostly white camouflage netting: 'He wasn't an in-patient, but he'd had a really awful time and he just used to come down every night and talk and talk for two hours, and I didn't need to say anything. The fact that somebody was there who'd listen to him several nights in a row actually meant that he did recover from it mentally. It took a toll, because it was hard sleeping, getting out of my mind all these different things, but the fact that Angela and I were both in it together was really helpful.' Morgan O'Connell recognised the value of what she was doing: 'In the case of one individual almost regressing into childhood, he was certainly saved for the Navy by this tremendous work being done with him. He was in part affected by her femininity as well as her professional skills, and getting the mothering he craved.'

Susie West, too, learned the value of listening when she examined an airman with a relatively minor facial injury, but raw mental scars. 'I said, "Tell me what happened," and nothing had prepared me for this ghastly, ghastly story. What he'd suffered was the psychological trauma of watching his oppo bleeding to death in his flying suit. It had a big impact on me, it probably made me a better doctor because I would now never underestimate what the answer would be if I ask, "What brings you here?" because it might be a very brief answer, or a very big, heavy answer.' The ship's company embraced the wounded men in their midst; there was no shortage of volunteers to help at mealtimes, or to sit and talk. As over dinner on the voyage south, the women were the most popular, whether from the Bureau, the cabin staff or Sue Wood chatting as she wheeled round a trolley from the shop. The graphic training films shown in the Crow's Nest had steeled men and women alike for what to expect, but even so, the plight of the casualties whose hurt and fears for the future were written in their strained faces and haunted eyes could be overwhelming. 'People are so used to Hollywood wars where people throw their hands up and die,' reflected Reed. 'You never see the wreckage that's in the background. Some of the people who volunteered couldn't keep going because it was so terrible. One girl really sobbed her heart out. She said, "I'll get used to it – please don't tell the others."'

Dealing with the Argentine wounded presented different and disconcerting challenges. The language barrier was a problem, though one of *Canberra*'s waiters spoke Spanish, which helped. The hard-eyed special forces lieutenant with perfect English refused to assist, remaining silent, glaring through his personal war of nerves. He relented only once; one of the most pitiful patients was a young man who had lost both legs, one above the knee, the other below, the victim of British wariness of suffering casualties when winkling enemy soldiers out of stone sangars. They found one solution was to fire an anti-tank weapon at the fortified positions; if the blast didn't account for the occupants, the collapsing stones would.

The wounded man had, with inevitable tasteless wit, been nicknamed 'Stumpy' when he arrived aboard *Canberra*. He was also suffering from a broken hip, and what remained of one leg needed to be put in traction, a metal rod having been inserted through it to make that possible. The problem was that never for a moment had the Bonito Club been contemplated as a hospital ward prior to early April, and there were no uprights around the beds that filled the dance floor to which traction equipment could be connected. Reed arrived with the bosun, a ship's carpenter and a supply of timber; after some deliberation, they began constructing a frame over the bed and its increasingly agitated occupant. 'Stumpy started screaming when he saw this gantry going up, because he thought we were going to string him up,' said Peter Mayner. 'They'd all been told they would be shot or killed by the British. He genuinely thought he was going to be topped by us.' From his own bed, the lieutenant intervened and calmed the near-hysterical man; he then returned to staring out the hated British.

Once more, *Canberra*'s spirit of improvisation and make-do-and-mend was at work; the patient had been lowered from the flight deck on the Heath Robinson casualty ramp made from a dock porter's trolley. Now, he would be treated using another cobbled-together contraption: a makeshift timber frame, ropes, and weights used for pressing meat in the butcher's shop on F Deck to provide the traction he needed. It appeared to work. 'We thought, "We've got it, absolutely perfect,"' said Reed. 'We all stood back to look at it, and the old ship rolled a couple of degrees and the weight moved. F**k; we didn't work that out.' More knots were tied and the unfortunate soldier carefully repositioned, his stump raised, the tension between the rod protruding from his flesh and the frame bringing a loud pop from his broken hip that the doctors assured the wincing chief officer and his men meant all was well; this time, nothing shifted and their patient settled. His nightmarish day that started with the conviction that he was about to be hanged had only just begun.

Reed returned that night to check that the frame was secure, only to find the bed empty, the ropes slack, and emergency surgery being performed, thanks to the alertness of a bandsman guarding the ward, who in the quiet of evening heard the persistent pat-pat-pat of something dripping, and went looking for what he thought was a water leak. 'It was blood coming from under his bed,' said Reed. 'There was another piece of shrapnel in him and it had nicked his artery. He was lying there unconscious, bleeding to death, and it had soaked the mattress and started trickling onto the floor. I shot round the corner into the operating theatre, and in the middle of it was the surgeon under this pool of light with his hand inside this bloke's wound picking out another bit of shrapnel. Oh, God. "Don't worry, Martin," he said, "This isn't surgery, this is butchery."' The operation, and blood donated by Marines and Paras stored in fridges formerly full of champagne, saved the young man; the following day, he lay in a fresh bed, what was left of his leg in traction with the butchers' weights, the wooden frame creaking slightly with the motion of the ship, but holding firm.

Indoctrination about British atrocities and the Argentines' susceptibility to their government's propaganda frustrated the doctors and nurses; it fostered fear and suspicion in their patients. There was no war here, in a converted theatre and adjoining nightclub, where Devine, Elsdon, Mayner, O'Connell, West and their colleagues treated them. But smiles were met with stony faces, friendly greetings blanked, especially by the officers. 'We had five of the most senior ones, and we didn't trust them at all,' said Elsdon. 'They didn't trust us either, and they couldn't believe they were on *Canberra* because they'd been told she had been sunk. We showed them plates with '*Canberra*' written on them to try to make them believe it, because they hadn't seen the ship when they'd come on board.' In the face of such intransigence, the nurses allowed themselves the gentlest touch of needling that did at least prompt a flicker of emotion in men from a football-mad nation. Straight-faced, they let slip that Argentina, reigning

World Cup champions, had been dumped out of the 1982 tournament then being played in Spain without even reaching the knockout stage, the ignominy compounded by star captain and national icon Diego Maradona getting himself sent off in the 85th minute against sworn rivals Brazil for kicking an opponent.

A breakthrough in relations with the Argentines came from an unexpected source. The special forces hard man was shifting about uncomfortably, his expression more distracted than deadly. He had gone to war dreaming of glory, fired by zealotry, determined to repel the reviled British from the beloved Malvinas, only to be shot up and taken prisoner before the landings had even begun, ending up here, confined to bed. Now his humiliation was complete: he was constipated. The doctors prescribed roughage, a daily bowl of All-Bran. The first was presented to him by one of the female cabin staff at breakfast. 'When she produced this for him he said, "I'm not going to eat that, I wouldn't give that to my dog",' said O'Connell. She was not putting up with any sour-faced tantrums; the air of menace was no match for the withering onslaught of an old-fashioned maternal scolding, whilst O'Connell looked on admiringly. 'She said, "Don't be so stupid, and stop behaving like a spoiled child. The doctors have said this is what you need for your constipation, so do as you're told. And while you're at it, why don't you help the doctors communicate with your countrymen?" He ate his All-Bran. Nobody in all his training had taught him how to deal with someone like his mother telling him to stop misbehaving, and she just broke down the barrier and he became much more willing to converse.'

A stroke of very British eccentricity reinforced the verbal clip round his ear. Amongst the more outlandish and un-warlike items of luggage that came aboard from QE2 at South Georgia was an accordion belonging to a major in the Scots Guards. O'Connell approached him, keen to grab any opportunity to take the patients' minds off their injuries. 'I said to this chap, "Would you mind playing and having a bit of a sing-song?" and he said, "Not at all".' The nightclub, empty of music since the evening crew donned gas masks and duffel coats to sing 'We Don't Want to Join the

Army, We Don't Want to Go to War', heard it again for casualties who had done just those things; the major pulled up a chair on what had been the stage, camouflage netting and blackout canvas instead of velvet drapes his backdrop, surrounded by bandaged men hurting inwardly as well as from their wounds, and played his accordion for an hour-and-a-half, getting them singing, hesitantly at first, starting to see a smile here and there, gradually bringing them out of themselves before they boarded the *QE2* for the journey home. The lieutenant, now altogether less clenched, turned to O'Connell. 'He said, "That would never have happened in our forces, no way would an officer have sat on the stage and entertained the troops."'

Canberra had been sailing the TRALA for more than a week by the time it became clear that the assault on Port Stanley was imminent, and thoughts turned to the young men they had come to think of as 'our lads', the teenagers with their skinhead haircuts who had pounded the Promenade Deck from dawn to dusk, queued patiently at the shop to buy nutty or even tights, swayed to tables with the food slopping about their trays in the swell and devoted so much energy to outwitting the rules allowing them only two cans of beer. Everything picked up from the signals and helicopter crews coming aboard pointed to an attack that weekend, confirmation coming when *Glamorgan* departed on the morning of Friday 11 June to join the bombardment of strongpoints. Days would pass before the scale of the sacrifice made by their lads became apparent to the ship's company, and as they tried to comprehend it, wondered which of them they knew had gone. The battles of the next few days would cost the lives of 25 Paras and Marines; 80 more were wounded, some so severely that their lives were transformed. Nine Scots Guards whose first sight of the Falklands had been from *Canberra* also died, and 43 were wounded. The fighting for the high ground around Port Stanley that claimed them all was vicious and merciless, giving the lie to complacent notions back in Britain that the Argentine forces were shambolic; the terrain was won only with sacrifice and bravery during a series of night attacks.

3 Para went into action first, against a position on Mount Longdon. The battalion had already endured much, marching across the hills in torrential rain, sleet and freezing storm-force winds to reach their starting point for the assault. Brian Faulkner, who had boarded *Canberra* with the advance planning party at Gibraltar, was now ashore with the regimental aid post, tramping up the hill weighed down by equipment including a GPMG. As he neared the top, he got the most cheerful of greetings; Sgt Ian McKay, his cabin-mate aboard, all smiles as usual. 'Alright, Brian, are you?' laughing as Faulkner struggled towards him under the load. He looked well, slimmer, the few additional pounds he habitually carried having dropped off on the march, and was in his customary high spirits. 'We hadn't seen each other for three-and-a-half, four weeks,' said Faulkner. 'We started chit-chatting and said once it's all finished, we'll get together and have a pint of beer.' They talked for a while, and then McKay went back to 4 Platoon. A few hours later on a frozen mountainside where men were fighting and dying, Faulkner watched his friend, who talked endlessly about his young daughter, Melanie, on the voyage south and what he planned for them both when he got home on leave after the war, being zipped into a body bag.

McKay, aged 29, was awarded the second posthumous VC of the Falklands War for his bravery during the brutal twelve-hour battle. As 4 Platoon attempted to clear a ridge, it came under heavy fire; its commander took McKay, a corporal and a few others forward to reconnoitre the enemy positions. He was wounded, and command of the platoon devolved to McKay, who decided that attack was the only option. He and three men broke cover and charged into a hail of fire; one of the men with him was killed and the two others wounded. He carried on alone, using grenades against the bunker from where the enemy had two platoons of Paras pinned down. At the moment he silenced the fire on his comrades, he was killed.

The toll mounted even after Longdon was taken; five men were killed by two days of Argentine shelling. When it was finally over, 3 Para had lost 23 men, including a Royal Engineer and a Royal Electrical and

Mechanical Engineer attached to the battalion. Two of the dead were only 17; they could not have served in Northern Ireland, but were allowed to come here, 8,000 miles from home, to this bleak and bloodied mountain. 42 Commando fought for Mount Harriet that same night, coming under heavy fire from determined defenders who in some cases had superior equipment, and lost two men. Yet more people were dying; four men of 45 Commando on Two Sisters. At sea, *Glamorgan* was hit by an Exocet fired from an improvised launcher on the islands, which killed 13, though the ship survived. In Stanley, shelling killed three women. Capturing Mount Tumbledown and Wireless Ridge on the night of the 13th/14th accounted for nine men of the 2nd Scots Guards and one of 2 Para.

All weekend, *Canberra* had monitored whatever military radio communication she could. It was frustrating; snippets here and there, impossible to form anything like a complete picture. Early on Monday the 14th, she was ordered to head towards the Falklands to transfer medical stores to *Hermes*, for airlift to *Uganda*. The sea was roughening, and she started to heave and crash through the waves, a gale driving spray across her that would freeze by nightfall. At 11.22am, shortly after sighting the carrier group, the radio room picked up an artillery net: 'Check fire, check fire, check fire. The enemy are surrendering in droves and putting up white flags'. The calm, unruffled voice coming out of the speakers was that of Lieutenant-Colonel Mike Holroyd-Smith, commanding officer of 29 Commando Light Regiment, Royal Artillery. More fragments of information followed as the radio officers searched the airwaves; Argentine forces walking back down towards Stanley from the high ground that had cost so many lives on both sides, weapons being dumped. Soon afterwards, confirmation in a signal to all the ships of the task force; white flag over Stanley, fighting ceased, surrender negotiations underway. There was a rider; the reaction from Argentina's government was unknown and all defences against possible attack must be maintained.

They reacted with relief, rather than jubilation. There were smiles and backslaps when Michael Bradford came over the loudspeakers to tell them that white flags had been seen over Stanley, but no whoops or cheers. 'I just thought, "Oh good, that's alright then",' said Elsdon. 'Whether we were all exhausted, or we'd seen what it had cost, so many people, to get to this, there wasn't any sense of elation. I'd been with so many people who'd lost friends and colleagues, and we could see what it had taken.'

Both Naval and P&O officers remained wary that this could be a limited, local surrender by forces on the islands; the uncertainty over the reaction from Buenos Aires was worrying. It was from the mainland that the worst air attacks had come, and still might. *Canberra* would remain blacked out and on high alert. Their concerns eased a little several hours later, with the arrival of a major who had the surrender document signed by Brigadier-General Mario Benjamin Menendez, appointed military governor of the Malvinas by the junta following the invasion. The single-page, typed instrument with the word 'unconditionally' prefacing 'surrender' crossed out and 'Her Britannic Majesty' misspelt as 'Her Brittanic Majesty' was handed to Graham Harding for transmission to London. He dialled and got the usual fax machine operator. Harding had developed an irrational dislike of the man, despite never having set eyes on him; over the course of weeks in their occasional exchanges, his sighing, bored, couldn't-care-less tone grated. Now, as the surrender ticked slowly out of the fax in front of him, he became animated. 'What do I do with this?' he asked. 'Try 10 Downing Street,' retorted Harding, and cut the line.

For the second time, a signal arrived to proceed with all dispatch; San Carlos again. *Canberra* had been on her way back out into the TRALA after the rendezvous with *Hermes*, and the fearsome swell caught her as she turned and set course for the Falklands, the gale howling through her upperworks, flinging sleet at the windows of the bridge and over decks now out of bounds, even with safety harnesses. The generators in the engine room whined ever louder as she wound up to 24 knots, no *Norland* to hamper her speed now, crashing through the waves pounding across her bow as she pitched onwards, her woodwork creaking and groaning. It was going to be an unpleasant night for the 600 on this black, daunting sea.

So be it; the Naval net had given the clearest indication of why *Canberra* was needed in such haste. Nine thousand Argentine prisoners of war were being held at Stanley airport without shelter from the foul weather. There were already exposure cases and every hour brought more; without immediate evacuation, the British forces could face a major medical emergency. She was going to become exactly what Scott-Masson had not wanted, a prisoner-of-war ship.

Here was yet another challenge to the ingenuity; *Canberra* must transform herself once more. Reed and Rudderham sat down and began working out how to accommodate the prisoners. Food would not be a problem; the 10 days in the TRALA had been used to re-stock the ship against the possibility of having to bring troops back aboard to shelter them. Space was the difficulty; as they discussed how many *Canberra* could take, Rudderham sent his bar manager to pace out the public rooms as he calculated how many square feet each prisoner could be allotted. He and Reed were certain about one thing: they could not take 9,000. 'We thought we'd better get a handle on this one quick, before it went up through the Navy and back down again, and we came up with a figure of about 4,000,' said Reed. Perhaps it was discomfiture at his ship having to carry prisoners, or maybe just annoyance at not being consulted about numbers, but Scott-Masson turned on the two officers. 'Maurice got hauled out to go see the captain and he came back very red, and said "Give me a very large drink",' said Reed. 'He said, "I've just been accused of total disloyalty to the command, because I said we couldn't take the prisoners." We never said we couldn't take them, the story had obviously got there the wrong way round. I got hauled out and had the same dressing-down.'

They pressed on nevertheless. Rudderham, the old hand at trooping, saw immediately that the ship had to be stripped of all its remaining soft furnishings. Mattresses and pillows needed to be taken out of cabins before Argentines who had been living in damp, filthy conditions came aboard if they were not to be ruined and unfit for *Canberra*'s lads when she took them home. The prisoners would have to sleep on the bare metal slats of the bunks or the floors; theirs was not going to be a comfortable voyage, but at least they would be warm and fed. Reed mobilised the crew to get every mattress out and forward for storage in the lockers, not an easy task as the ship pitched through the winter night. 'Everything we could think of to move, we stripped out,' he said. 'Then we did the same with the William Fawcett and the Meridian Room.' The ship's company had to move up to C Deck and above, leaving everything below for prisoners; the passageways were busy again, mattresses being hauled about, crew shifting their belongings.

Signals were flashing back and forth constantly now; Lieut-Col Andy Keeling of the Royal Marines was coming aboard as PoW commandant, along with interpreters and a company of Welsh Guards. *Canberra* signalled back; this number of prisoners and the scale of the ship, with its multiple passageways and stairwells, needed more than a single company of men to guard them. Very well, a company of their old friends from 3 Para would also be sent. Work to clear the ship to her most spartan yet continued for much of the night. By morning, the gale had blown itself out, and *Canberra* headed towards San Carlos in bright, bitter weather, teams out on the upper decks with ice scrapers shifting the night's frost as they passed *Uganda* in Falkland Sound. Her crew came to the rails, waving and cheering, and *Canberra* gave them two blasts of her booming whistle in return; no need for stealth now. She was anchored by mid-afternoon, the guardsmen on board. There was another arrival; a short, rotund Swiss representative of the Red Cross to oversee the treatment of the prisoners, Hugo Berchtold, who had been aboard *Uganda* where he was the object of some hilarity, thanks to his imperfect appreciation of the nature and current plight of the Falklands, asking the chief officer to book him a car and a room at the Hilton most convenient for San Carlos. He was, however, charming and helpful, offering genial advice to ensure that the Geneva Convention was adhered to.

Canberra had been darkened by the time the approaching engines of the first landing craft full of prisoners were heard across the calm waters of the anchorage; it emerged out of the dusk, heading for the open galley doors, the faces of 140 men aboard turned upwards, taking in their first sight of the huge white ship as they came alongside. Scrambling nets were down, and they began climbing, bandsmen helping them up as the Welsh Guards, rifles ready, watched for any sudden movement or signs of threat. Soldiers herded the prisoners along the passageway and up to the Promenade Deck, taking it slowly because some limped, grimacing with each step, especially on the stairs. The searching of each man got underway, all of them patted down, their outer garments taken off if necessary. Contraband began to pile up on the deck: bayonets, ammunition, a pistol from what appeared to be a chaplain, spare parts for weapons, eventually enough of them to assemble a machine gun, and food, odd bits of sheep that had been clumsily butchered, some raw and stinking, others blackened from being cooked after a fashion over open fires. Once the Guards were satisfied, the prisoners were taken into the Meridian Room, where trestle tables had been set up, at which sat senior NCOs as well as *Canberra*'s Bureau staff, ready to process them under the guidance of the Red Cross man.

Only now, under the subdued lighting, was it possible to take a proper look at the captives as they were formed up into lines; thin, pinched faces ingrained with dirt below steel helmets that seemed too big, frightened eyes taking in the room and the men and women looking back at them curiously, filthy battledress, some with no socks, a few shifting from foot to foot, wincing with pain, others involuntarily scratching at their groins. A smell began to seep through the room as the men warmed up; stale sweat, but something else too, a musky, earthy undercurrent that set the British sniffing, trying to catch what it was. It struck all of them simultaneously: peat. The paperwork began as each man came forward to the tables; his name, rank, age, regiment. The process had a touch of the absurd. 'They all had to be identified so their details were taken down, their names, and the Red Cross said they had to be labelled,' said Rudderham. 'Well, the only thing we had were P&O baggage labels so they all went off with "Travel P&O", "Cruise the sun" and all this sort of thing – baggage labels as their identification.' The labels were tied to their epaulettes, the different colours for each deck bright against the grimy olive combat jackets.

Medical screening began, and the more the doctors and nurses saw, the grimmer they became; these men were in shocking condition, most apart from the officers malnourished, all caked with dirt. The ones who limped gingerly removed boots to reveal severe cases of trench foot, the flesh dead and white, coming away with socks if they had them or starting to blacken around sores. Some had relatively minor shrapnel injuries, but their treatment had been botched; sepsis was setting in and surgery was needed. 'These butcher surgeons had just stitched anything up,' said Mayner. 'I don't know how many cases of gangrene they would have had if we hadn't opened up so many wounds. The way they had been treated was shameful.' The soldiers scratching themselves had lice around their pubic area, and dozens were suffering from stomach cramps or diarrhoea, possibly as a result of drinking untreated water from streams on the islands, which carried the risk of liver fluke infection. 'They looked pathetic, absolutely pathetic,' said Angela Devine. 'It was like something from the Russian revolution seeing these poor guys, and while we were treating them they had guns trained on them. I found that awful, these poor injured guys with a gun on them.'

They needed food and washing. Ever the cruise ship purser concerned for the welfare of his passengers, whether blue rinses or ravenous prisoners of war, Rudderham had put considerable thought into what to serve. 'We did think "What would they like?" because the Argentinians are very mixed, like us, Italian, German, British, Welsh, various nationalities, but we did think if there was a lot of Italians they might like some of the rice that we had for our Indian crew. So they had been living on lamb, beef and mutton around the Falklands with no other rations, so they fell upon our idea of a nice risotto with fish and rice and tomato, as they thought this was a lovely change.' They were escorted down to the Atlantic Restaurant in batches under guard, and the hot meal dished up on the tin mess trays the Marines and Paras had used, the risotto coming with a bread roll, tea, small bar of chocolate and plastic cutlery so no knives or forks could be secreted as weapons. There was a touch of trademark *Canberra* hospitality; each man was given a cigarette for after his meal. This led to some misunderstanding on the part of at least one green-faced, retching young man. Reed said, 'One poor kid had never smoked in his life, and he came out honking all over the place; he thought he was forced to smoke the cigarette.' Washing needed to be tightly controlled, especially when all 4,000 prisoners came aboard, if *Canberra* was not to run short of water; there was further confusion amongst prisoners jumpy after lectures from their officers about how the British would mistreat them if they were captured. 'We reckoned they could have twenty seconds under the shower each and we wouldn't run out of water,' said Philip Pickford. 'So all the sergeants were lined up at the shower blocks and they had a stopwatch, and they said "You have twenty seconds, starting now" and some of these guys were so traumatised that they'd go under the shower with all their clothes on and come out dripping wet.'

The last of more than 1,000 prisoners from San Carlos were aboard by about 10pm, but processing them continued until the early hours. At first light, *Canberra* weighed anchor and departed for Stanley to pick up the rest, with the frigate *Andromeda* and the destroyer *Cardiff* as escorts. The mountains over which so much blood had been shed in the past days came into view, snow-capped now, as did plumes of smoke from fires. Soon, the crew gathered on deck muffled against the cold for a sight of the capital, more like a village than a city, small, single-storey buildings with red-painted tin roofs, bright in the clear afternoon. *Canberra*'s draught made it too risky to take her all the way in, so she anchored at Port William, a couple of miles north-west. An hour-and-a-half later, as dusk fell, the sound of cheering came from the water, drawing crew back to the rail; C Company of 3 Para, here to help guard the prisoners, delighted at coming back aboard their beloved great white whale.

An exhausting night lay ahead; a biting wind whipped spray into Reed's eyes as he took the first of *Canberra*'s boats towards the dark jetty to start ferrying the prisoners aboard. The blackness was unnerving, Stanley's electricity supply having failed; everything was shadows and silhouettes. The line of prisoners stretching back from the quay as far he could make out in the gloom were more shapes than men, hunched figures with their heads down against the sleet that dripped from their steel helmets or peaked forage caps, sodden woollen blankets wrapped around their shoulders. Along the road from the jetty, British silhouettes; military police guarding heaps of Argentine weapons. Reed and his officers armed themselves with pistols from the stockpile, which made them feel them a little safer. Loading the boats would be difficult enough, but the darkness made it hazardous. A captured Argentine ship was anchored at the end of the jetty, and *Canberra*'s men went aboard. It had a searchlight, and they managed to get it working, which helped as the transfers began, the prisoners moving slowly along the jetty towards the solitary patch of light, each boat filling up and heading away across the choppy water as the weather grew steadily worse. 'I was absolutely frozen,' said Reed. 'It was blinding rain, cleared up, torrential downpour, cleared up, snow, cleared up, sleet, cleared up, and the wind never stopped. I got wind burn on the right cheek, and ever since then if I go out in the sun or the wind, it reddens up and reminds me.' It was even harsher for the men in the boats, soaked by spray as they ferried back and forth. One of *Canberra*'s cadets began to shake uncontrollably as he developed hypothermia, needing to be hospitalised alongside the casualties. Reed imposed a 30-minute limit on men working the boats, the crew revolving between stints in the cruel night and periods back on board to get warm. The line of prisoners seemed never-ending, the fear in their eyes plain under the harsh searchlight. 'These guys were terrified, they all had that wide-eyed look,' said Pickford. 'They thought they were being put on board *Canberra*, taken out to sea and then thrown over the side.' He was lucky; an Argentine major who spoke English was in the line, and Pickford held him back from boarding to translate and soothe anxieties.

Loading continued all night, and as dawn broke the boats were still criss-crossing between the jetty and *Canberra*, fuller now of people than she had ever been. Every square inch was taken; eight crammed into each four-berth cabin, sharing bunks or sleeping on the carpet, jammed shoulder to shoulder in the William Fawcett and Meridian Rooms, every one of them wearing a luggage label, their clothes so dirty that stains were left on whatever they leaned against or sat on. The aroma of peat was over-powering; thousands upon thousands of bodies saturated in it from the moorland and sods cut and burned for warmth or cooking slaughtered sheep. Something else permeated the ship; the sound of thousands of shuffling feet, scuffing and scraping along the hardboard towards the next meal or shower, a constant sandpapering undertone seeping up from the lower decks. The prisoners' bootlaces had been removed, along with their belts, so they could not be used as garrottes or to commit suicide. It also reduced the risk of mutiny against the 200 guards, a meagre force if they were charged; without laces, the Argentines' boots fell off if they walked normally and so they shuffled.

The dangers of a riot had to be taken seriously; there had been trouble ashore late the previous night far back in the queue from the jetty when jeering between islanders and the prisoners developed into scuffles, before a group of Argentines broke free, letting the handbrakes off two vehicles that careered into buildings and set fire to a store that had ammunition inside. Guards also needed to be alert to officers being attacked by their men, as had happened at Stanley airfield where some had been allowed to keep their handguns for personal protection against conscripts seeking revenge for being forced into this vicious war. Those officers probably deserved the hatred directed at them; they had continued to eat well as their men went without rations. As Reed had ashore, Michael Bradford armed himself with a pistol, even though he considered the majority of the prisoners were in no mood for a fight. 'They were young lads who were happy to be out of a terrible war,' he said. His opinion was widely shared. These prisoners were in an even more pitiful state than those taken aboard at San Carlos, gaunt, hollow-cheeked and starving. The cases of trench foot were even worse, the consequence of weeks in the mountains as winter closed in. It was impossible to picture most of them as part of the army that had put up such stiff and costly resistance to the Paras, Marines and Scots Guards in those final, brutal days.

The layer of dirt that covered the faces and matted hair of the youngest gave them the appearance of urchins, an impression reinforced by wide, uncomprehending eyes. The medical team and bandsmen carrying out examinations and searches thought that the weeks past had hardened them to whatever horrors this war could produce; what was becoming apparent, though, was profoundly disturbing. Amongst the soldiers, swamped by uniforms several sizes too big, were boys. 'In some of their packs, we discovered children's crayoning books,' said John Ware. 'These were not soldiers. At one point we discovered some of them had been taken straight out of their classrooms at school and deposited on the Falklands. It was really quite heart-rending. These so-called Argentine soldiers were mainly kids, very young teenagers.' The thought of these starving boys who should have been at home with their families trying to find comfort in colouring books whilst dug into foxholes on frozen mountainsides brought crew to tears. Some had descended into feral behaviour, dropping their trousers and defecating wherever they were, until the guards and older prisoners intervened. Substantial numbers had no idea they were in the Falklands, believing they had been caught up in a border war with Chile. 'You couldn't help but feel sorry for them,' said Sue Wood. 'They were so young; they had clothes that didn't fit them, boots that didn't fit them, no socks, and they'd been made to go; it was just awful.'

Others, though, were more formidable; a hard core of tough, well-trained and professional fighting men who carried themselves with pride, even in defeat. These were the soldiers who had inflicted deaths and injuries on the British. They had the same ailments as the rest, but bore them more stoically because they were altogether more relaxed, knowing they were in the hands of armed forces that did not inflict atrocities on prisoners of war. These men were, however, not well led; the demeanour of some of their officers was so arrogant and aloof that it sparked instant dislike. 'All the officers were concerned about was why they hadn't got a single cabin,' said O'Connell. 'We told them that the ship was designed for 1,500 people, not the numbers that were on board, so be grateful you're here at all.' The officers' dismissive refusal to help with the mammoth task of screening the prisoners led to them being regarded with contempt by the medical team. 'We knew there were a number of doctors on board, and we showed them where the medical facilities were, but they weren't interested,' O'Connell added. 'We relied on a staff sergeant who fortunately spoke English as our main point of contact.'

Communicating with the prisoners threw up surprises. Ware was startled to be accosted in a London accent by a dishevelled prisoner. 'He said, "Here, mate, what am I doing here?" It transpired he was from Enfield, his father was English, his mother Argentinian. The marriage had split up and his mum had taken him back to Argentina, and he'd ended up in the army as a conscript, which was bizarre.'

Sue Wood's husband, Graham, was similarly taken aback as he dished up food. 'All of a sudden he heard this "Alright, mate?" and it was a young lad from Manchester of Argentinian descent who'd gone back to visit relatives and got conscripted into the war,' she said. Guardsmen were thrown by some prisoners speaking to them in Welsh. A quirk of history had seen a ship full of settlers from Wales land in southern Argentina in the 19th century, and their native language had survived in the region. Paras on guard duty in the Meridian Room managed to get their message about not littering across with a dollop of pidgin Spanish, writing on refuse sacks, 'Puto el Rubbisho in el Bags, Rapido'.

Feeding and exercising the prisoners became a non-stop operation. It took between seven and eleven hours to get them all through the Atlantic Restaurant; two meals a day would have to suffice if the cooks were not to be working around the clock. Risotto was abandoned in favour of hot, bulky stodge that could be cooked up easily in huge quantities, like the rice and corned beef served on the morning of the 17th. The food was basic, but filling. Eduardo Ortuondo was a 19-year-old conscript in an infantry regiment: 'For the first time in my life, I had a potato, baked in the oven, wrapped in aluminium foil. On the islands, we had uncovered potatoes when we were digging trenches and ate them raw.' An hour's exercise followed, and once again the Promenade Deck was filled with soldiers, not pounding round for mile after mile this time, but shuffling slowly, the scraping of their boots on the cracked and crumbling decking compounding the damage done by the troops on the way south.

If the ship's company regarded with curiosity the men and boys they had brought troops 8,000 miles to wage war on, the prisoners were no less intrigued by their surroundings. There was a stir aboard each of the boats ferrying them to *Canberra* when her name became visible; the prisoners believed the propaganda that she had been sunk. The absence of malice on the part of the crew and soldiers helped to calm the apprehensions of some as the guards sought to find common ground. 'We got on well with them,' said Ortuondo. 'We got by with a mix of English and Spanish, and we talked about music. I liked Phil Collins and Sting, and so did they.'

Music was also on the mind of Sergio Vainroj, aged 19, whose piano studies at a conservatoire had been interrupted by conscription into an infantry regiment. He had taken his recorder to war with him, to try to cheer his comrades, as well as keep his own spirits up. Vainroj needed all the optimism he could muster; he had lost twelve kilos, not washed in 65 days and watched as wounded men were brought past him from the battles in the mountains, wondering if he would be sent forward to replace them. He could not contain his excitement when he saw the piano in the Meridian Room, and approached a Para on guard asking him with broken English and gestures if he could play. The soldier, amused by this thin, grubby prisoner reeking of peat whose nervousness had vanished at the sight of a piano, nodded and smiled. Vainroj sat down, lifted the lid, rubbed his hands together to warm them and flexed his fingers. 'I started to play Bach, Mozart, Piazolla, the music I knew,' he said. The prisoners sitting cross-legged on the floor all turned towards him, their disbelieving laughter at hearing music in the midst of all this growing louder. The guards grinned too. 'Suddenly a companion shouted to me, "Play the national hymn" and many other voices came, "Play the hymn, play the hymn." As I played the introduction, an officer shouted, "Soldiers, stand up. The national hymn" and 200 soldiers stood up together.' It was doubtful if the Paras recognised the Argentine national anthem, but they knew the threat that a roomful of men suddenly fired up and leaping to their feet represented. Vainroj was hoiked off the piano stool by the soldier who had allowed him to play and dumped on the floor as order was restored.

The last of the prisoners was on board by lunchtime on the 17th. The Red Cross tally was 4,144, of which 40 were classified as 'reserved persons', it not being clear where they fitted in to the Argentine forces. They might have been political officers, special forces or very senior officers who had lied about their rank; the uncertainty meant that they were guarded especially closely. In all, there were 5,400 people aboard, more than twice as many as she had ever carried; once again, she was grossly overloaded. Reed began to worry; *Canberra* simply did not have enough lifeboats or lifejackets. If she was attacked, or fire broke out, and the order to abandon ship given, more than 1,800 people would be going into the icy waters of the South Atlantic without a chance of survival. A signal was sent around the fleet asking for additional lifesaving equipment; the response was negligible, a 25-man liferaft and 100 lifejackets. Officers were faced with an unavoidably callous calculation: if the lives of the ship's company and the embarked military were to be saved, prisoners must die. Once they were in the boats, along with as many Argentines as possible, the guards would have to start massacring captives to give themselves a chance. Orders were not given to that effect, but the soldiers had been briefed about the shortage of lifeboats. They understood what would be necessary. Reed was aghast at what he was thinking.

'I'm still a passenger ship chief officer, I'm not this thing. It was something that I just had to bash on with, even though it's not normal. The guards would be at the stairways bringing the people up from the various cabins and when the time came when there was nothing left except for the guards, then they would have to back out onto the boat deck and get into a boat, hoping that the mad rush of 2,000 people left behind wasn't going to mow them down. You can't say to them, "You will then shoot as many prisoners as you can to block the alleyway," but that's basically what you are going to have to do to get out alive.'

The rest of that day was spent waiting, as the Red Cross attempted to broker a guarantee of safe passage to Argentina and a suitable port was identified. Scott-Masson, Burne and Bradford were discussing possible destinations when Pickford knocked at the captain's cabin door bearing a volume of the *Lloyd's List Ports of the World*, which he had been leafing through on the bridge. A place called Puerto Madryn, on the Patagonian coast in the southern province of Chubut, had caught his attention; an aluminium smelting town, close to the heartland of Argentina's population of Welsh ancestry. 'It had the right depth of water, a good port for bulk carriers and we could go alongside,' he said. 'It's also out of the way of Buenos Aires, because for a ship to go into one of their big ports and land a defeated army would be political suicide, but this would suit the Argentinians because it was very remote and we could get them ashore very quietly.'

He was not to know it, but *Canberra* was bringing at least some of her prisoners full circle; a few miles south of Puerto Madryn, Argentine marines had rehearsed the invasion of the Falklands because of the coastline's similarity to that around Stanley. The command team immediately recognised the port's merits; so did the Red Cross and Buenos Aires, where the junta was crumbling. Crowds that gathered outside the presidential palace to cheer Galtieri after the invasion had returned, this time chanting, 'Son of a whore', as the doors to the balcony where he had basked in the acclaim remained shut. On the 17th, he was forced to resign as president and head of the army. The price of his hubris had been terrible: 255 British dead, 655 Argentine, hundreds more wounded. His fall prompted a few scuffles amongst the prisoners, in which conscripts attacked hard-line officers and NCOs who had preached the junta's greatness at them from the moment they were forced into uniform. The guards let them get a punch in and then stamped out the trouble. The next morning, Argentina guaranteed the Red Cross safe passage for *Canberra*.

She sailed early in the cold, bright afternoon of the 18th, large sheets of canvas with the letters POW painted on them fixed to her rails, and a trail of debris littering her wake when she reached the open sea; helmets, webbing, bootlaces and heavy blankets, foul from being huddled under for weeks, taken from the prisoners and dumped over the side by the bandsmen, the trappings of a beaten army stretching away for miles astern, buoyant for a while as their spirits had been after the invasion, before being swallowed by the South Atlantic. There was a touch of apprehension within the ship's company; they were not worried about the passage to Puerto Madryn, reasoning that the 4,000 prisoners aboard kept them safe from attack, but betrayal on the return journey. *Canberra* was now classified as a 'cartel ship', unheard of in modern warfare, giving her inviolable status to pass between belligerent nations. Even so, there was concern that rogue elements within Argentina might try to launch a last, spectacular blow against Britain, as the World Service told of a country in turmoil, consumed by injured pride, public fury being directed at the Argentine Navy for failing to join the war after the *Belgrano* was sunk, hawkish voices urging the nation to fight on. The medical staff also worried about what would happen to their patients. Some, like the double amputee, remained very frail and in need of specialist care. Those who worked in the hospital, staff and volunteer alike, had redoubled their efforts, securing them better food than the rest of the prisoners to try to build up their strength. Whilst thousands shuffled towards the galley for a gloopy dollop of rice and corned beef, the patients had been given sausage, egg and chips; tonight, their last aboard, they were having steak.

Possibly the most bizarre order of the entire Falklands campaign was issued as *Canberra* entered Argentina's territorial waters at about 10am on the 19th. 'There was to be no whistling or singing of "Don't Cry for Me, Argentina",' said Graham Harding. 'We were warned very firmly that if there was, there'd be trouble and we'd be on a charge.' Everything possible was being done to demonstrate that *Canberra* came in peace; at her masthead, in keeping with Merchant Navy custom of flying a courtesy ensign on entering foreign ports, was the flag of Argentina, albeit one

265

captured in Port Stanley. The morning was glorious; cloudless and so sunny that for the first time in what felt like months, those on deck could feel warmth on their backs. Away on the port horizon, there was a plume of smoke. A call came in, 'Canberra, Canberra, this is Argentine destroyer D2 – over', the voice speaking perfect English with a light American accent. A polite acknowledgement went back, with the enquiry if the warship would prefer to speak Spanish, an offer declined with equal politeness.

She gradually came into view, which caused a stir on the bridge; a sister ship to the doomed HMS *Sheffield*, a Type 42 destroyer built at Barrow-in-Furness, painted not in battleship grey but as white as *Canberra* once had been. Muxworthy noted that the Spanish-speaking Lieutenant-Commander Bill O'Shaughnessy who had come aboard at Port William recognised her as the *Santissima Trinidad*; only months before as the junta laid its invasion plans, she had visited Portsmouth where he had been her liaison officer. The courteous radio exchanges continued as he asked after officers he knew, as the destroyer took up station half-a-mile away and escorted *Canberra* through the sweeping bay towards the long wharf at which no other vessel lay. Stretching back along its three-quarter mile length towards the shore was a line of lorries and ambulances. She came alongside for the first time since Sierra Leone as Argentine seamen scurried to secure her lines; her gangways were down by 2.15pm, and the formalities began.

The Argentine reception committee of several dozen officers and a group of Red Cross officials was headed by a white-haired, hatchet-faced general in sunglasses and immaculately pressed olive battledress. Burne welcomed him aboard. 'I thought we might as well be civilised – war's war, and now we're getting over it,' he said. 'I was giving him coffee in the cabin I used, and he kept looking around saying, "Where's all the damage?" which corroborated that they had gone for *Canberra*.' Burne offered a tour of the ship, which the general accepted, the hatchet face growing longer as it became clear that she was intact; evidently, the junta's propaganda had been swallowed by even very senior officers. The first Argentines disembarked were the most seriously wounded from the hospital, unloaded through the sea doors and taken to ambulances under Red Cross supervision. Rosie Elsdon watched sadly: 'Some of them were really badly injured and would need months of specialised care, and I was thinking they weren't going to get that. If they'd been brought back to Britain they'd have had really good medical care.' Happily, her concerns proved to be unfounded; the men were well looked after. The young soldier who had lost his legs and came so close to dying survived, his life ending as a result of a car crash a decade later.

The walking wounded went next, being helped down the gangway, at the top of which Burne shook each man's hand. The special forces lieutenant had thawed to the extent that he smiled and exchanged a few words of cordial farewell; he even clutched a souvenir, a *Canberra* menu card bearing a picture of the ship and the signatures of the doctors, nurses and volunteers who had looked after him and made him eat his All-Bran. The prisoners began to shuffle towards the exits, saying their own goodbyes to the guards, who had established a good rapport with them. In the William Fawcett Room an Argentine sergeant major got to his feet and thanked the Paras for the fairness they had shown. Many grabbed menu cards as keepsakes as they left, waving goodbye, the luggage labels on their shoulders fluttering in the breeze as they stepped back onto home soil. The white-haired general greeted those coming off, but then tired of it. 'He went and stood by the gangway and kissed some of them and shook hands, but then after the first 50 he pissed off,' said Muxworthy. 'We felt sorry for them: there they were, beaten, bloody glad to be home, and there was nobody there, no families, no publicity; their general had lost interest and buggered off, and they're just trooping away to these lorries.'

There was a last glimpse of the enmity between some of the officers and their men. 'A squaddie was detailed to carry an officer's bag for him,' said O'Connell. 'He followed the officer along the jetty to the far side and then chucked the bag in the water, and all the ship's company gave an almighty cheer.' The disembarkation continued quietly but steadily, all pretence of welcoming the troops back to Argentina abandoned now as each man reached the bottom of the gangway and made his way towards a truck where there was a space. One of the last men off was Milton Rhys, a 20-year-old teacher from the Welsh-speaking town of Trelew, not far from Puerto Madryn, who had acted as an interpreter. Burne said, 'I thanked him, and he said, "Oh, I may see you again, I'm off to Cardiff University next year," which I thought was a nice touch.' Within three hours, they were all gone, the trucks heading towards the shore, the men on them looking back towards the big, rusty cruise ship that had brought them home as they wondered what awaited in the country at the end of the jetty. The Argentine general reappeared and came back aboard to sign the Red Cross documentation certifying that the prisoners had been handed over. The formalities were brief; ten minutes later, as he adjusted his sunglasses and was driven away in the wake of the trucks, *Canberra* was getting ready to sail. The *Santissima Trinidad* waited in the bay to escort her. The polite and subdued mood of the Argentines at Puerto Madryn had eased fears of an attack; they showed no aggression or appetite for a fight. Even so, she remained on alert as land slipped away over the horizon and the destroyer turned back at the limit of Argentina's territorial waters.

The prisoners had left calling cards; as portholes were opened to blow away the now-fading smell of peat and the crew set about cleaning the ship, they were touched to find dozens of notes in cabins, on menu cards, odd scraps of paper, luggage labels. All said the same thing: thank you. There was another memento, testament to an admirable resourcefulness amongst the Argentines determined to take advantage of this oddest of floating prisoner-of-war camps; a collection of empty champagne bottles. The night before arriving at Puerto Madryn, a stern but baffled sergeant major appeared on the bridge where Pickford was officer of the watch. 'He said, "I've got a very disturbing report, sir." Oh, yes? "All the prisoners are f**king pissed."' Nobody could fathom how it had happened; the smelly, underfed men settling down for the night on the floor of the Meridian Room were the happiest they had been in weeks. Rudderham found the answer. At the forward end of the lounge was the Century Bar, one side of which had been partially hidden from the guards. There was a seven-inch gap between the top of the locked shutters and the ceiling; being half-starved at last had its uses. One of the prisoners managed to wriggle through the gap; inside, he found an unlocked cabinet full of half-bottles of champagne, which were passed out, passed round, and then put back. It was the perfect crime. 'We all took our hats off to them,' added Pickford. 'Good on them.'

A rather more unpleasant reminder of the prisoners was the stomach bug many had been suffering from. The bandsmen, in close proximity as guards and medical orderlies, had picked it up. Against his better judgement, John Ware was persuaded to give a concert as *Canberra* headed back to Port William: 'Every time I looked around, one of the musicians would be diving out to the loo in the middle of one of the pieces. I can't say it was the best concert we ever gave, but we managed it.' The Paras were also feeling the effects of the last few days, following on from the horrors of Mount Longdon and the march into Stanley. They were utterly exhausted, collapsing gratefully into cabins, many sleeping for much of the journey back. *Canberra* was spotless again by the time she anchored late on Sunday the 20th, prepared to embark more prisoners. The new week dawned cold and clear, and with it came the best possible news: she did not have to return to Argentina. She was going home, and taking her lads with her.

CHAPTER FOURTEEN

Bringing Her Children Home

NICK VAUX SMILED as she came into view from the helicopter, rustier, dirtier, more salt-encrusted than when he had seen her last, on May 21, looking back from the landing craft as the waters of San Carlos erupted around her and wondering how she could possibly survive. The women assistant pursers who had seen him off that day were waiting, doing their best – and failing – not to blanch at how badly he smelled. 'I walked into that immaculate entrance and the same girls came out and said, "Oh, how wonderful", and gave me a great hug, and I could see them recoiling.' He had been touched to find a letter from one of them hoping that 42 Commando had not suffered too many casualties waiting for him when his men arrived in Stanley. Vaux made his way up to C Deck, and along to his cabin; all was exactly as he had left it, clean, tidy, his clothes packed away. Except there, on the table by the window, were cards and a bottle of champagne with a note welcoming him back from Geoffrey, the steward from the Crow's Nest, who had drawn him aside to wish him well on D-Day. 'I looked round and thought, "You're back, and you're going back to England in this wonderful cabin" and I couldn't think of a better conclusion to the war.' Vaux opened the bottle and finished it as he stayed in the shower until the smell of the last 30 days had gone.

Mattresses and pillows were being moved back into cabins in readiness for the soldiers. The ship's company had shaken off its fatigue, the announcement that they were going home freeing them to celebrate after their cautiousness over the surrender. 'There were lots of smiles, whereas they were few and far between before that,' said Reed. 'The low spot was

270

being told we were going to get prisoners, but the high spot was being told, "That's it, go and pick the troops up".' A debate was underway within the military over which units she should carry. All aboard *Canberra* hoped for the same men who had come south, but then word came that 3 Para would not be among them. They were sailing for Ascension with 2 Para aboard *Norland*, and then flying back to Britain. *Canberra* would embark her lads from 40 and 42 Commando, plus 45 Commando. It was disappointing; the buzz claimed worries over scrapping as the reason; traditional rivalry between Marines and Paras, held in check on the way to war by a common enemy, might result in fighting now that it was over. In reality, the Parachute Regiment, which had suffered the worst losses of the land battles, wanted its men to return together so there could be a co-ordinated reception with the families in Aldershot. Even so, both Marine and Para commanders greeted the decision with a degree of relief that any potential flashpoints had been avoided. The Paras, raw from their losses, were tense and angry; the two battalions, 40 dead between them, brawled aboard *Norland* on the way to Ascension.

John Ware's thoughts turned to bringing the Marines back aboard with a flourish. He went ashore to 3 Brigade headquarters with the suggestion that the band played them through Stanley. The idea was rejected. As he returned to the jetty, Ware met Captain Peter Babbington with K Company of 42 Commando. 'You could see that they were still very disciplined, but very tired, there wasn't a spring in their step. Peter said if they'd had the band in front that would have been fabulous, their shoulders would have been up, their heads high, and I should just have done it without telling anyone.' Stanley was off-limits to all but a handful on official business from *Canberra*; it had been judged too hazardous for civilians. Piles of captured weapons and ammunition were everywhere, debris littered the streets and basic services including sanitation and electricity were failing. Landmines posed another risk; after the fighting had ceased, a British major's vehicle had been blown up, breaking his back. He was brought aboard *Canberra* for the journey home. The last thing the military needed was sight-seeing crew from a cruise ship, and so for most, the nearest they came to the islands they had sailed 8,000 miles to help liberate was standing at their ship's rails, gazing across the anchorage towards the moors and mountains. A few made it ashore, officially or otherwise. Scott-Masson and Bradford went for a look round when the prisoners were being embarked, and Devine and Elsdon visited the field hospital at Ajax Bay, where they found the medics who had trained them in preparation for the casualties of war grey with fatigue and somehow older. One of the least official landings was by Leslie Jenkins, the shop manager, determined to see Stanley after coming halfway round the world. He hitched a lift aboard a boat and after walking around the battered capital went into the Upland Goose Hotel, where he was greeted with surprise by Jeremy Hands of ITN. As they talked, Jenkins told him how annoyed the ship's company still were at the fuss made over *QE2* at home. 'He said to me, "Don't you worry about a thing, you've seen nothing yet." He said we'd get the most spectacular welcome there has ever been in Southampton.'

On the 23rd, *Canberra*, with most of 42 aboard, sailed to San Carlos to collect 40 Commando from their positions defending the anchorage, an operation officers thought would take the whole of the next day. They were all aboard by lunchtime, neither flagging nor pausing for a second in their desire to escape the cold and damp, scrambling up the nets and through the sea doors, clattering delightedly through the familiar passage-ways towards allotted cabins, laughing and greeting crew who tried to hide their anxiety as they watched for familiar faces. They were hoping that men with whom they had become friends were not among the dead or injured. 'There was one young lad who I'd really got to know, and I only knew him as Bud,' said Sue Wood. 'He was only about 17, and I'll never forget that when I saw him and he looked at me, I just said, "It's good to see you" and I couldn't say anything else.'

The return of the Marines further lifted the crew's spirits; it was good to hear their chatter in the bars where that evening they downed their two cans, to see the Atlantic Restaurant filling up with men in buoyant mood instead of frightened prisoners. As they ate, *Canberra* sailed back to Port

William to embark her remaining passengers. Friday 25 June was even colder than the day when she had taken the Argentines aboard, a cruel wind once more soaking the boats in freezing spray; as before, Reed had to rotate his crews to minimise the risk of exposure. Graham Harding watched as men came aboard, rubbing their hands and stamping their feet after the transfer from the shore; each saying the same thing as they felt the shelter of *Canberra* embrace them, 'Oh, it's warm.' The flight decks were as busy as on D-Day, helicopters shuttling constantly, lifting men, stores and gear aboard as the line at the jetty gradually diminished, those waiting their turn warming themselves against the blustery squalls with the thought that every boatload away brought them a few minutes closer to home. Burne was scrutinising the arrivals by helicopter from the bridge wing, now and then ordering the master-at-arms to investigate if he suspected a stowaway. A passage on *Canberra* had not been as eagerly sought since her maiden voyage, and there were a few who chanced their arm in getting on board without permission, gambling that once she put to sea little could be done about it. They reckoned without Burne's eye for the shifty and his alacrity in sending them straight back ashore. One of them turned out to be Ewen Southby-Tailyour, and even this distinguished officer who had contributed so much to the success of the campaign faced expulsion until Vaux intervened on his behalf. Burne acted from the best of motives; *Canberra* had been grossly overloaded on her way to the Falklands, and the number of prisoners aboard on the way to Puerto Madryn might have resulted in a bloodbath in the case of fire or attack. He said, 'With the war over, there was no point taking unnecessary risks by overloading the ship beyond the limits of our lifesaving capacity, and P&O were keen on that, too.'

The strangest arrival was *Canberra*'s solitary cruise passenger. Jack Abbott was a widowed 78-year-old retired trapper, who had resolutely refused to budge from his wooden bungalow in Stanley even though artillery shells screamed overhead and Argentine troops had ransacked it when he ventured out one afternoon to his only remaining neighbour for a cup of tea. His was a lonely war; in his isolation, watching a video of the Royal wedding between Prince Charles and Princess Diana amidst the overturned furniture had been a comfort, at least when the electricity was on. When it was not, he reflected on the apparent happiness of the young couple as reassurance that the proper order of things would surely be restored. He had been due to fly to Britain to visit his three sons two days after the invasion, and upon hearing that *Canberra* had been requisitioned wrote to P&O expressing his confidence in a British victory and his wish to sail aboard her. Somehow, the letter found its way through the tortuous postal chain to London in time.

Derek Hudson, of the *Yorkshire Post*, had been aboard with three other journalists in the hope of securing berths, only to be told the ship was full. His consolation was an invitation to a 42 Commando celebration at which upturned Argentine helmets were being used as ice buckets for the rationed beer. Producing a bottle of whisky made Hudson especially popular as the mood swung from raucous, to sombre, to sentimental. The bastardised version of 'Summer Holiday' was sung, there was remembrance of the lost, and the National Anthem. Best of all was a warm comradeship. 'I was very touched when two of the Marines gave me a miniature *Canberra* lifebelt from the souvenir shop that they had customised into a 40 and 42 Commando Falklands Task Force memento,' Hudson recalled. '"Hang onto it," said one of the pair, "You've been through the same as we have." Not quite, I thought, but it was a much appreciated kindness. And I did hang onto it.' Only one reporter, John Shirley, would sail with the Marines. *The Sunday Times* was producing a book about the war, and asked if he was willing to make the voyage in order to gather as much information as possible, arriving home much later than the other journalists, who were flown back. He said, 'I'd lost a lot of weight, about two-and-a-half stone. I was very tired indeed; I hadn't got family to go back to, my girlfriend was speaking to me again but it wasn't a big deal, and I liked the idea of taking two weeks sailing home, eating some decent steaks and it would be a great place to get a story.'

Throughout the day, *Canberra*'s showers were in constant use as men sluiced away the stench of foxholes, trenches, yomping and battle, lingering and luxuriating under the first hot water they had felt in weeks. 'From the minute I landed to the minute I got back on board, I was cold and wet,' said Chris Sheppard. 'I stank to the skin. When I took my clothes off, they all smelt of piss and shit, so I had a good wash and fortunately they had very good washing machines on board and I threw everything in.' There were 2,500 troops all doing the same thing. *Canberra*'s water consumption shot up. 'Blokes were so pleased to stand under a shower that they just stood there and stood there,' said Reed. 'Clear running water was such a wonderful thing that they weren't turning off taps or showers, the daily consumptions went potty, and we had to shout at them quite often. We had to persuade them to take it easy. If you can make water that's fine, but if the making system goes wrong, then we're buggered.' Getting clean was part of a readjustment to normality; men found that the smallest of everyday things had become novel, even alien, after a month at war. Sheppard said, 'My big thing was that I sat down on a chair, and it was a really nice experience, just sitting on a chair felt really good.' In common with many others conditioned to living in a dugout, he found it initially hard to settle in a bed with a mattress, tired as he was; it was just too comfortable. The warmth of the ship, despite being so welcome after the bleakness of rain, sleet and snow, caused unexpected problems. 'All our feet were badly damaged,' added Sheppard, 'and as they got warm in bed, they started hurting. The cold had kept them a bit dead from the pain.' K Company was suffering particularly severely. The freezing conditions had damaged the feet of nearly every man; small wonder that there was little spring in their step when Ware met them in Stanley. Concern over possible long-term effects led the Navy to fly specialists on board at Ascension to carry out examinations. Bungy Williams said, 'They were doing tests on us for how long it took for the feeling to return to them after being frozen, and it was taking four or five times as long as it would for a normal person. A lot of people were in a lot of pain with their feet when we got back on.' The compensations of being back, though, far outweighed the discomfort. Tin trays were mopped clean in the Atlantic Restaurant as men who had lived on ration packs wolfed down hot food and fresh bread rolls by the basketful.

The entry in the deck log yearned for for weeks was made at 5.22pm. *Canberra* weighed anchor and got underway for home. There were no fanfares or cheering send-offs; nobody was out there to wave goodbye as the wind drove rain across the decks and down the windows of the bridge, the night too black and overcast to see the mountaintops where friends had fallen, though lights were visible from the tin-roofed buildings they had climbed the slopes to reclaim. That first black night when she had crept into San Carlos seemed both an age ago, yet vivid; the howl of jets bearing down still sounded in their minds tonight, when all they could actually hear was the sea and the rain as the Falklands slipped away. In the darkness ahead, they could picture *Ardent* burning herself out, in the chill wind feel the cold of South Georgia, in the fading aroma of uniforms being stripped and washed, scent the frightened boys they had taken home. The clatter of helicopters all day had evoked thoughts of men pallid with pain being winched down to hospital, the throb of the landing craft the hours when they watched a clearing sky and willed nightfall to come. Hardly any aboard, irrespective of uniform, had known anything of these islands at the turn of the year; now, as they left them behind with dead comrades who had shared the surprise at how familiar they seemed, their mark would remain always. *Canberra*'s course was eastwards, a final precaution against the now extremely unlikely possibility of attack, taking her beyond the reach of even the longest-range Argentine aircraft, before turning north. Admiral Sandy Woodward summed up all she had done as he signalled his congratulations.

'Very much regret I was unable to visit in the general exodus to say goodbye personally. P and O service as an LPH [Landing Platform (Helicopter)], floating Harley Street, maritime Wormwood Scrubs, and great survivor of San Carlos Bay, was in the true style. Well done. Bon Voyage Great White Whale.'

There were echoes of the Easter weekend when she had left Britain in the days that followed. Men found their way about the ship once more and the commanding officers of the three units discussed how to occupy them. 'We had an early conference to decide how we were going to run this show,' said Vaux. 'One was conscious that there had to be a certain discipline because otherwise the whole thing would unravel very quickly, we could have problems with girls and particularly with alcohol. You could also have problems if we said we're not going to do anything, that would have been a mistake, so it was decided that we would have the minimum amount of restrictions on what you couldn't do, one of them being you couldn't have unlimited drink in the men's canteens. We also decided we must have some sort of mustering of people each day and a programme of some sort; the whole idea was to say you've done a really good job, we want you to relax and enjoy the voyage home.'

The crew smiled and exchanged glances as they heard the thud-thud-thud of feet pounding the Promenade Deck once more, no longer with the relentless lockstep that made the upperworks tremble, nor the heavy thump of men running in boots and full fighting order, but a gentler, more relaxed drumming as the men jogged, enjoying their training sessions. They were keen to stay in shape. 'Nobody wanted to look like a lard-arse when we got back,' said Lou Armour. 'Everybody wanted to look fit for the birds.' The correspondence with girls who had written to the soldiers held out the prospect of the happiest of leaves. Men had thoughtfully daubed their letters with Falklands mud or a smear of blood to emphasise the privations of combat and how much in need of comfort they were at its end; the promise of it came in the next mail drop. Armour was typical of many of the troops; he had seven penfriends and photos of them all. One would be waiting to meet *Canberra* when she docked, another in Berkshire counted the days until he reached her, a third in Kent made arrangements to take time off work so she could devote herself to soothing the scars of battle, and a fourth in Yorkshire had bought tickets for a Rolling Stones concert. He needed to be as fit as possible when he got back to Britain.

The band played night and day, after fulfilling what Ware had tallied as 39 different roles. Music filled the ship as it gave concerts and small groups split off to tour the decks and bars, getting sing songs going and accompanying men who got up to perform. They played at the smokers each commando held, and for a Naval tradition, a 'Sods Opera', in which the men took the mickey out of each other, their officers, and 40 Commando, which was mercilessly ribbed about not moving from the landing grounds at San Carlos.

There was a touch of overgrown schoolboy high jinks about it all; a competition to eat the most plum duff, won by the band's bass player, George Tate, who forced down 14 helpings, and a ship's electrical officer called to free 20 hulking Marines from a jammed lift with a capacity of 12, the men tumbling out in fits of laughter. Efforts to outwit restrictions on drink were as vigorous as ever and Muxworthy worried about running out. His concern was not eased when a consignment of beer was airlifted aboard and soldiers helped load it into a lift to take it below: 'I saw one load go in and watched the lights on the lift go one, two, three, three, three, three, four, five. They were stopping it and chucking off boxes for their lads. I should have seen it coming.' One of two buoys in the Crow's Nest took the fancy of the brigade air squadron after a glass too many. They decided to present it to Brigadier Julian Thompson as a mark of respect. It was half the height of a man and twice as bulky; after wrestling it down the stairs, and, convulsed with laughter, getting wedged in a passageway, they abandoned it dented on the flight deck at 2am. Reed established who the ringleader was, and called him in. His war had seen him constantly in danger; at its end, he found himself being ticked off like a naughty fourth-former. He had the good manners to keep a straight face as the chief officer raged. 'I had the hero of the whole bloody thing in front of my desk, giving him this mammoth bollocking, and afterwards he marched out. He'd been risking his life for months and I was tearing him off about nicking a buoy. I went outside and he's collapsed against the wall, doubled up laughing, and he said, "That's the funniest thing I have ever seen, you being so f**king angry." We've stayed friends ever since.' Buzzes came and went: *Canberra* was heading for Spain so they could go to the World Cup final; she would stop at the Canary Islands; there was definitely going to be shore leave in Gibraltar.

The laughter, the wheezes, the sing songs masked some fragile emotions. Men found themselves unexpectedly and easily moved to tears; a letter or a record over the loudspeakers could do it. A certain trigger was the Rod Stewart song 'Sailing', with its words about going home, which was played often. Evenings drew gatherings of soldiers to the bows where they quietly stood, just looking ahead over the empty sea towards home, remaining until darkness fell. Marines still in their teens who had seen more suffering than most lifetimes bring went over and over what they had done and witnessed, their comrades listening until it was all talked out, nothing left bottled up; the time and space of sailing 8,000 miles proving invaluable in reconciling themselves to all that had happened. Everybody needed to talk; as on the way south, the hospital was a magnet for those popping in ostensibly for a coffee and a chat. Its doctors and nurses knew what over-bright smiles hid, and had learned how to listen. Some were agonised. Reed was alerted to a young medic the crew had found hopelessly drunk in the middle of the night on more than one occasion. He asked to see him, gently pointing out that they were worried he might come to harm, even go overboard. An appalling story emerged; the doctor had been among those treating Guardsmen brought out of the inferno aboard *Galahad* after she was bombed. Every man he came to died. His fate brought him those beyond help, as around him colleagues saved lives. 'He couldn't cope with this, had this horrific guilt complex, thought he was the kiss of death,' said Reed. 'It was a huge problem for him and the only way he could get round it was by drinking himself to sleep and he'd wake up in the middle of the night and stagger about, not knowing where he was.' Reed listened to another doctor. He had worked at Ajax Bay, where an unexploded bomb was lodged in the building. The thought of it gnawed at him until his nerve went in the middle of an operation and he fled outside; he did the bravest thing of all in returning and continuing, but was nevertheless consumed by shame that fear had overtaken him.

Morgan O'Connell was kept busy. 'Sometimes a junior officer would just sidle up saying they wanted to talk to me about two or three of their men, but would end up talking about themselves. I think it was because on the way down, they had already got used to the shrink, he didn't have two heads and didn't have a paddy wagon waiting to cart them away and he wasn't going to prescribe major tranquilisers, so most of what I did was listening. There was none of the depressive symptoms that one would expect; there was a lot of anger and guilt, and, "If there's a God, why was this allowed to happen?" Then, as we got closer to home, "What would the people there be like?" Because we had changed, we presumed they had too and what would it be like to be home? Many of us, the one thing we didn't want was a great big party, we just wanted to go home and shut the front door and maybe a week later have the party, but for the first 24 to 48 hours we just wanted to be at home with the ones nearest and dearest to us, and in our own time start to tell them how much we wanted them to know about it.' O'Connell saw in both the Marines running the Promenade Deck and the P&O crew moving back into cruise ship service people taking comfort from routine and using it to readjust to normality.

Vaux and his fellow commanding officers could see their men dealing with the psychological consequences of fighting this war, and gave thanks for the decision that had brought them back aboard *Canberra*. 'This period was the best thing that could have happened,' he said. 'There was no post-traumatic stress in 40 or 42 Commando. The reason was we had three weeks of chilling out, having the chance to just relax and talk about things, and there were band concerts and company banyans, which just released all the tensions.' His officers, close anyway, savoured each other's company; they knew that when they arrived back, other postings awaited. 'It was the last time we'd all be together so we made a lot of that. I've heard other units say that 42 officers were very group-ish on the way back, and if we were, that's why. We just made the most of the success and our own company before it came to an end.'

The P&O crew showed little sign of stress beyond a few incidents of drunkenness. People were sleeping again and talking about having 'the channels'; off duty, they kept their own company, fond as they were of the Marines. *Canberra* was home and their friends a family, with all the kindnesses and quarrels that brought; they understood closeness in that controlled, hierarchical world below decks. The ship herself was returning to what she knew; as June turned to July, and the jagged peak of Ascension came over the horizon, sunshine brightened her grubby public rooms as the blackout canvas was torn down and dumped over the side, another trapping of war discarded to sink in her wake like the prisoners' blankets and bootlaces. Her lights shone over the sea as they were meant to; the crew were back in whites and shorts, the heavy woollens and waterproofs of days scraping ice and nights alert for a dash to the lifeboats packed away. The Marines stripped down to swimming trunks, sending the camper stewards into a swoon, and sprawled everywhere to sunbathe; on top of the chacons, in whatever space they could find on the Sun Deck, around the Alice Springs Pool, on the small flight deck forward of the funnels, getting a tan for the birds waiting for them; reading, dozing, talking it out.

Spoof memos and cartoons began appearing outlining proper procedures for lying in the sun; badges of rank must be worn on the trunks, and nobody below lieutenant-commander to use chairs with striped upholstery. A ship full of sunbathers, even lying out on salty, rusty cargo containers instead of loungers, was familiar, and looking after them fulfilling. Rudderham, biding his time and holding back stores left aboard for cruising until exactly the right moment, produced tubs of ice cream. The men laughed delightedly as they were handed out, sitting up cross-legged as they ate raspberry ripple or mint choc chip with the wooden spatulas that came with it, another step towards normal life. More guests were arriving, and *Canberra* would make sure they were as pampered as if she was newly out of Southampton. As she passed Ascension, John Turner flew aboard with two Ministry of Defence officials to carry out an inspection of the ship. 'Not only did I get a decent cabin, it was decked out in exactly the same way as it would have been when cruising,' he said. 'The bed was turned down, the lights were dimmed and there were some drinks there and chocolates. The standards had been maintained even in those circumstances, which was remarkable.' Rudderham conjured even more from stores loaded at Naples. Waiters back to their poised best in the Pacific Restaurant took evident pleasure in serving smoked salmon, venison, turkey and pheasant, the reaction of the officers not so very different from men with reddening shoulders finishing their ice cream as the sun set.

A party of entertainers sent by P&O also arrived at Ascension; evenings began to take on the flavour of a voyage through the Mediterranean as singers and dancers staged shows. Scott-Masson gathered his crew together for drinks to thank them for all they had done and braved; they gave him three cheers. They cheered an old friend as well: *Elk*, who had shared so much with them. She fired off flares and a volley from her Bofors gun in salute as *Canberra* passed; in reply, the defence teams returned to the GPMGs on the bridge wings and fired the last shots of her war into the air. Countless other weapons were aboard; pistols looted from prisoners and the stockpiles at Stanley as souvenirs. The order was issued that under no circumstances must these guns be taken back to Britain, and an amnesty declared. Hundreds appeared from the recesses of packs where they had been hidden, and thrown overboard from the Promenade Deck. The men would have to make do with Argentine helmets as keepsakes.

Turner and the MoD men found a ship battered but in remarkably good condition given that by the time of her scheduled arrival in Britain she would have been at sea for 94 days with no shore support. The only mechanical defect was the failure of one of her stabilisers. There was, though, evidence of how overloaded she had been; a twisting of her steel was visible at the same point throughout several decks. Once the landing pads were removed and the chacons unloaded from the Sun Deck, complete refurbishment would be required. Soldiers hauling packs and weapons through her passageways had left bulkheads and woodwork scuffed; despite the hardboard to protect her flooring, new carpets would have to be laid throughout. A decision on what furniture could be salvaged must wait until it was cleaned and examined. Fumigation was also recommended because of the state of the prisoners. New washing machines were needed after the onslaught of Marines cleaning their kit; engineers had deployed all their ingenuity in cannibalising failing machines to keep others going, but the wreckage was accumulating on deck, to be chucked over the side as the coast of England neared. The survey confirmed what had been obvious since before *Canberra* reached Ascension on the way south; the Promenade Deck had to be completely relaid.

There was a discussion about how to commemorate her service in the war, Turner writing in his report, 'We, in the end, rejected the renaming of rooms (San Carlos Bar and Island Room becoming Falkland Islands Room) on the grounds of the sensitivity of the Latin temperament and our regular calls in Spain and Italy. However, it was agreed that a small museum on board containing memorabilia would be appropriate.' The astonishing scale of her achievement in carrying an army to war, the men it defeated home and then the victors back to Britain was becoming apparent, as well as the sheer hard work the ship's company had put into looking after them. Rudderham, deputy purser Nigel Horn and ship's accountant Helen Hawkett compiled a list of the food and drink used, noted by Muxworthy. The galley had turned out 646,000 meals, going through 65 tons of meat and 17 of fish, 11 tons of eggs and 74 of potatoes, blackened or otherwise. Some 660lb of instant coffee had been used and 38,750 sachets of tea, each of which made half a gallon, some of the 10 tons of sugar consumed being stirred into those hot drinks. And then, of course, there was the beer – 460,000 cans or pints of it drunk by men who had followed the rules or found a way round them, in bars as they sang along to the bandies or in the smoky fug of jammed cabins on the lower decks turned into speakeasies.

A fractious exchange of signals had passed between *Canberra* and Northwood over where she would dock. The MoD ordered her to Plymouth, close to the Marines' bases, a decision that caused exasperation. She was too big to go alongside there; getting the returning troops off would be a major exercise involving boats. 'The reality was that every single Royal Marine wanted to go back to Southampton,' said Vaux. 'Everybody knew that if we disembarked in Plymouth it would be disorganised and we'd have to get off in landing craft. Having seen the departure from Southampton, everybody knew that was where we should return.' The ministry was not budging, even in the face of a signal from Julian Thompson emphasising the closeness between 3 Brigade and *Canberra* and the wish of all aboard to return to her home port. Abruptly, without explanation, the MoD changed their minds; to the relief of all, Southampton it would be.

They had little idea what to expect when she arrived there. A suspicion lurked in their minds that *QE2* had claimed all the glory for the merchant ships of the task force. Even the arrival of television crews and reporters by helicopter for her last night at sea failed to persuade many that her welcome would not match the fervour of her send-off. 'Because we'd been so preoccupied with the operation, we knew no more than that the nation was supportive,' recalled Vaux. 'We had absolutely no idea of what was in store. I was interviewed, and the reporter kept saying to me, "I suppose you're really excited about coming into Southampton," and I said, "Well of course we are, because our families are going to be there," and at the end, she said, "I don't think you quite understand what's waiting in Southampton".'

After three months that had changed them forever, the men who gathered at the bows to gaze homeward caught their first glimpse in the middle of the afternoon on Saturday 10 July. As *Canberra* closed on The Lizard before sailing along the south coast, they began to have an inkling of what awaited. 'It was all green, green pastures and lots and lots and lots of people, black like little ants all the way along,' said Muxworthy. An RAF Nimrod approached and passed low and slow in salute, the thunder of aero engines now sending thrills through the ship's company rather than terror. Other clues appeared; for the first time in weeks, she could pick up television, and here was the weatherman in kipper tie and check jacket sticking sunny symbols on the south coast and making a point of saying that it would be a glorious day in Southampton for *Canberra*'s arrival. The signals that wished them well as they departed that cool Good Friday evening beckoned them home; as dusk approached, a sparkling chain flickered along the coast, as drivers parked their cars facing out to sea and flashed their headlights. Dignitaries flew aboard as well as the press; the high command of P&O, Lord Inchcape and Rodney Leach, still wrangling with the government over compensation, with word that the morning would bring the most distinguished visitor *Canberra* had hosted, the Prince of Wales.

Britain lay to port, the tiny figures swallowed up by the gathering night as the tattoo of lights spelled out the message of welcome as vividly as the Morse lamps of the foggy approach to the Falklands had relayed orders. Aboard, all made their way up to the midships flight deck, finding whatever vantage point they could; Scott-Masson, the guests and the remaining wounded up on the Captain's Deck, the rest grouped around, at the rails, on Monkey Island, at the emergency conning point. Out they marched, the now worn and scabby improvised anti-slip surface of green paint and sand crunching beneath boots polished to a mirror gloss: the Marines band, *Canberra*'s band, men who had not flinched amidst air raids as they operated the creaking ramp lowering the wounded to hospital, shrugged off tiredness to take their music around the bars to bolster the spirits of young men nursing a beer and worrying. They comforted sailors whose ship had been lost, prepared the dead for committal to the sea and treated boys, sent to war with colouring books in their packs, compassionately. Marines had sniggered when it was announced that the band was going with them to the Falklands; now, as they roared their acclaim, it was inconceivable that it should have been anywhere else. The band played for half an hour, the old favourites that had echoed around the frozen anchorage of South Georgia as *Ardent*'s survivors waved goodbye, and boosted morale in the gloomy, edgy days of sailing the TRALA, setting 3,000 pairs of feet stamping and *Canberra*'s superstructure vibrating in time with them. With pinpoint timing, 'Sunset' was played as the ensign was lowered. 'They wouldn't let the band go, kept shouting "More, more, more",' said Ware. 'Obviously, I had to do something and there was one piece of music which had become a favourite in all our concerts, so I simply said, "Here we go, 'Hootenanny'" and the reaction was absolutely amazing, the stamping and the cheering.' This was the band's night, its men splitting into groups to play for the most joyous party the ship ever knew.

The Marines sensed the welcome that awaited and set about making banners to hang over the rails as *Canberra* entered Southampton. Camera crews caught the ebullience as the men sang, did their party pieces and cheered; Jeremy Hands decided to get a shot of himself amid a raucous group. He should have known better; within seconds, every stitch of his clothing had been stripped and he was hoisted aloft, his crew dutifully filming it all to be shown at ITN's Christmas party.

Sore heads were jolted from sleep by a bugler blasting out 'Reveille' over the loudspeakers at 5.30am that Sunday, 11 July. The voice of assistant purser Lois Wheeler that followed was altogether more soothing, the ship smiling at her poker-faced smoothness in heralding this extraordinary day as if they were arriving from a routine potter around the Mediterranean. Muxworthy noted what she said.

'Good morning ladies and gentlemen. It promises to be a fine day, with every prospect of a warm welcome when we dock. Now if you would care to make your way to the dining halls, you will find an early breakfast awaits you. We hope you have enjoyed your cruise, and that we might have the pleasure of your company again. Good morning.'

Everybody felt something in the air; the early-morning radio bulletins were full of *Canberra*'s arrival, the roads around Southampton packed, crowds piling into the port and onto the foreshores, the local stations they could pick up reporting Mayflower Park already busy with people bagging the best pitches to watch her come home. The most perfect of English summer days was blooming as the light sea mist cleared. Even at Ascension, the sky had never seemed as blue as this, nor the waters as sparkling. Boats were already out to greet her as she steamed slowly past the Isle of Wight, small craft bobbing in her wake, their occupants waving and cheering, as were people lining the shore. Just before 9am, the ship's company straightened its shoulders and took a deep breath as a Wessex helicopter in the red of the Queen's Flight hovered in and settled gently onto the midships landing pad, swept as clean as it could be after three months of lifting and loading. Scott-Masson, pumped up with pride, was waiting. A smiling Prince Charles stepped down onto the deck, shook his hand, and was escorted to the Meridian Room to meet crew, spending an hour chatting, bantering and joking, explaining that he would depart well before they docked as this was their day and he did not wish to distract any attention from them.

No prospect of that; The Solent began to fill with boats, more and more of them, dozens at first, then scores, then too many to count, hundreds upon hundreds of pleasure craft and yachts, even a ferry, all hooting, their men and women standing, waving with both arms, hurrahing, every one of the craft garlanded with 'Welcome Home' banners, a joyous, gathering clamour that brought two thousand troops to *Canberra*'s rails. There was not a spare inch of space at her starboard side as the men and P&O crew packed it, a fusillade of wolf whistles going up at groups of girls aboard motorboats who bared their breasts as a taster of what awaited the soldiers they had written to. 'I leaned over the bridge wing, and looked aft, and all I could see was legs all the way along the boat deck,' said Reed. 'I thought, "What's the hell's that?" and the boys had all jumped in the lifeboats and were dangling their legs over the side. No, no; but I thought I can't do anything about it, so I just left them there.' A roar of acclaim greeted a line of canoes paddled by sea scouts, the cheering so loud that it could be heard above the boom of *Canberra*'s whistle replying to the flotilla that surrounded her, yet more small boats joining with every passing minute. She slowed to a crawl as they chased around, the Marines waving down at them from 80ft above. 'I was just stunned,' said Reed. 'All these boats, just extraordinary; I was sure something was going to get squished, but the pilot was quite cheerful. Seeing them all, so pretty, just overwhelming.'

The shoreline was as jammed as *Canberra*'s rails, shoulder to shoulder, no break in the crowds anywhere, only endless lines of waving, cheering people. Muxworthy formed up Naval Party 1701 around the edge of the forward flight deck. 'I thought, "Sod it, we'll get the best position" and there were yachts and motorboats around us, singing, shouting, and just people wherever you looked, this sea of people.' There with them was the band, her band, its music woven through the shouts and the cheers and the wolf whistles, playing 'A Life on the Ocean Wave', 'Rule Britannia', 'Heart of Oak', 'Land of Hope and Glory', as the waiters came out onto the fo'c'sle and danced. It seemed hardly possible that any more craft could surround her, but still they came as she headed up Southampton Water, fire boats now, plumes fountaining from their hoses, the sea churning under so many boats, setting *Canberra* rocking gently. From up ahead, a roar rolled across the water towards her, the exultant shouts and cheers of tens upon tens of thousands. 'I had no idea this would happen,' said Nick Vaux. 'I shed a tear at some point because I was so overwhelmed that all these people would come to cheer us on when we got back. Everybody shared in it, everybody felt they were being given more than the recognition they deserved, and that was just magic.'

A seething mass of red, white and blue filled the dockside, an endless crowd of people stretching away as far as anyone aboard could see, in Union Jack T-shirts and plastic hats, waving flags and banners, dancing, jigging, waving, shedding tears of happiness. There was not an empty foot of space anywhere; on and on they went, those at the back cheering ever louder, waving their flags ever higher to be heard and seen. The tears were flowing in millions of homes, too; impossible to hold them back as the tumult of *Canberra*'s homecoming became apparent, the massive, spontaneous celebration on water and on land coming unedited and unpackaged, live on the BBC and ITV. Cameras aboard helicopters caught the flotilla of boats filling the Channel, ahead and astern; on land, the sea of men, women and children thronging the dockside, too many to count. The police stopped trying after 35,000 had passed through the gates, eventually estimating as many as 120,000; it was anybody's guess how many tens of thousands more lined the approaches to the port, or the numbers aboard the boats. Amid the clamour, the reporters picked up quiet, perceptive moments of reflection. Burne told Jeremy Hands, 'Each young man who fought in this war deserves every cheer here today.' Each civilian, too; the acclaim was for the men and women of this battered, magnificent ship also. 'It was the scale of the emotion,' said Susie West. 'Everybody's little individual bubbles of celebration grouped together to make an explosion, an incredible high.'

As she drew nearer, the crowds took in every detail of the great white whale, unbowed and all the more affecting for her careworn appearance; the mottled, salty, fading paintwork, the vivid streaks of rust the length of her hull. From the dockside, they craned upwards at the wall of cheering men in khaki with their banners of canvas and bed sheets draped over the rails: 'WE WENT, WE FOUGHT, WE CONQUERED.' 'LOCK UP YOUR DAUGHTERS, THE BOOTNECKS ARE BACK.' 'MAGGIE RULES OK.' A jibe at a threatened stoppage on the railways, 'CALL OFF THE RAIL STRIKE, OR WE'LL CALL AN AIR STRIKE', and the most personal of all for those who had sailed 25,245 nautical miles on this epic and hazardous voyage, '*CANBERRA* CRUISES WHERE *QE2* REFUSES'. The tugs nudged her to the berth; at 11 o'clock, on the dot, she was home. The Marines band from Portsmouth played on the quayside; from high above, *Canberra*'s band joined in, both striking up 'Land of Hope and Glory', the troops and the mass of people ashore coming together to bellow out the words as a cloud of red, white and blue balloons soared into the sky.

There had been no homecoming like this in living memory; *Canberra* had come to embody a finest hour for an age that thought such moments belonged to the past. Her role in this strange, savage, unexpected war over a land that most of Britain had never heard of only months before made her the focus for an outpouring of affection, emotion and patriotism. They came to salute the armed forces in the shape of the young men she had taken to war and brought home again, and to hail her and those who had served aboard; stewards, cooks, cleaners, butchers, bakers, carpenters, men and women just like themselves, who could never have imagined being caught up in conflict as ships were sunk and soldiers, sailors and airmen lost, but when called to do so found within themselves extraordinary reserves of courage and determination. This had been their finest hour too.

A relief P&O crew made its way through the crowd, ready to come on board to take over the moment the gangways were down; most of *Canberra*'s company had been at sea for more than six months and leave was to begin with immediate effect. Yet, even though exhausted, they did not want to go. She was theirs; they had endured so much together that to hand *Canberra* over to others seemed wrong and unfair to her. 'We felt terribly guilty at just walking off the moment the ship docked,' said Philip Pickford. 'Martin and I discussed it, we were saying we don't want to leave now, we wanted to stay on board another week and make sure she was all set up for the reconversion, but they insisted we went and that was quite traumatic in its own way.' Reed felt impelled to stay. 'Dear old P&O, it was based on kind-heartedness, they didn't realise it was still our ship and we had to wind it down and make sure everything was done. I suppose we were a bit psychotic at that stage, but we couldn't just give up and go away, so we stayed that night on board and packed up properly the next morning.' Hugh Williams went with him, the urn containing his ashes having spent the war in Martin Reed's locker. 'He was a radio officer, and when he died, it was in his will that he wanted his ashes scattered off the *Canberra*.' Then war had intervened, and he had been overlooked; his wishes would be fulfilled now that peace had returned.

The joy of reunions remained with men and women ever after. Rosie Elsdon glimpsing the brother she thought was in Germany here on the quayside waiting; Susie West catching sight of her sister and hurling her hat across, seeing it caught; Graham Harding picking out his wife-to-be amid the mass of people because she was waving his big, brightly-coloured golf umbrella; John Ware's 13-year-old daughter confessing that she had tried so hard not to cry but couldn't help it when she heard *Canberra*'s whistle; John Muxworthy finding his wife in the crowd and leading her back aboard; Dennis Scott-Masson's midday pinkers the best of all since sailing three months before, for being shared with his wife. Soldiers and sailors held wives or sweethearts in lingering embraces, and the parents of the youngest hugged them closer than ever before. Safe at last; *Canberra* part of each greeting. 'She was looking so forlorn, this lovely white ship that hadn't been painted for a long time,' said Sue Wood. 'She looked worn out, but she was like a mother figure, bringing all her children home.'

CHAPTER FIFTEEN

Britain's Favourite Ship

A VAST, EMPTY dry dock filled the television screen, the sun chasing away the shadows, clouds rolling overhead. A beautifully modulated male voice began speaking as the camera flitted about, picking out the hooks of cranes in silhouette. 'This giant dock has been waiting, waiting for a very special message; the SS *Canberra* is home from the Falklands.' A pause, hammers against metal clanging on the soundtrack. 'Soon, a different army will clamber over her decks, to reappoint her in the style to which she was previously accustomed, a style that can produce a superb five-course meal washed down by a Madeira sunset, or a late-night band in a mood to match the moonlight dancing across the Bay of Naples.' A snatch of crowds cheering and a ship's whistle replying. 'When *Canberra* resumes cruising on the 11th of September, such unforgettable moments will again become everyday events.' The camera pulled back and upwards to take in the whole of the dock as the image of *Canberra* slowly faded up until she occupied it, overlaid on her the caption, 'SS *Canberra*. She'll be ready when you are'.

It was 15 July 1982, four days after she arrived home, and the television advertisements that began to punctuate prime-time shows were matched by a campaign in the newspapers, where full pages were taken out. An army was indeed preparing to clamber across *Canberra*'s decks; in Southampton's King George V dry dock, the Vosper Thornycroft men who converted her for war had returned to make her fit for peace, beginning work on 9 August. As in April, showers of sparks spilled from her upper decks as the flight pads were cut away and the mushroom of girders were lifted by crane out of the Bonito Pool. The thicket of scaffolding supports was removed from the Crow's Nest and The Stadium cleared in readiness to become a theatre once more. Hardboard flooring and the carpets beneath were ripped out from bows to stern. The Promenade Deck was relaid, and the teak of the Sun Deck renewed and polished. Her hull was cleaned and inspected, the rusty streaks that had become a trademark scoured away. On the dockside, thousands of gallons of paint arrived; she would be brilliantly white once more. Refurbishing her took three weeks, at a cost reported by *The Sunday Times* of £8m, paid by the government. The taxpayer was also picking up the bill for the dancing moonlight and Madeira sunsets after P&O's most audaciously successful round of wrangling. Restoring *Canberra* to make her fit for cruising had always been part of the agreement when she was requisitioned; paying for a costly and flamboyant advertising campaign was not. Nevertheless, P&O prevailed, and a bill for £689,981.70 was presented to the Department of Trade on 21 October.

Her men and women were adjusting to the changes that war had wrought in them, some preparing to return, others wishing to leave her behind. They had watched the Marines on the way home talking out the trauma, and found their own journeys still had some way to go. The attention and admiration that serving aboard *Canberra* brought could be disconcerting. Strangers wanted to buy them drinks, expecting stories they did not feel like sharing in return. The reserved, undemonstrative Dennis Scott-Masson, dealing with the months past in his own way, enjoying his family, home and high summer in the Somerset garden from which his wife had sent pressed flowers in her letters, was put out to find people he did not know intruding, coming to his door, wanting to congratulate him. 'He was rather hounded – we almost had to put up the barricades,' said Anne-Marie Scott-Masson. 'People were walking up the drive and sticking their noses against the windows trying to see inside the house. There was nothing nasty about it, but he was a rather private person and he didn't like it.'

Martin Reed was also uncomfortable, especially after being interviewed by his local newspaper and posing, smiling, for a photograph with a shell casing from a naval gun that he kept as a souvenir. The paper used its article about him at the top of a page; below it, was the story of a grieving family whose son, a helicopter pilot, had been killed. Reed found his thoughts going back to childhood whenever a loud noise made him start: 'I suddenly realised why my mother used to jerk and jump if a car backfired when I was holding hands with her as a kid. She'd lived through the Blitz and been bombed out twice. It's not until it happens to you that you realise how these things burn their way in.' Jumpiness at sudden noise was common. 'I couldn't cope with going to firework displays for a very long time afterwards,' said Susie West. 'I just couldn't see why it was a form of entertainment.' Returning to normality after the intensity of their experiences left others restless, unsure of how to move on with their lives. 'I felt quite unsettled,' said Rosie Elsdon. 'I didn't know whether I wanted to stay at sea because I thought normal cruising would be really tame, so I had three months off and then went back to sea because I was unsure what to do.' Kevin Mountney was flat, uncertain about how he felt. 'I talked to my father, who'd been in the Second World War, and I decided it would be better to go back to *Canberra* for a little while longer, maybe a year, and work through how I was feeling on there, where it had all happened, instead of trying to settle somewhere else.' Angela Devine wanted to break the ties to *Canberra*, joining a ship sailing from the West Coast of America. 'I'd kept a diary and all the newspaper cuttings, and made a scrapbook. After about a year, I threw it all away. I was petrified that it was going to take over my life, and I didn't want what had happened to become what my life was all about.'

For 129 men, there was no chance to return. Their reward for going to war was to be thrown out of work. These were the deck and engineering crew drawn from the pool of unemployed to cover the gaps left by the Asians who, at the National Union of Seamen's insistence, did not sail south. The day after sharing in the joyous homecoming, the men were told they had no jobs. P&O could point to contracts to justify itself, that the men had signed on only for the duration of *Canberra*'s requisitioning and could also point out that it had obligations to its long-serving Asian crew.

The overriding obligation, though, was to the balance sheet; the Asians were paid only a quarter of the wages of the men the NUS had insisted P&O employed. A P&O spokesman quoted by the *Guardian* on 13 July missed the point as he bleated, 'It is an unhappy situation that these seafarers now find themselves unemployed, but it is not something that we as a company can take responsibility for.' Such a statement was at odds with the mood of Britain; the talk was of fairness and decency having triumphed in the South Atlantic, of core values of doing what was right coming out on top. The abrupt sacking of more than a quarter of the ship's company who had served with such courage was at odds with those sentiments; for them wrong, not right, had prevailed. P&O had the afterglow of *Canberra*'s euphoric arrival at Southampton to thank for avoiding a public relations disaster over its shameful treatment of men dumped onto the dole even as the country celebrated; their dismissal went largely unnoticed.

The triumphant atmosphere produced exceptional business. *Canberra*'s remaining three scheduled cruises of the year were fully booked and the phones were ringing from passengers determined to sail on her as soon as possible. The Falklands factor, which would propel Margaret Thatcher back into Downing Street with an increased majority in 1983, turned *Canberra* into the country's most sought-after cruise ship. Every cabin was full. Regular passengers and newcomers alike wanted to be part of her story, to be able to tell their friends that they had sailed aboard the ship that took our lads to war, and braved the dangers of Bomb Alley, wanted to hear the crew's stories, stroll the circuit pounded by Marines and Paras, wonder which of the men had occupied their cabin and what they had done once *Canberra* had landed them. The days when she had sailed half empty were gone, never to return; Britain was prouder of her now than she had been in 1961.

She was back to her elegant best as the passengers boarded on 11 September for 14 nights that would take them to Gibraltar, Corfu, Palma and Vigo. The public rooms were pristine once more, freshly carpeted and decorated, the furniture new, the drapes, plants and flowers back in place, the piano in the Meridian Room played by a scruffy young Argentine prisoner tuned and polished to a high gloss. The passengers had seen the pictures of the midships landing pad and went up to the Bonito Pool to try to visualise it, looked down from the Crow's Nest and pointed out to each other where the forward flight deck had been. Her farewell that day was full of affection; crowds came down to the dockside and there were waves and cheers from the shore as she made her way down Southampton Water, the fireboats with her once more, sending up plumes of spray. All the passengers wanted to talk about was the Falklands; Reed, in common with others, found himself giving away more than he intended: 'Going back to work was fine, but people always wanted to know what it was like. We had this saying, "Whatever you do, don't talk about the war," because once you started, it was non-stop, one story would trip another and before you knew what was happening, you'd see this glazed look appear.' Scott-Masson addressed his passengers' fascination by delivering an hour's lecture. The Stadium was packed, the setting a usefully dramatic backdrop for what he had to say, standing on the stage where the X-ray machine had been, looking out an audience which knew it was seated where wounded men had been treated only weeks before. He told the story of requisitioning, the voyage south, San Carlos and the prisoners, again and again stressing the bravery and hard work of his crew, lightening the narrative with anecdotes; problems with the blackout, worries over beer running out, rigging up traction for the prisoner who thought he was about to be hanged. At its end, there was enthusiastic applause.

There were official thanks a month later, when the special Falklands honours list was published. Scott-Masson was awarded the CBE, as was Christopher Burne, waiting to take command of HMS *Glamorgan* once she was refitted following the Exocet strike that killed 13 men two days before the war ended. There was another notable award; an MBE for Rosie Elsdon, glibly dubbed 'The Nightingale of the *Canberra*' by the tabloid newspapers. She was working aboard the P&O ship *Island Princess* in the Caribbean when the award was announced. 'It was a huge surprise, and I was embarrassed really because I didn't do anything that other people didn't do,' she recalled. 'I do feel it was on behalf of all the P&O people and all the girls who were there, it wasn't just for me, it was for everybody.' Word of her work in the hospital during long night shifts had spread whilst *Canberra* was in the South Atlantic; senior officers also knew how vital she had been in helping the traumatised Naval man who appeared every night, simply by listening to him. It seems likely that Scott-Masson recommended her for possible recognition. John Turner, in his report on *Canberra* compiled after he joined at Ascension, noting, 'Captain Scott-Masson was asked to put forward about ten names for commendation by the Senior Naval Officer.'

The links between *Canberra* and the forces she had taken to war remained strong; in November, she hosted a dinner for the senior commanders of the task force. The following summer brought the happiest of reunions; the Marines band under John Ware came back aboard to play throughout a two-week cruise to the Atlantic Islands, performing all the old favourites, 'Hootenanny' among them, though this audience was far too sedate to set the superstructure trembling with stamping feet. There were no ad hoc performances around the public rooms, even though the band split into smaller groups to play for dancing or as a backdrop to polite conversation over afternoon tea. Ware, in common with so many aboard, found that he had been marked by those dangerous, uncertain days in the Falklands. 'I had occasion to visit the Portsmouth band, and I was in their library when a low-flying aircraft suddenly shot over. After it happened, the two guys who were with me were looking at me in rather a strange way, and I said, "What's the matter?", and they said, "Don't you realise what you've done? When that aircraft came over, you were almost under the desk".' Nick Vaux was also to return in the years that followed, attending a reunion dinner on board at which a number of senior politicians were present. He had told his wife about the magnificent stateroom in which he sailed to war and so gratefully returned to once it was all over. 'I said to her, "I wonder if I'll be given the same stateroom I had before?", and we were given a little two-berth, one-up and one down. The stateroom had gone to a politician.'

Gradually, the numbers of officers and crew remaining to tell eager passengers their stories of taking *Canberra* to war dwindled, as they moved on to join other ships. Early retirement was beckoning Scott-Masson, who departed in 1984. 'They were opening up trade on the West Coast of America on smaller ships, and that didn't really appeal to him, so he was happy to go early,' said his wife. 'The Falklands was the pinnacle of his career, and it all seemed pretty tame afterwards. He did say that some of the usual passengers weren't as nice as those he'd had going south and coming back again.'

Canberra sailed serenely on through the remainder of the 1980s and into the 1990s, a British institution to which devoted passengers returned year after year. They were not only the elderly; families came too and long-serving crew watched children grow from toddlers to teenagers, summer by summer. As the Falklands War grew more distant, bookings declined from the peak of the years immediately afterward, but she remained immensely popular, periodic refits bringing her up to date, even if her interiors had wandered away from Hugh Casson's 1960s vision of cool elegance into garishness. Journalist Jan Moir, aboard in the mid-1990s, winced a little, writing, 'If you must have nautical decor, then I suppose a ship is the place to have it, but the orange chairs decorated with anchors, the blue sofas with cockleshells, the woven compasses and the flotilla of clipper ships foaming across the curtains seems – to me, anyway – to be one seafaring motif too far.' No matter; her passengers loved their surroundings, Moir noting, 'The real joy of the *Canberra* is that she allows the British to be British, in all their eccentric, picky, happy-go-lucky glory, no matter where in the world she sails.' The affection in which she was held made her the natural choice to take D Day veterans to France for the 50th anniversary of the Normandy landings in June 1994. She took her place at Spithead to be reviewed by The Queen aboard *Britannia* before a lone Lancaster bomber swooped down low, releasing hundreds of thousands of poppy petals, the flowers drifting over her decks, where the old soldiers had gathered for a service of remembrance.

That summer of commemoration brought a reminder that she was now an old ship, suffering a complete power failure that left her adrift in The Solent. There had been increasing mechanical problems in recent years but this was the worst yet. A new generation of cruise vessels was appearing, bigger, more comfortable, more fuel-efficient, needing fewer engineering crew; they were the ships of the future. As *Canberra* had made a generation of liners that preceded her appear to belong to a bygone age, so she was being left behind by these floating hotels to which passengers were increasingly drawn. The end of her career was announced on 25 June 1996. She would be withdrawn from service the following year after a farewell world cruise and a season in the Mediterranean; the spectre of scrapping had loomed once before, and P&O was at pains to point out that it would be avoided if possible, its managing director, Gwyn Hughes, telling the *Independent*, '*Canberra* is now an elderly lady and though she remains a much loved ship, no vessel can continue indefinitely. We very much hope the vessel will not be scrapped. Various organisations have approached us about possible uses for the ship. These include her becoming a floating hotel or a visitor centre.' Inevitably, as the captain who had taken her to war, a comment from Scott-Masson was put out by the company: 'We are all mortal. There has to be a time when she comes to the end of her life. For a ship like that to last for 35 years is quite remarkable.' His philosophical tone hid his true feelings. 'He was devastated,' said his wife. 'He thought it was totally unnecessary and that she could have gone on longer.'

This would be a year of nostalgia. She departed from Southampton on 6 January, through the Mediterranean and the Suez Canal, bound for Bombay and then Singapore. Sydney awaited, with all its memories; of her first arrival there in 1961, the last of a breed of great liners, after the swiftest of passages from Britain, her Ten Pound Poms at the rails taking in the sight of their new country, excited yet apprehensive about what it might hold. The city put on a show to welcome her; flotillas of small boats, fountains of spray and cheering. The West Coast of America and Panama followed, before she arrived home in Southampton on 7 April, to be readied for her final programme of cruises that took her through to the autumn. The crowds came to the port once more on 10 September to see her off on the last of them, bound for 20 days in the Mediterranean. A band played, balloons were released, the cheers followed her down the Channel, along with dozens of boats. Everywhere she called – Haifa, Istanbul, Athens, Naples, Cannes, Palma – there were salutes. In Cannes, her passengers watched tearfully as a ceremony was held to hand over the 'Golden Cockerel', a metal silhouette on a pole carried by the fastest ship of the fleet, to P&O's new flagship, *Oriana*.

Fog shrouded the south coast on the morning of Tuesday 30 September as she brought her last paying passengers home, her arrival delayed until lunchtime so that as many people as possible could come out to welcome her. Memories of her return from the Falklands were everywhere; the crews of a flotilla of warships on exercise manned the decks in salute. The frigate HMS *Cornwall* took up station at her stern to escort her, as slowly the fog began to clear as she entered Southampton Water. Gradually, the outlines of boats could be made out, all around her, following her in, hundreds of them, as they had on that sunny Sunday morning 15 years earlier. Then, soldiers had made banners to hang from the rails; now, the passengers did likewise. The day was clearing rapidly, the cheering of crowds in Mayflower Park overlaid by the sound of approaching aero engines; a single *Canberra* bomber, followed by two RAF Sea Kings and a formation of army Lynx helicopters flying low overhead. The Paras were there to salute their great white whale, the regiment's Red Devils display team skydiving into the park, trailing red, white and blue smoke that matched the cloud of balloons released from *Canberra* as she berthed to the accompaniment of a military band. She had sailed three million miles in 36 years, including her most epic journey of all, southwards to danger; a million passengers had boarded, among them brave men scrambling through galley doors after fighting a war and frightened boys wanting to go home. Now, there was one more journey to make.

The ten days that followed were full of uncertainty as to *Canberra*'s fate. P&O remained silent. The day after she arrived, under cover of darkness, she was moved to the eastern docks to make way for the *Oriana*. As before sailing for the Falklands, she was stripped. Paintings, furniture, fixtures and fittings were removed. Talk of her becoming a floating hotel or visitor attraction was brought to an abrupt end on the morning of Friday 10 October. A terse press release announced that she had been sold to a scrap merchant in Pakistan and would sail that evening. By the time the news was printed in the morning papers, she would be gone. It later emerged that the breaker had paid $5,640,818. BBC Radio Solent invited Julian Thompson and Nick Vaux to the docks to see the ship that had meant so much to them, and the men under their command, for the last time. 'It was the most forlorn thing, it was so sad,' recalled Vaux. 'It was a miserable day, squalls and rain, low clouds, and there was this sadly shabby-looking *Canberra*, and I thought, "Absolutely the end of an era".'

The captain given the task of taking her to destruction was Mike Carr, who had known her since 1968, when she was still making line voyages to Australia. His connection to her ran deep; he had met his wife on board, but could not allow sentiment over *Canberra* to get in the way of the job that needed to be done. He was told to keep everything low-key; this was not an event to celebrate. For the first time since the return voyage through the South Atlantic, her lights were dimmed as the lines were cast off at 9pm and the tugs took her into the channel, a skeleton crew of 72 on board. On the quayside as the rain came down, a crowd of a few dozen, mostly former crew members, began cheering and whistling. She could not be allowed to leave in silence, not after a lifetime of bands playing her away. The chief radio officer, Freddie Lloyd, a Scot, had a cassette of pipes playing traditional airs, and he sent the music blaring from the loud-speakers: *Flower of Scotland, Dark Isle, Flowers of the Forest*, the melancholy of the laments appropriate for this sad, wet autumn night. They were drowned out by three long blasts of *Canberra*'s whistle, booming and echoing across the port for a final time as she said goodbye. Along Southampton Water there were cars flashing their headlights, a water salute at Fawley and the sirens of other ships. The land to which she had been first an emblem of a new age, and later a symbol of national pride, slipped away from her forever.

Carr moved his crew into the best cabins. They would be comfortable on this voyage; they would also make sure that *Canberra* looked her best, because she deserved no less, even on the way to be scrapped. 'My big concern was fire breaking out, so I said to them "Pick cabins you want to be in, and I want you all on a phone, so if the worst comes to the worst, I can get hold of you." We made the Bonito Club the ship's wardroom, which everybody could use, and then we set about really cleaning her up. By the end, she looked fabulous.' The Bonito Pool had been kept full, and a warm afternoon was filled by the laughter of a competition to build rafts out of drums and planks; it grew all the more uproarious when the only one that capsized was the deck officers'. 'We all got as fat as pigs,' said Carr. 'She was virtually fully stocked with everything, and we had two chefs, ate very well, put a lot of weight on and had a very good time.' There was simply no point in being gloomy as the voyage progressed, even though *Canberra* was a ghost ship. All the crew knew her well, and the still, quiet emptiness of deserted stairways, restaurants stripped bare and darkened decks was eerie, the quiet only broken by the banging of doors that came unlatched, swinging open and shut with the motion of the sea.

The final negotiations over scrapping were ongoing as the voyage progressed; *Canberra* had been at sea for two weeks before it was confirmed that she should make for Karachi, where she anchored on 28 October. Amongst the paperwork, Carr noticed a clause making it clear that P&O was determined that its last great liner must never sail again under another flag: 'P&O to retain title to the propeller until the blades have been cut and removed and also the main engines until they are removed and the vessel has been cut up to the extent that it is not practical to rebuild.' On 30 October, *Canberra* weighed anchor and sailed 30 miles north-west to Gadani, then the biggest ships' graveyard in the world. She was to be beached and then dismantled.

On the morning of Halloween, Carr was ready to hand over to a beaching master to take her in. He could not handle a ship the size of *Canberra*; Carr would have to do it himself. At 8.39am, he weighed and turned for the open sea, heading ten miles out to gather speed before bringing her back round at 20 knots, the draught that caused such problems when she first began cruising trimmed to the angle of the beach. The pipes were playing over the speakers as she came in, the shoreline growing closer and closer. She beached at 9.40am, all but silently, no juddering impact, 2,100ft out. After all the emotional outpourings of the final homecoming, the weight of history and pride that sailed with her, it was an anticlimactic end. 'It was very smooth, and none of us felt it,' said Carr. 'There was no feeling of going ashore, the only thing was a huge stern wave developed, just slowly as we got into shallow water, and that eventually just rolled onto the beach. In fact, we had to check with bearings to see if we were aground.' There was a bottle of champagne on the bridge; Carr and his officers toasted *Canberra* until it was empty.

Her destruction was long and messy. Dismantling scheduled for three months dragged on for well over a year. The men of Harland and Wolff who invested years of themselves in her had done their job well; the toughness and resilience that withstood the ferocious seas of the South Atlantic hampered the poorly paid workmen scrapping her by hand, cutting the bridge and its streamlined wings away bit by bit, then the funnels, slowly but inexorably erasing the profile that had once been so futuristic. Anne-Marie Scott-Masson kept from her husband the newspaper photographs of his ship being torn apart. 'We always avoided it,' she said. 'He absolutely hated seeing that.'

Those last few pictures were no longer of the *Canberra* that meant so much to her men and women. They could never supplant the snapshots in the mind's eye of all who shared in the comradeship of 94 days at sea on a strange and perilous voyage through war. Each held their own image that embodied her spirit, commemorated at crew reunions, an annual black tie dinner for officers who were at San Carlos on the day she landed her troops, in the remembrances of Marines and Paras at get-togethers. Pristine, elegant, loading young soldiers burdened with heavy packs at Southampton on an Easter weekend; plumes of spray erupting around her as she rocked under the impact of explosions; looking in disbelief along that rusty hull at Britain cheering them home. Every personal picture, all that they had seen and done, was bound up with her.

'There was something special about *Canberra*, the way that she drew people together,' reflected Philip Pickford. 'She was an old-style liner, and they don't exist today. But *Canberra* looked like a ship and behaved like a ship. She was a great ship, one of the best.' Only grudgingly did she yield to the breakers, fading from view gradually, as she had into the fog that cloaked her approach to war; her superstructure slowly disappearing, next her hull, for a while enough jagged shards of it left sticking out of a long, open beach to hint at what she had been, then finally, nothing.

Acknowledgements

I owe a debt of gratitude to two men in particular for helping to make this book possible. Captain Martin Reed RNR displayed unstinting candour, insight and kindness. Commander John Muxworthy RN demonstrated a warm generosity of spirit and I readily acknowledge how helpful his book, *The Great White Whale Goes To War*, published shortly after *Canberra* returned from the Falklands, was to me.

Two more men have my special thanks: Major General Nick Vaux for his frankness and Lieutenant General Sir Hew Pike, not only for sharing his thoughts but for opening 3 Para's battalion log from the period.

The late Graham Harding and his wife, Linda, showed exceptional kindness in sparing precious time and allowing me sight of his privately published memoirs. Anne-Marie Scott-Masson was equally generous in permitting me to draw from a recording of a lecture by her late husband.

John Shirley, aboard *Canberra* for *The Sunday Times*, shared his recollections and opened doors that otherwise might have remained shut. A valued colleague, Derek Hudson, provided both memories and background material. Steve Matthews, webmaster of sscanberra.com, helped with contacts and made much useful memorabilia available.

My thanks to all the following, who displayed great patience in sharing their memories: Lou Armour, Lawrie Ashbridge, Laurie Bland, Steve Brabham, Christopher Burne, Mike Carr, Don Chapman, Don Cole, Angela Devine, Brian Faulkner, Lyell Guthrie, Sue Ingham, Leslie Jenkins, Roger Lancaster, Peter Mayner, Norman Menzies, Kevin Mountney, Rosie Norman, Morgan O'Connell, Eduardo Ortuondo, Roy Paddison, Roger

Patton, John Perry, Philip Pickford, Norman Pound, Kim Sabido, Chris Sheppard, Aldo Solari, Mick Southall, John Turner, Sergio Vainroj, John Ware, Susie West, Guy Williams.

Susie Cox, curator of the P&O Heritage Collection, went out of her way to help, as did the staff of the Caird Library of the National Maritime Museum, Greenwich. Grateful thanks also to the staff of the Sound Archive, the Imperial War Museum, London, for kind permission to draw on interviews with Michael Bradford (catalogue number 11764), Maurice Rudderham (catalogue number 12141) and Dennis Scott-Masson (catalogue number 12206).

I would have been lost without the help and support of friends. Peter Charlton, editor of the *Yorkshire Post*, was characteristically good humoured and tolerant. Author and journalist Duncan Hamilton offered wise advice. Karen Johnson was tireless in transcribing interviews, Robert McFarland also contributing. Sheena Hastings and Duncan Stephenson lifted a weight of worry by conducting interviews on my behalf with former Argentine army soldiers. Jim Pybus and Tom Richmond did greatly appreciated favours.

Special thanks to Graham Coster, Louise Tucker and Melissa Smith at Aurum.

Last, but never least, my thanks to Carole for her love and encouragement throughout.

Bibliography

Adams, Valerie, *The Media and the Falklands Campaign* (Macmillan, 1986)

Arthur, Max. *Above All, Courage: Personal Stories from The Falklands War* (Cassell, 1985)

Bicheno, Hugh, *Razor's Edge: The Unofficial History of the Falklands War* (Weidenfield & Nicolson, 2006)

Bilton, Michael and Peter Kosminsky, *Speaking Out: Untold Stories from the Falklands War* (Andre Deutsch, 1989)

Bishop, Patrick and John Witherow, *The Winter War: The Falklands Conflict* (Quartet Books, 1982)

Boyce, George, *The Falklands War* (Macmillan, 2005)

Clapp, Michael and Ewan Southby-Tailyor, *Amphibious Assault: Falklands: The Battle of San Carlos Waters* (Leo Cooper, 1996)

Colbeck, Graham, *With 3 Para to the Falklands* (Greenhill Books, 2002)

Dale, Iain, ed; *Memories of the Falklands* (Politicos, 2002)

Ethell, Jeffrey and Alfred Price, *Air War South Atlantic* (Sidgwick & Jackson, 1983)

Fox, Robert, *Eyewitness Falklands* (Methuen, 1982)

Freedman, Lawrence, *The Official History of the Falklands Campaign, Volume I: The Origins of the Falklands War* (Routledge, 2007 (Revised))

Freedman, Lawrence, *The Official History of the Falklands Campaign, Volume II: War and Diplomacy* (Routledge, 2007 (Revised)).

Hammerton. A. James and Thomson, Alistair, *Ten Pound Poms: Australia's Invisible Migrants* (Manchester University Press, 2005)

Hanrahan, Brian and Fox, Robert, *I Counted Them All Out and I Counted Them All Back: The Battle for the Falklands* (BBC, 1982)

Hastings, Max, *Going to the Wars* (Macmillan, 2000)

Hastings, Max and Jenkins, Simon, *The Battle for the Falklands* (Michael Joseph, 1983)

Higgitt, Mark, *Through Fire and Water: HMS Ardent: The Forgotten Frigate of the Falklands* (Mainstream Publishing, 2001)

Jennings, Christian and Adrian Weale, *Green-Eyed Boys: 3 Para and the Battle for Mount Longdon* (HarperCollins, 1996)

Jolly, Rick, *The Red and Green Life Machine: A Diary of the Falklands Field Hospital* (Red & Green Books 2007 (Revised)).

Kerr, Michael, ed; *Bon Voyage; The Telegraph Books of River and Sea Journeys* (Aurum, 2010)

Leach, Admiral of the Fleet Sir Henry, *Endure No Makeshifts* (Leo Cooper, 1993).

McCart, Neil, *Canberra: The Great White Whale* (Patrick Stephens, 1983)

McCart, Neil, *SS Canberra 1957–1997* (Fan Publications, 1998)

McGowan, Robert and Hands, Jeremy, *Don't Cry For Me, Sergeant Major* (Futura, 1983)

McManners, Hugh, *Forgotten Voices of the Falklands: The Real Story of the Falklands War* (Ebury Press, 2007)

Middlebrook, Martin, *The Fight for the 'Malvinas': The Argentine Forces in the Falklands War* (Viking, 1989)

Middlebrook, Martin, *Task Force: The Falklands War 1982* (Penguin, 1987 (Revised))

Muxworthy, John, *The Great White Whale Goes To War* (P&O, 1982)

Pike, Hew, *From the Front Line: Family Letters and Diaries 1900 to the Falklands and Afghanistan* (Pen & Sword, 2008)

Reynolds, David, *Task Force: The Illustrated History of the Falklands War* (Sutton, 2002).

The Sunday Times Insight Team, *The Falklands War: the Full Story* (Sphere, 1982)

Thatcher, Margaret, *The Downing Street Years* (Harper Collins, 1993)

Thompson, Julian, *No Picnic,* 3rd edition (Cassell, 2001)

Thompson, Julian, *Ready for Anything: A History of the Parachute Regiment* (Weidenfeld & Nicolson, 1989)

Vaux, Nick, *March to the South Atlantic: 42 Commando Royal Marines in the Falklands War* (Buchan & Enright, 1986)

West, Nigel, *The Secret War for the Falklands* (Little Brown & Co, 1997)

White, Rowland, *Vulcan 607: The Epic Story of the Most Remarkable British Air Attack Since WWII* (Bantam Press, 2006)

Wilsey, John, *H Jones VC: The Life and Death of an Unusual Hero* (Hutchinson, 2002)

Woodward, Admiral Sandy with Patrick Robinson: *One Hundred Days: The Memoirs of the Falklands Battle Group Commander* (HarperCollins, second edition 2003)

Index

Index page.

Index